Ruth Zweifle

# FRACTURED

90
94
102
118
122 —

'No Angel' =
'objective' article
144 - 'a real
conversation'
requires
listening to &
hearing 'the other'

This book is part of the Peter Lang Education list.
Every volume is peer reviewed and meets
the highest quality standards for content and production.

PETER LANG
New York • Bern • Frankfurt • Berlin
Brussels • Vienna • Oxford • Warsaw

**HELEN FOX**

# FRACTURED

## RACE RELATIONS IN "POST-RACIAL" AMERICAN LIFE

PETER LANG
New York • Bern • Frankfurt • Berlin
Brussels • Vienna • Oxford • Warsaw

Library of Congress Cataloging-in-Publication Data
Fox, Helen.
Fractured: race relations in "post-racial" American life / Helen Fox.
pages cm
Includes bibliographical references.
1. Post-racialism—United States.  2. United States—Race relations.
3. African Americans—United States—Social conditions—21st century.
4. Minorities—United States—Social conditions—21st century.
5. Racism—United States.  I. Title.  II. Title: Race relations in "post-racial" American life.
E184.F65    305.800973—dc23    2015010727
ISBN 978-1-4331-2370-2 (hardcover)
ISBN 978-1-4331-2369-6 (paperback)
ISBN 978-1-4539-1619-3 (e-book)

Bibliographic information published by **Die Deutsche Nationalbibliothek**.
**Die Deutsche Nationalbibliothek** lists this publication in the "Deutsche
Nationalbibliografie"; detailed bibliographic data are available
on the Internet at http://dnb.d-nb.de/.

The paper in this book meets the guidelines for permanence and durability
of the Committee on Production Guidelines for Book Longevity
of the Council of Library Resources.

© 2015 Peter Lang Publishing, Inc., New York
29 Broadway, 18th floor, New York, NY 10006
www.peterlang.com

All rights reserved.
Reprint or reproduction, even partially, in all forms such as microfilm,
xerography, microfiche, microcard, and offset strictly prohibited.

Printed in the United States of America

# CONTENTS

Introduction      1

Chapter 1: "This Town Is So Liberal, There's No Such Thing as Race."   7
Chapter 2: Are We Post-Racial Yet?   25
Chapter 3: "Santa Just *Is* White, Kids."   51
Chapter 4: Racism by Any Other Name   71
Chapter 5: Dumping On the Poor   89
Chapter 6: Racism as a Complex System   113
Chapter 7: The Way Forward   135

Notes   159
Bibliography   171

# INTRODUCTION

As a white child growing up on Chicago's South Side in the 1950s, my small world was surprisingly diverse. My earliest playmates were our Japanese and Chinese neighbors, the newly resettled German Jews who lived down the block, and my Irish Catholic cousins who lived in a tough neighborhood across town. I went to a predominantly black high school, chafing at the unspoken rules that kept black and white students apart: the dating taboos, the color-coded classrooms where the "college-bound" students—white—were separated from the "regular" students—black—regardless of promise or effort. My friends were a mix of rich and poor. My rich friends lived in stately homes near the university; my poor friends lived in dark, overheated apartments near the train tracks. We never discussed this much; in our world, class, like race, was not a topic of polite conversation. My mother had told me that we were "middle-middle class," which was probably more wishful thinking than reality, for she was a single mother earning a high school teacher's salary, paying off a mortgage on a ramshackle house and barely keeping up with repairs on our clunky old car. Nevertheless, she always found a way to pay for music lessons, fill our Christmas stockings, and have just enough cash left over at the end of the summer to buy groceries before her regular paycheck started up again in the fall.

When I was accepted at two top universities—Chicago and California—I knew it was not because of my grades, which were modest, or my SAT scores, which were pretty dismal, compared to what is expected at top schools today, but because of my ability to talk enthusiastically about books and my unusual interest, for a girl, in science. I understood that my acceptance at these schools was based on some form of affirmative action, though they didn't call it that in 1960, and that this declaration of faith in my potential was not so freely offered to my black classmates. This, too, was never discussed in my family or circle of friends. I accepted my good fortune as my destiny.

When I went to India as a Peace Corps Volunteer in 1964 I was confronted for the first time by deprivation so extreme that it defied all of my previous notions of poverty: huts made of straw and mud that collapsed in the monsoon rain, skeletal people who existed on skimpy meals of rice and dal with a bit of chili for spice if they were lucky; cows that could find so little grass that they ate discarded newspaper. When I returned to the United States, stunned by my new awareness of human degradation, I took a job in an urban ghetto where I ran a small preschool for children who had been cast aside by the public schools. Visiting my young students' homes, I witnessed a different kind of poverty: a young mother of seven, so distraught over the death of her infant that its spirit had appeared to her in the form of a pigeon; a sad-eyed, mute youngster who, if it weren't for his race, would have been an ideal candidate for scholarship to a specialized private school; a young black, nurse's aide struggling to care for her profoundly disabled 5-year-old after working all night but too ashamed of her "failure" to apply for public assistance. In India, I had thought I had seen the worst of the human condition. But now I realized that what was happening in my own country was even more disturbing. Somehow, America had the resources to send college graduates abroad to improve the life chances of the world's poor but could not do the same for its own people. I attributed my country's appalling acceptance of poverty and racism to political blindness, or at best, the lack of a vision of a just society. It was only much later that I began to understand the working of systems that keep hierarchies of privilege in place, the ways that long forgotten history continues to shape the present, the tenacity of race and class privilege that has gripped our nation since its founding.

I began to teach about race at the University of Michigan's Residential College in the 1990s at the request of a white student who felt that the silence about race left our social science concentration incomplete. I spent the summer reading stacks of books and articles on the history and sociology of race, the biographies of famous people of color, the novels and personal experience stories written by people of African, Asian, Latin American, Native American, and Middle Eastern descent that I had somehow missed in my

INTRODUCTION 3

previous education. In the fall, with some trepidation, I embarked on my first undergraduate discussion seminar, which I called "Unteaching Racism"—the idea being that since racism is taught, as it was to me, it can also be untaught. My students took to the study of race with enthusiasm and good heart. As my confidence grew, I began to anticipate students' reactions to the material and to each other, understand their confusion and resistance, and find the articles, books, and videos that would help them open up in the classroom. During that period, I wrote a book for teachers—the book, in fact, that I wished I'd had in hand when I plunged into this new territory myself. *When Race Breaks Out: Conversations About Race and Racism in College Classrooms* has now gone into its second revised edition (Peter Lang, 2014), with a new emphasis on how today's college students, the "Millennials," can be brought into discussions about interpersonal and systemic racism, even when they feel, as they often say they do, that race is "no big deal" for their generation.

As I researched the latest revisions for *When Race Breaks Out,* I became interested in the idea, touted in the media, that with Barack Obama's election, the United States had entered into a "post-racial" period where race mattered less than ever before in our history. From my reading of the academic literature, and perhaps more importantly, from my years of teaching and interacting with students, I knew this wasn't true. Yet something was different about this time period, something I couldn't quite put my finger on. My students were more polite to each other in the classroom, more willing, it seemed, to interact across racial lines. Gone were the days when an emotionally charged comment sent a student from the classroom in tears. Yet in conference and in my informal social interactions with students and faculty of color, I learned that many were battling intense emotions in class and on campus. My white students, on the other hand, seemed open, relaxed, and completely unaware of the effect of their naïve comments and uninformed opinions on their peers of color. What had happened? My questioning quickly turned into this new book project. I wanted to get beneath the surface, not only at my own university, where I had previously interviewed students and faculty about race, but across the country. What did people make of this supposedly "post-racial" era we had now entered with the election of our nation's first black president? What do they think other people mean by that term? What were their own experiences with race? How had they seen race relations change over time? If they were teachers, how would they describe racial dynamics in their classrooms, on campus, and in their larger communities? How do they see socioeconomic class interacting with race? Which is more important in today's society, in their view? If they were students, what did they think about the racial climate on campus, in their classrooms and living spaces, their clubs and extracurricular activities? My interviewees for my previous books had identified mainly as black or white. What was the feeling in parts of the country where Latinos, or Asians, or Native Americans predominate?

As I refined my ideas and interview questions, I planned interviewing trips to the East Coast, the Northwest, the Midwest, and the South, arranging to stay with colleagues and old friends who would put me in touch with their students, fellow faculty members, and local acquaintances who were willing to talk with me about race and class. Letting my interview pool develop organically meant that I would probably miss some areas of the country and some important voices, but it also ensured that I would get the honest, reflective stories I was looking for. I knew I could not just ask people randomly what they think and feel about race. I would need time and space for conversation and go-betweens who would assure my interviewees that I could be trusted. Nevertheless, that trust was not always there. As a white interviewer, I knew that my background, my experiences, and my racial identity would affect what people would decide to tell me. This was brought home to me most strikingly when I interviewed three women on a Native American reservation in the Midwest where I had extended family. Despite my family connection, the comfortable setting, and the ease I felt interviewing in a location I had enjoyed many times in the past, I was startled by the pointed question the tribal historian put to me before the interview began:

"Are you a racist?"

I fumbled for an honest answer. Could I say, truly, that I hadn't internalized the racist stereotypes about Native Americans that I had learned from movies and television as a child? Could I honestly say I had not been taught throughout my education—and indeed, my career—that my own European American culture, "the dominant culture," was superior to anything that "non-whites" had to offer? Could I say that I understood, viscerally, that the impoverishment, substance abuse, and suicide on so many Native American reservations are directly related to the history of extermination and its partner, the "Indian schools," and are not simply the fault of individuals who make poor life choices? No, I could not. But if I agreed that I was indeed a racist, what was I doing there?

Seeing my confusion, the tribal historian went right to the heart of her concern: "I mean, are you going to look down on Indian people and write racist things about our community?"

INTRODUCTION 5

"No, certainly not," I answered, with some relief.

"Okay then. We just needed to know. Because we've dealt with too many people like that before."

With white interviewees, too, interviewing is not a straightforward thing. Whites are often reluctant to talk about race at all, and when they do, they try very hard to say what they think the interviewer wants to hear, especially if they have little understanding of how race works in this country and how they themselves are implicated. My being white may have given my white respondents confidence initially, but they were also on the lookout for my political stance, my inclination to judge them for their views, my motive for writing this book, and my own experience with race. It would be better to be open about these things, I thought. If I were to simply ask them objective-sounding questions without divulging a hint of my personal background or point of view, they might be even less likely to give me honest, detailed answers. And to add to the complexity, I knew that my gender, age, profession, dialect, accent, regional identification, socioeconomic class, and immigrant status would also play into these perceptions. So to make the interviews as real as possible, I conducted my one- to two-hour interviews more like intimate conversations than straight question and answer sessions. And while I know that my respondents' remarks would have been different if I had been a different person, my interviewees, all 87 of them, have given me some remarkable material. I have foregrounded their stories, their words, and their emotions as much as possible throughout the book. To preserve privacy, and in some cases, to protect job security, I have avoided mentioning specific institutions, departments, or workplaces, and I have used pseudonyms unless a respondent specifically asked to be identified by name.

I have been delighted at the variety of areas of the country I was able to cover in my travels. I soon discovered that many of my interviewees had studied, worked, or lived in several different areas of the country and the world, so they were able to compare their diverse experiences with race. They talked about life in a great variety of places: Michigan, Massachusetts, New York, New Jersey, Pennsylvania, Maine, North Carolina, Florida, Georgia, Arizona, Colorado, Idaho, Washington, Hawaii, Puerto Rico, Saipan, Haiti, Costa Rica, China, Britain, Senegal, and South Africa. I interviewed people mostly as individuals and occasionally in groups of three or four, almost always in person and occasionally by Skype. I talked with 53 females and 34 males: 27 identified as African American or black; 5 as Native American; 7 as Latino, Hispanic, or Latin American; 2 as Asian; 12 as biracial or multiracial; and

# 6 FRACTURED: RACE RELATIONS IN "POST-RACIAL" AMERICAN LIFE

34 as white. They were undergraduate and graduate students at colleges large and small around the country. They were graduate student instructors, professors, deans, program directors, and administrative staff. They were community relations specialists, community organizers, international students, and primary school educators. They were high school students, high school teachers, moms, and dads. They ranged in age from 16 to about 80. There was no way I could pack all their wonderful stories into this book. But each of their observations and personal experiences added to my own understanding of how race and class work in this country, and this has made the book more nuanced, more informed, and I hope, more convincing.

In addition to these interviews, my explanations of racial history, current racial incidents, and the new civil rights movement that you will find in this book, have been informed by the writings of scholars of race and law, by historians and philosophers of color, and by videos, Internet blogs, news reports, lectures, student activist meetings, political demonstrations, conference proceedings, and reports from human rights organizations. Above all, my understanding of race and my evolving political point of view have been formed by my 22 years of teaching about race, racism, human rights, international development, and nonviolent social movements at the University of Michigan. My beliefs about race and class and my social justice orientation will, I hope, be evident throughout this book.

I began my interviews in the summer of 2013. One year later, as I was about halfway through the writing, Michael Brown was shot, Ferguson exploded, and a new civil rights movement took off across the country. My last two chapters, Chapter 6, "Racism as a Complex System," and Chapter 7, "The Way Forward," are centered on these events.

My profound thanks are due to each of my interview respondents, my hosts at various institutions, and the patient readers of my drafts as this book took shape. But most of all, I want to thank you, the reader, for your courage and open heart as you begin reading this book. I hope you discuss it widely, in class, in book clubs, in religious institutions, with your parents and friends, with your roommates, your teachers, and the higher-ups at your schools and workplaces. Feel free to disagree with me. But listen closely to the voices that speak to you of things you may not have heard or thought deeply about before.

Helen Fox
Gainesville, Florida
February 2015

# · 1 ·

# "THIS TOWN IS SO LIBERAL, THERE'S NO SUCH THING AS RACE."

Kay has been cooking the last two days: fried chicken, collard greens, macaroni and cheese, sweet potato casserole. "Really stereotypical," she laughs. "But good. Fantastic, in fact." How does she identify racially? "I'm black (*confidently*). And white (*jovially*). I think (*hesitantly*). Actually, that's a really good question," she says, piling the crispy chicken onto a platter. "I generally identify myself as black. But I acknowledge that my mother is white, or if you want to look at it ethnically, our family's white side is Russian, German, and Austrian. On my dad's side, we don't know. We can't trace it. Somewhere in Africa, of course. Our people were probably slaves."

Kay is curious about my interest in this "post-racial" era and eager to tell me what she's been thinking. Race has been on her mind as long as she can remember, she says, but only recently has she begun to make sense of it. Tonight, two of Kay's high school friends, Emma and Troy, along with their moms, have joined Kay's family and me for dinner before I interview the teens. We load up our plates at the kitchen island and eat quickly, standing up, murmuring our approval. The moms have to go soon; they've got evening meetings. The rest of us grab huge oatmeal cookies and settle ourselves on the living room couch. I turn on the recorder and explain my project: I'm asking people all over the country to talk about their experience of race and racism in what some commentators are calling "post-racial" America. I'm starting my journey in September 2013 in a small, middle-class, college town that prides itself on its progressive politics, its ardent support of education, and its friendly, low-key, community life. "Multiculturalism" is a given here. Although the town has been traditionally white since its founding in the early 1700s, the local public high school, one of the best in the nation, has recently achieved a diversity quotient of 40% students of color.

"Like one in five kids in our school is black," Kay explains. "But that doesn't mean we're 20% African American. We've got a lot of Cape Verdean students, and a lot of 'half' kids, like Puerto Rican and black."

"And then we have around 10% Asian," adds Troy.

"Asian is a huge category, right?" I remind them. "What's the largest Asian group at your school?"

"Maybe Chinese?" Troy says. He doesn't really know. Troy identifies as white; his European roots, he suggests, are not particularly relevant.

"I think they're Korean," says Emma. "Or maybe Japanese?" Emma says that she considers herself to be white. She says *white* crisply, as if she has recognized the significance of the term only recently and is still a bit uncomfortable with it. She would prefer to talk about her "two halves"—her father's people are German and Russian Jews, she says, and her mother's great grandparents came to America from Ireland to escape the potato famine.

"I'd guess another 10% of the kids at our school are Latino," adds Troy. "And then there's a few Indians—Asian Indians, maybe two in each class. And some Vietnamese and some uh—Cambodians, maybe like 3%, total."

"What about the teachers and the administration?"

"Ninety-five percent white," says Kay, after some thought. "And the staff, I mean the custodial staff, is a hundred percent black."

"Interesting dynamic, don't you think?"

Kay nods. She has been thinking about what this occupational disparity means for the black students as they consider their future. And not just the black students, she says. There's a message in it for everyone.

"So how would you describe the racial climate at your school?" I ask.

Kay laughs. "This town is so liberal, there's no such thing as race. Supposedly."

Emma takes Kay's hand affectionately. "Okay, this is interesting," Emma says. "I guess this is going to sound really bad, but before I got to know Kay, I had mostly white friends. And I actually thought that was fine, you know? Our school has always been proud of its welcoming environment. That's what

## "THIS TOWN IS SO LIBERAL, THERE'S NO SUCH THING AS RACE." 9

our school is about, inclusiveness and diversity. So before this year I would have said we had no racial problems at all. Even though I didn't see any particular interaction between whites and students of color, it seemed so normal it was hardly noticeable. And the way I used to think was, 'Oh, we're all just friends with whoever we're friends with—color has nothing to do with it.'"

"But then?" I ask.

"But then I followed Kay into a world that I had not experienced before, and I was shocked to find out how many students of color at our school are angry."

"Angry or really, *really* frustrated and discouraged," says Kay. "Some of them are so fed up, they're not even angry anymore."

"Fed up with what?"

Troy and Emma both reach for the microphone at once.

"The white kids," says Emma. "And the teachers. And the curriculum."

"The silence about race," says Troy. "And our liberal town that thinks it's so 'kind, safe, and fair,' as my middle school motto goes, that we don't have any racial issues."

"Kind, safe, and fair?" says Emma, incredulous. "Is that what they said?"

"Yeah," Troy says, laughing self-consciously.

"Mostly the students of color are angry at the way they've been excluded at every turn," says Kay. "But the white students are generally unaware of this, like Emma and Troy were before we started having a lot of intense conversations about race."

"So there are different opinions about the racial climate, then?"

"I think it's more accurate to say that there are groups of students with different levels of awareness about what's really going on," says Kay. "Let me try to break it down for you. First, there's a large group—the white kids, basically—that thinks there's no problem. Not that they think race isn't pertinent, but that our school—it's welcoming, it's good, we're diverse, so—it's fine. Then there's a population of kids whose second language is English, and they're stuck in classrooms way off in the back of the school and I have *no* idea what they think, to be frank. Then there's a small group of black kids who are integrated among the white kids who take more honors classes. And basically, they go along with the idea that everything's fine, even if they kind of sense it's not fine, you know? I guess before this year I would have been seen as part of that group."

"You *were* part of that group," says Emma gently. "Or that's what it seemed like to me." "True," Kay admits, laughing a bit sheepishly. "But then there's a group of black kids who only hang out with other black kids, or Indian kids, or Latino kids, who are very, very *angry* at *everybody* in our school."

"That's what's so weird," says Troy. "I never knew this before Kay started talking about it."

"These are the kids who are frustrated and fired up all the time," continues Kay. "Basically, their thing is that they've wanted to take honors classes and they've had encounters with staff where they've been told they're not good enough, and they're *sick* of it. And then there's another group of black kids, mainly the black males at our school, who have had those racialized experiences and kind of want to talk about them but instead, they've internalized their frustration. So that creates a situation where there's a portion of the school that's fed up and the other portion that doesn't think there's a problem. And that's a really weird disparity that shouldn't exist if there was any real communication among the different groups. Not to mention a welcoming environment."

"Tell me more about the frustrations of students of color," I ask Kay. "How have they been told they're not good enough?"

Kay sighs. "Honestly, our school is so segregated, you can glance into any classroom and know whether it's an honors class or not. It's that simple. A non-honors class will be mostly black and Latino with a few white kids. An honors class will be mostly white kids with one or two Asian kids, maybe one black kid, maybe not even one black kid. And the result is that a lot of the kids of color in our school end up going to community college—if they go to college at all. And this in a town that is *obsessed* with sending kids to college! Our school has sent students to *amazing* colleges, but then there's that disparity, that division by race. Yet all you ever hear is, 'Oh no, discrimination doesn't happen in our town.' That's the one that really drives me crazy: 'Prejudice isn't relevant here. We're colorblind.'"

"So this might be a difficult question, but I've heard people say, 'Well, those kids who aren't going to college just didn't work hard enough to get into the honors classes or even to get into college at all.' What's your take on that?"

Troy raises his hand as if he is in class. "I can answer that," he says, ignoring Emma and Kay, who are laughing at his earnestness. "When I was in middle school, the teachers there—and I *loved* my teachers—they always gave me encouragement to go above and beyond what I thought I wanted to do and often above and beyond the assignment. But I didn't see the same attitude towards people who weren't white. What I noticed was that teachers automatically put the kids of color with the white kids who didn't want to do any work. That's not to say that there were no kids of color that teachers paid attention to. But in order to be one of those kids, you had to be really excelling and really showing interest in your school work. But the *second* you were like, quiet, or didn't seem to show interest, then you were sort of relegated to a lower level. And even though I'm pretty sure the teachers did this unconsciously, that lack of encouragement ends up making a big difference to kids of color for a long time. Because if you haven't been challenged or successful in middle school, you're probably not going to get into honors classes in high school."

"That's right," says Kay. "And since there are no role models to help them deal with the ways they've been ignored and excluded, those kids either turn off or use up a lot of emotional energy getting angry, which can get in the way of their getting any work done. So when junior year comes around and the kids in the honors track are applying to top colleges, most of the kids of color are left behind. And what's making them so mad is that they *know* they didn't start out any different from their middle school peers."

"So it might *look* like they didn't work hard enough," says Troy, "and it might be true that some of them actually *didn't* work hard enough, but it's really more complicated than that."

"So it's kind of subtle," I say.

"Maybe it would be subtle to white people," says Kay. "But not to the people who have to experience it."

"Mmm, good point," I say, conscious for the first time in the conversation of my race. "Great point, in fact."

"So right now, there are all these lost teenagers at our school who just get together and *vent*," continues Kay. "And when they complain to the administration, which they do periodically, the response is always, 'Oh, not in *our* town. You're overreacting. You're being overdramatic.' And of course, that makes them even angrier. I think this process of teachers separating white kids from kids of color has been going on in our town for a long time. It's never been addressed in an intergenerational way. And what scares me most is that if nobody's talking about it or doing anything about it, then maybe they think that's the way things are *supposed* to be."

"That *is* kind of shocking," I reply. "You're saying that if people in this town really believe they have achieved equality and equal opportunity but at the same time they ignore the disproportionate results they might actually believe that students of color just can't cut it?"

"Yeah," says Kay. "What else could they be thinking?"

"They might point to you and say, 'Why can't the others be like this great student?'"

"My parents are both professors," Kay reminds me. "They've always pushed me to learn, learn, learn. So I guess I've been one of 'those kids' that Troy was talking about who were motivated and on top of things from day one. My teachers have always liked me. But I'm a little afraid to think too deeply about *why* they like me so much. Is it because I'm more like them? Is it to prove to themselves they're not racist? I honestly don't know."

A moment of uncomfortable silence follows this remark, as I think back on the high achieving students of color I've taught over my university career. Have I been one of those teachers, I wonder? Have I been partial to students of color who show unusual initiative without asking myself what I might have been doing to further discourage the silent ones, the poor writers, the absentees, the unprepared? I have learned, mostly from what I've read, that the achievement gap between whites, who tend to have more resources, and students of color, who are disproportionately poor, is caused by inadequate schools in low-income neighborhoods, poorly trained teachers, the demands on parents who work multiple low-wage jobs, and the lack of "cultural capital" in impoverished homes: the sophisticated dinner table conversations, the access to computers, the number of books on the living room shelves, the educational achievements of the parents and their ability to help with homework. It's harder, at least for me, to see how teachers' unconscious racial biases might contribute to the problem, or even cause it, in this case. This beautiful, little East Coast town is not plagued by poverty. Its schools are all top-notch. Its politics are progressive. Teachers earn above-average salaries and are excited about their work. Yet the achievement gap persists. Students of color are furious about it. And Troy, who has only just begun to reflect on his experiences as a young white male, is a witness to the way teachers' unconscious attitudes sort kids by race. I agree with Kay; it's disconcerting to think too deeply about these issues.

So I forge ahead: "Kay, I'd like to go back to my earlier question about racial climate. You're saying that the main issue for students of color is about getting into honors classes and the different educational outcomes by race, right? But Emma is focusing on the social things: who she knows, who her friends are, who interacts with whom. That seems really different from the issue of academic segregation."

"Maybe the whole honors/non-honors thing is how the social separation begins as well," says Emma, laughing nervously. "Since I'm in all honors

"THIS TOWN IS SO LIBERAL, THERE'S NO SUCH THING AS RACE." 13

classes, I almost never interact with students of color, except for the few I see in class every day, like Kay. We have honors classes with the same kids year after year. So I never see the majority of the kids of color except in the halls, or at lunch, or in an afterschool club if I decide to join one. So that sets up this whole idea of, 'Oh, we must be different because we live in these two different worlds.'"

"Once I started thinking about it, I realized how few friends of color I really have," says Troy. "In fact, I have very few that I can name. Like three?" Troy's honesty is so comical that Kay and Emma begin to giggle uncontrollably.

"But then I have *so* many white friends that I can name," continues Troy, undaunted. "I mean, I used to think, 'This school is so diverse, and I have this friend of color and that friend of color! *Ow!* I'm set!' But just having a few friends of color who— "

"Never mention race," says Kay.

"Because race isn't supposed to be an issue," adds Emma.

"Yeah," agrees Troy. "Having a few friends like that is really different from knowing what most students of color are thinking and experiencing at our school. So there's this huge separation. And as I've become more aware of what's going on, I've started noticing how I'm actually helping to keep that separation going. When I walk by, say, a group of Latino students, I'm sub-consciously saying to myself, 'Oh, that's the Latino group. I don't know them. I don't really need to know them.' And I know it's like, bad, but whenever I walk by *any* group of culturally different, or I guess racially different people, I'm ignoring them. I'm telling myself, 'They're not like me, so I don't even know how I would talk to them.' And I don't think I'm alone in thinking that."

Kay nods. "So there's a barrier that's been set up between the honors kids and the non-honors kids for a long time and that's developed into two dif-ferent worlds. And that means the amount of time that white kids and kids of color actually get to communicate is very small, unless they're making an active effort to be part of the other group, and people almost never try to do that."

Emma sighs deeply and takes Kay's hand again. "I hate to say this, but for a white student, it feels *strange* to make that effort in our school. You don't want to be that first one. And because race is never talked about and the racial separation is never addressed, if you try to actually make friends with a group of kids of color, you feel like you're not, like, in the right *place*. And if you're not in the right place, you feel awkward and uncomfortable. So obviously there must be an issue there. But in our school there are no racial issues, right?

So it's kind of terrifying. Because trying to integrate a lunch table brings up what you don't want to think about, which is that in fact, race is a *central* issue at our school. If you have to *force* yourself to approach an unfamiliar racial or cultural group, then *obviously* there's an issue." Emma says this with great intensity, as if both her anxiety about race and her need to say something genuine about it are compelling her to explain what's been roiling inside.

"So tell me more about how kids are raised here. I want to understand how this all gets started."

"Basically, from day one, little kids in this town are seeing racial stereotypes on TV," Kay explains. "Like on some sitcom there's the Indian friend with an accent that makes him sound like he's an idiot. Or the Korean girl who ignores her nice, white roommate for no reason and only talks gibberish with her Korean friends. And then of course there's the perennial favorite, the black gangbanger. But when the kids start playing off these stereotypes, they pick up this vibe that says, 'Oh no, you can't say things like that. You can't even *think* that. Like that's not right.' But those stereotypes are still so deeply engrained that the kids end up confused. They have these stereotypes about people of color that they've been conditioned to believe, but nobody's explaining how they learned them or why they're on TV in the first place. People are just telling them that they *can't* think those things because our community is so post-racial."

"Do they tell kids that overtly?"

"Not necessarily overtly, since most adults are so uncomfortable talking about race," says Kay. "But subliminally, *definitely*. The kids get the message. It gets so ridiculous in this town that even the word 'black' is an offensive term. Which it's *not!* And that shuts off conversations people could have because they're afraid of saying the wrong things. That's the best I can explain it."

Thinking about Kay's comments, I try to imagine what it would be like to be born in, say, 1998, into a progressive, white family in this community. You would have no direct experience with the themes and symbols of racism that were so prevalent in the past, and most likely, no serious discussion in your family about their connection to our country's racist history. You know that the link between blacks and fried chicken is supposed to be funny, but you don't know why. You might figure out that mimicking an Indian accent is rude and avoid it out of civility, but you might not understand why the pain of ridicule and exclusion among many Asian American families runs so deep. You suspect that asking questions about these things makes people uneasy. So if your whole town, or at least the white majority, can act as if race doesn't exist, you can avoid racial drama altogether.

But this tactic has consequences you might not expect. "One of the things I realized recently," says Emma, "is that by ignoring race and ethnicity, you're stripping people of color of some of the most important ways they define themselves. So the community might *look* diverse, but if you insist that color is not important, you're actually making it even *more* white, culturally at least. In fact, you're basically *forcing* the people of color to submit to your kind of white community, which is one where race and ethnicity don't matter. And if you can't ever talk about race, you aren't going to be able to gain enough perspective to see what's happening."

"Another consequence of the whole post-racial political correctness thing," says Kay, "is not only are you erasing people's cultures, you're also ignoring the history of oppression that people of color have faced and their strength in confronting it. That experience is where a lot of our culture comes from! So if we can't talk about cultural and racial differences, then all that music and art and literature and philosophy that has come from struggle is being undermined, too. And that's almost as harsh and cruel as oppressing people in the first place. Like, even though I can't trace my roots to a specific place in Africa, those centuries of slavery and Jim Crow and all the ways my ancestors resisted are a big part of my identity. I wouldn't want someone to be saying, 'Oh, we don't see *you* anymore!'"

"Speaking of oppression, what an issue it would be in this town if you took the Holocaust away from the Jewish community!" says Emma.

"Great example," agrees Kay. "I have a friend whose father writes books about the Holocaust, and I don't hear any of our friends say, 'Oh, he's obsessed with it; he's talking about it all the time; he needs to just get over it.' But when I talk about race, it's like, 'Not everything is about race, you know? Like, stop talking about it.' And how many people do you think died on the slave ships coming over to this country? Where did *they* all go?"

Emma and Troy nod reflectively.

"Kay, I'd like to ask you something," I say finally. "Judging from this conversation, it sounds like you've broken through the barrier of silence about race with at least some of your white friends. How did that happen?"

Kay laughs. "One thing you have to understand about this town is that even though you're not supposed to talk about race, *everyone* makes racial jokes. All the time! Including me!"

"Even against your own racial group?"

"Yes! In fact, I was the *worst!* I made the *worst* jokes. I guess at that time it was my only way of talking about racial issues. And that's how Emma and Troy and I started this conversation. With really dumb racial jokes."

"How does a post-racial town make racial jokes?" I wonder.

"It's kind of interesting," says Kay. "It's not the blatant kind of racial joke that you might find online or a joke that an outright racist might make. A post-racial, racial joke is more devious. What you do is push some stereotype to the point of offensiveness, and then you go, 'Well like obviously I don't believe that!'"

"So you make your joke and then distance yourself from the racism it implies?"

"Exactly," says Troy. "What you do is put some stereotype out there and then try to make it sound ironic or say it the way a racist would but like you *never* would. I used to do that all the time."

"Where did you learn these jokes?" I ask.

"Honestly, from just about every other white kid at our school," says Troy. "It's so common it's unbelievable. Like we would do these stereotypical things like flash gang signs or talk like drug dealers we saw on TV."

"Or you might introduce your black friend as 'my black friend' just to show how much you're not noticing that she's black," says Emma.

"Okay, here's another example," says Kay, laughing at my quizzical expression. "Last year Emma and I sang in a choir together that was all white kids with maybe three black kids and a couple of Latinos. And we sang a lot of songs from the black gospel tradition, even though we were primarily white, which I still think is hilarious. But while we would be singing, some friends in my section and I—we would do these stereotypically black things that we saw in the movies, like slapping one hand on top of the other, which I actually have never seen black people do. So we would make jokes like that and play off the black stereotypes because we thought we were above it all."

"We know it's stupid," says Troy. "But we do it *all the time*. Because there's no space to talk about race, it's the only way we can bring it up. And since we're such a liberal, PC town where everybody knows what everyone else thinks, or so they say, it's fine to make jokes about race because obviously no one is racist."

"But that's not necessarily true," Emma breaks in. "Because jokes are only funny when they're smart. So there must be something in that joke that

## "THIS TOWN IS SO LIBERAL, THERE'S NO SUCH THING AS RACE." 17

*means* something to people. Otherwise, why would the whole lunch table be laughing?"

"Yeah, if they're so amused, they must all have this common belief about the people that they're making fun of," says Kay. "Like, okay, here's a really bad one: 'What's the difference between a black man and a pizza? Answer: A pizza can feed a family of four.' Funny, huh? But then if anyone would object, you could say, 'But *obviously* I don't believe that black men can't feed their families.' So it becomes a way to get away with being racist by refusing to admit it, if that makes any sense."

"So how did telling these jokes lead to serious discussions about race?" I ask Kay.

"Well, I had sort of developed this idea in my head that if I joked about race a lot, then talking about race would become more accessible to the white people I spent time with. And in some ways it did work. I mean, that's how Emma and Troy and I started talking about it. But once I got through my joking phase, I started reading books and listening to people who know how to speak *authentically* about race. I mean, people who take the issues head on and *tell the truth* about them. So I was educating myself. I was thirsty for knowledge. And then I wanted to educate others as well. But I didn't know how to do that with people who are so deep in denial. So I used to carry books around with provocative titles. Like there's one—I don't know if I can say this...." Kay gestures toward my voice recorder hesitantly.

"Say it."

"Okay, well, the book's called *Nigger: The Strange Career of a Troublesome Word*. It's by Randall Kennedy, a Harvard law professor who's black. I don't agree with all of it, but I think it's pretty interesting. Anyway, I got the book from the library and I said, 'I'm going to carry this around wherever I go.'"

"You did that on purpose to shock people?"

"Yeah! Because at that point I had gotten past my joking phase, and I was intensely wanting my white friends to know that race was a serious issue. So I would carry that book around school and leave it prominently on my desk. I guess that was my way of trying to be authentic. Race is all around us, in our culture, on the Internet, on TV, at our school, everywhere! So let's deal with it! And that's how Emma got involved."

"Yeah," Emma breaks in. "Once we started talking, I got really fascinated. And by just listening to what Kay had to say over the past couple of months, I've realized that race is a really big issue at our school and that students of color are really upset. But when I mention what I'm learning to my white friends they say, 'Oh, they're being overdramatic about it. Not everything has to be about race! I just don't think it's that big a deal here.' And I tell them, 'Well, okay, you can say that, but I'm beginning to see and hear what that unhappiness is about, and even though I haven't been able to truly understand the root cause of that unhappiness, partly because I'm not a person of color in this school system, I just want to talk more about it. I want to get more involved. Because it's frightening to learn what people in our school are experiencing when all you ever hear is that we have such a welcoming environment. And to only find that out when I'm a senior—I've been going to school in this town since third grade! Why am I only learning about this problem now?'"

"I want to understand how there can be no mention of race in your classes if your town has such a progressive education system," I tell the teens. "Aren't you learning anything about the cultures or histories of the people of color who go to your school? Aren't you discussing current events that are all over the media like the Trayvon Martin shooting or the Redskins mascot issue?"

The three friends all shake their heads. "Most of our teachers seem really uncomfortable about bringing up anything remotely racial," says Troy. "And I think the last time I had a course centered on a culture that was not European or European American was in like third grade. And that wasn't even a culture we'd recognize today. I think it was, like, ancient Egypt."

"Really!"

"And the only other class that touches on other ethnic groups is English Lit," Troy continues. "And there we learn by reading novels, so even if it's about a different culture, you don't really think about it too deeply. It doesn't really affect you."

"Are you saying that if it's not about *you* it's not relevant?"

"Um, yeah," says Troy. "I know that sounds really bad."

"Maybe that was a bit harsh, the way I put it."

"Not really," says Troy. "I mean, it's true."

"What about in your history classes? I would think that a school that prepares students for top U.S. colleges would want you to know quite a bit about the rest of the world."

"We *are* taught a lot of history," says Kay. "But I think most of those classes are very Euro or American based. Even World Civilizations, which is mandatory, is still primarily focused on Europe, especially on the Greeks and Romans, which is where 'our' civilization, as they call it, comes from."

## "THIS TOWN IS SO LIBERAL, THERE'S NO SUCH THING AS RACE." 19

"Well, what have you learned about the histories of people of color in the United States? Like how did Chinese people originally get to this country, or the Koreans, or the Hmong, who I've seen around town?"

"I don't know. I have no idea!" laughs Troy. "It's really not funny, but...."

"Not only that, we study almost no African American history," says Kay. "We have no modern African history. I know *so* little about Asia. I don't mean only East Asia. I mean every *part* of Asia. Western Asia, South Asia, Southeast Asia, I don't know *anything*. I wish I did, but I don't. And then we study ancient African civilizations for about two seconds."

"You *must* learn something about the civil rights movement."

"Sure, we study that," says Troy. "For about two and a half weeks."

"What I remember about U.S. history, which I took in 10th grade, so that's two years ago, is about the Japanese Americans during World War II," says Emma. "And that was like a *big* thing in our class, maybe even bigger than the civil rights movement. I remember people being like, 'Wow!' That was probably the only time we addressed race relations in the U.S."

"But people didn't really care about it; they didn't like, relate," says Troy. "We just sort of said, 'Oh, that's not us, and we don't really understand their culture and we don't really understand them so why should we really care? I mean, it's terrible that Americans sent Japanese Americans to internment camps, but so what?' Like I said, it doesn't really affect our lives, you know?"

"U.S. history was really hard for me," says Kay quietly. "I was the only black kid in my class. We started with the Reconstruction era after the Civil War and moved through industrialization at the end of the 19th century and then the Harlem Renaissance, which was pretty prominent. We talked about that quite a bit. In fact, we watched a whole video on it. So you might think that's a pretty good attempt at being multicultural. But what I've realized looking back on it is that basically, in U.S. history, we study blacks in a white context. You know, like how blacks were fitting in to what was going on for the white majority."

"Yeah, Kay and I talked about this," adds Emma. "It's always like white is the default. And then we study, 'Oh, and black people were there too.'"

"In the Industrialization unit, we watched a film made in the 1940s about the 1880s that didn't mention an African American soul," says Kay. "Actually, I think my teacher did that on purpose, because she was an *excellent* teacher. I *loved* the way she taught that class. She did a lot with what she could. The video was all about—industry! Happy times! It didn't mention blacks, who were being horribly persecuted under Jim Crow. It didn't mention Native

Americans, who were being wiped out. And even though we didn't really talk about it much in class, I think she chose that film to give us a sort of clue as to how most Americans saw this country back then, which was—*white*, completely and totally. And then later, when we watched a film about the black power movement, that was very emotional for me. But I didn't really have anybody to look to or talk about my feelings with because I was by myself in that class."

"Why was it emotional for you, Kay?"

"I think it's because watching that video, it suddenly hit me that all along I had been learning about how I didn't fit into this country."

"Wow," says Troy.

"But it's true," says Emma. "That's the way history is taught. This country is basically white, and everyone who isn't white is kind of an add-on. But if I were to tell that to my white friends, they would reject it right away. I think the scariest experience I've had over the last few months is that when I initiate a conversation about race with only white people, I start to change my ideas back to what I thought before. Because the white kids start saying, 'Yeah, but not everything has to be about race. What about poverty issues? Some people just aren't focusing on their schoolwork.' And then what I've learned from Kay all goes out the window, and I start thinking, 'Hey, I'm white too. Shouldn't my views be fitting in with what these kids are saying? Isn't that a better way for me to look at it?' And that *terrifies* me, because there shouldn't be a 'white way' to see things if we're ever going to build community. But even though no one will admit it, there *is* a 'white way' of seeing racial issues. And to agree with that way is like coming back to your home base, like your *safety*. It's what you've been learning all your life."

Kay is nodding. "It's a relief to hear someone say that, even if it's depressing."

"So guys, if you were in charge of your school, how would you change things?" I ask.

Kay brightens up immediately. "I have *so* many ideas about that," she says. "I would untrack all the classes in each and every discipline. And I would physically integrate all the classroom areas. Like my teacher was telling me about how students with mental disabilities are in the back of the school? The back corner, the oldest corner. These are the kids who need para-professionals with them at all times during the school day. A lot of teachers apparently don't want them anywhere near their classrooms because they can be disruptive. But I think it's weird and kind of upsetting that they're kept in the back

# "THIS TOWN IS SO LIBERAL, THERE'S NO SUCH THING AS RACE." 21

where almost no one goes, except the English Language Learners, the ELL's, who are also in that back corridor."

"I don't even know the room where the ELL students are!" says Emma. "And I thought I knew this school inside and out."

"Doesn't that kind of send a message?" asks Kay. "And then, I would make—this might be kind of painful for them, but I would make every single teacher in our school, including administrators, facilitate a conversation about race in their classroom. And I think a lot of them would miserably fail," she laughs. "In fact, I'm very confident that a lot of them wouldn't be able to do it. At least then, they'd know that race *is* an issue at our school and that they should start thinking about how to deal with it professionally. Also, I'm sure that honors and non-honors kids can learn in the same classroom. We've already had a demonstration of that. Can you believe this? The English Department had an honors African American literature class, which was all white, right next door to a non-honors African American literature class, which was all black. They were separated by folding doors? And so one day the teachers opened up the doors and mixed all the kids together because they were *sick* of that ridiculous situation. And it went fine."

"What about you, Emma? What would you change?

"I'm not sure. Right now, I'm so new to these conversations, I can't tell what the school should look like. I just think there should be space for people to talk about it. So I love the idea of having facilitated conversations about race, and I think they should happen a lot."

"Troy?"

"Well, for me, the wake-up call was a very emotional meeting of students of color that I ended up at a few months ago—long story. But at this meeting, a lot of kids were crying—I mean seriously, *crying* about the situations they had been put in at school. And I had *absolutely* no idea. I mean, Kay had told me before that kids were upset, but I had sort of disregarded it. But then I actually heard them talk about the tough situations they were experiencing, like the white people at this school disrespecting them and then saying there are no problems here, and teachers not giving them the same opportunities as others, and all the things we've been talking about tonight. And that one meeting had such an impact on me. It made me want to change my ways. Not necessarily change other people, but change myself. That's why I'm trying to stop making racial jokes. And I'm trying to be more conscious about what goes through my head when I see groups of students of color in the halls. At least that's a start. So I wonder, if everyone had the opportunity to hear these students' stories firsthand in a space where kids feel comfortable talking honestly about their experiences, I think there could be a noticeable change in the school environment. Because even though I've said a few times tonight that we have a hard time really caring about people from different backgrounds because we think they're not like us or because they have nothing to do with our lives, we're really not that coldhearted. Actually, I think if I can change, so can a lot of other white kids at this school. I mean, you can kind of see that a lot of them really *want* to talk about race, even if they do it unproductively."

Kay smiles at her friends. "To have people around like Emma and Troy is really encouraging to me," she says. "Because there's a sort of energy and fire people get when they start to see what's really going on. I know that I can get kind of relentless about it, but things are so much better since we've started talking about this stuff in an authentic way. I tell them about the things I've been reading and recommend books. And that opens up new doorways and new conversations, which are always so interesting! I like that new sense of vigor. The fact that Troy and Emma and I have been friends for a long time has helped make these conversations possible. So I think if people can build trust, and I'm not saying that's easy, but if they do, then when they talk about race, it can be exciting."

The more I thought about this interview with Kay and her friends, the more I realized that what was happening in this small college town is emblematic of our country's so-called post-racial era that began in earnest with the Obama presidency. Like so many students at this progressive high school, the majority of white Americans, whether liberal or conservative, believe that we're pretty much over race in this country, that we don't need to agonize over it, that it's time to move on. Obviously, racial incidents still do happen, they say, but mostly in other people's towns, on other people's streets, not their own. They might have friends or coworkers of color who they see as individuals, not "as a color," but with whom they have never had a serious conversation about race. They believe that the fair thing to do is to treat everyone equally, as if race no longer exists, regardless of anyone's racialized experiences or their racial group's history, which, after all, happened long ago. If anything, many whites believe that *they* are the ones who are discriminated against through laws and practices that give people of color an unfair advantage. If people of color suggest that racism is keeping them in poverty, or blocking them from advancement, or contributing to their failure at school, many well-meaning whites will shake their heads silently, thinking how politically incorrect it would be to state the obvious: Such explanations are a way of denying responsibility. While this message is phrased in a variety of ways, depending on a person's background, their politics, the extent of their vocabulary, and their state of mind, the common view among white folks around the country is not too different from the one held by white adults and teens in Kay's liberal college town: "No one here is racist. Jokes about race are amusing, or perhaps juvenile, but in any case, they shouldn't be taken too seriously. Racial explanations for student success and failure are beside the point. And since we're so inclusive and multicultural these days, we have no need to talk about race."

Meanwhile, in communities of color, especially on college campuses, in high schools, in the workplace, on Native American reservations, in immigrant enclaves, and in the distressed urban core, the conversations, the experiences, and the emotions that I encountered while conducting these interviews have sounded strikingly different. Even though I have studied and taught about race, racism, and culture for over 20 years, I have been astonished at the extent of the separation between people of color and whites in this country. Physical separation, experiential, economic, emotional, conversational, you name it, we are living in worlds as different as those inhabited by white students and students of color in this progressive high school.

But regardless of the ways whites dismiss the significance of race, they are still encountering it, still commenting on it, still embarrassed by it. In their private conversations they might mention the personal failings of people whose lives and choices they disapprove of and who also "happen to be" people of color. They might point to poor study habits, or inadequate parenting, or lack of respect for authority. They might mention the violence and misogyny of rap music, the backwardness of a particular culture or religion, or the need to obey immigration laws like their own ancestors surely did. When people of color take to the street in protest, whites might shift the conversation from the grievances that sparked the demonstration to the violence of the few. They might claim that economic class is the villain these days, so it would be better to focus our efforts at reform on the outrageously wealthy 1%. They might point either with pride or alarm to the new diversity in parts of the country that were formerly white or to the efforts at bringing more students of color to elite high schools and colleges. No matter what their politics, they tend to equate the mere presence of people of color in formerly white spaces with a fully integrated community.

But what is remarkable to me, and hopeful, is that Kay, Emma, and Troy are beginning to examine such racialized assumptions and practices more deeply—if largely on their own. They are reflecting on their experiences as children, recalling the ways they were affected by media images, and realizing how their peers were treated differently from themselves. They are noticing that their groups of friends are not as diverse as they once thought, and they are tracing the details of how that happened and why. They are beginning to see how racial inequality is unintentionally promoted at their school: how smart, caring educators set a social and political agenda that excludes students of color; how they design and teach curricula that minimize minority histories; how they decide, consciously or not, which racial groups will go on to college; and how they silence frustrated students who see the situation all too clearly and want to speak *authentically* about it, as Kay would say.

The dawning insight of these teens mirrors what scholars of race have been saying for a long time: Racism is an insidious system of control that is held in place by white-normalized procedures and practices and by the attitudes, both conscious and unconscious, of well-meaning people who are unwilling to think deeply about how race privilege works. And now that we've been declared "post-racial," facing this uncomfortable fact as a nation has become even harder. For if we don't see race, how can we see injustice?

# · 2 ·

# ARE WE POST-RACIAL YET?

With the election of Barack Obama as the 44th president of the United States in 2008, the media seized on the term *post-racial* to highlight how far our nation had come since the turmoil and struggle of the 1960s. By the time President Obama gave his 2010 State of the Union address, the theme of unification and racial healing had become so widespread that commentators were beginning to report transient moments of color blindness. As he watched the address, MSNBC's Chris Matthews told his audience how startling the moment was for him. The speech was so broad-ranging in scope, he said, so in tune with so many problems and aspects of American life, that he forgot, for an hour, that the president was black.

"It's interesting," Matthews mused. "[President Obama] is post-racial, by all appearances... I was watching and I said, wait a minute, he's an African American guy in front of a bunch of... white people and there he is, the President of the United States and we have completely forgotten that [he is black] tonight, *completely* forgotten it."[1]

Had we really forgotten the president's race, I wondered? Who, exactly, was the "we" Matthews was referring to? Was he thinking of people like himself, liberal whites who long for the day when race no longer matters? Or did he really believe that the whole country had achieved, if only for an hour, the dream of a color-blind society? Regarding the latter, I was doubtful.

For one thing, I didn't imagine that African Americans had forgotten they had elected the nation's first black president. And I didn't think people who were so deeply skeptical about the president's birth certificate,[2] or his middle name—*Hussein*—or his "socialist" plans for taking over the country[3] found his race irrelevant. Even the idea that young, white Obama supporters who had worked so exuberantly for the election of this smart, progressive guy with an international consciousness and an African father could see the president as raceless only 14 months later seemed deeply suspicious to me, especially after my conversation with Kay, Emma, and Troy about what was going on in their town where "there is no such thing as race." I wondered if anyone actually believes our country is completely "over" our racial problems, or if not, that at least we are heading in that direction. Or is a post-racial society an achievable goal?

"What do you think is meant by the term post-racial, and how far do you think we've come, as a country, toward achieving it?" I asked variations on this question to 87 high school and college students, scholars, teachers, administrators, community leaders, tribal members, and ordinary folks in my travels across the country. Literally everyone I talked to laughed at the idea— some hilariously, some derisively, some, especially the younger people, more politely.

"I think the idea that this country is post-racial is some kind of fantastical wish-fulfillment," says a white woman who worked for years as a community organizer in Brooklyn. "The pain of racial inequality is always with us, and that is hard for people of color to bear. But white people don't want to bear it either. So I think that there's a rush, at least on the part of white folks, to plant a flag every time we possibly can, that says 'Hey, we're at the post racial moment; we've actually *healed* this thing.' But clearly, it's not true!"

An art educator at a New York City college agrees. "I think what people mean by post-racial is this whole colorblind business," she says. "'Oh look. We've solved it. Done and done!' But then there's the flip side to it. I have a brother-in-law—a white guy—who still uses the n-word. And his take is that things have just gotten worse. 'I'm working hard,' he says. 'Why can't *they* work hard?' '*They*' meaning anyone who is black or brown and poor."

"White students, in particular, have that attitude of 'what's left to talk about?'" says a white instructor of women's studies at a university in the Northwest. "When I ask them what they think about racial disparities, they'll say, 'Oh, we're *so* much further now! It's *so* much better now. We've come *so* far!' But when I ask them about the conditions on the Native American reservations in our area, they say, 'Oh, *they're* not suffering. Look at all the money they make off all those white people with the casinos. We give them all our money!' That kind of mentality. So they think Native Americans are doing just *fine* for themselves, when in fact there is chronic poverty on the reservations in our area. But it's funny; they'll claim everyone's equal, but then they'll immediately follow that with examples of discrimination against white people. White students get *real* upset about scholarships because they think they're not going to get any since they're all going to minorities. They don't realize that minority-specific scholarships make up less than 1% at this school. And even when I give them the facts, it doesn't seem to shake their conviction much."

"*Oh* my goodness, this country is *definitely not* post racial!" says a Chinese American graduate student who has lived and worked on every continent. "You can see it the minute your plane lands in the U.S. You just look around at the work force! I step out of the plane in say, New Jersey, and who's working in the restaurants? Who's taking my luggage around? You've got the South Asians, you've got the Hispanics, you've got African Americans, all in the lowest paid jobs. And going back to my old neighborhood in Florida where I used to teach in a community college, you see *so* much more neighborhood segregation nowadays. The African Americans are on one street, Cubans on another, the Chinese on a third. And just listening to my college friends, white families from Alabama, defending the 'Southern way.' They're on the defensive. They feel they're being attacked and looked down on. They want to retain 'their way of life,' as they call it. So I do see people who are interested in race. They're not running away from it. But I really don't think they're that interested in solving it. Yeah, I don't think this country is post racial at all."

It's not only Southerners who harbor nostalgia for a racist past. A white woman at a fish fry in Northern Michigan expresses her relief at moving home from multi-ethnic California: "We came back to America!" A teacher who grew up in a wealthy white enclave in the Midwest describes her parents' neighborhood: "These people don't see themselves as antiquated or racist, but rather, as protecting a 'way of life.' That bland, inoffensive phrase blurs over the negativity and hatred at the core of their philosophy and disguises it as a kind of nostalgia. Wealthy Conservatives are much quieter than the Confederate flag wavers in the South, but they're equally protective."

"I do think that in my lifetime, huge progress has been made," admits a white, senior, English professor at a small Jesuit college. "It would be silly to not say so. Same thing for women, same for gays, huge progress has been made, especially in relatively liberal areas of the country. But all I have to do is turn on the radio or the TV and listen to one of the Neanderthal newscasters, and it's so clear that *nothing* has changed! *Nothing!* But whether they like it or not, some aspects of America *are* changing rapidly. Just look at the demographics—by midcentury, people of color will outnumber whites. It's the old truism, fear of change, fear of losing power. Whites are feeling threatened. So they hold on to the old idea that even if you're the poorest white man in the land, you can still look down on *somebody!* Even if you're middle class, you can still think, 'Oh, I'm better than *that* person. They wouldn't even *be* here if it weren't for affirmative action.' And you can do this at the same time you're insisting that you're color-blind. That's post-racialism in a nutshell."

"Why do you think people hold such contradictory attitudes these days?" I ask her.

"I think for the vast majority of people there is a very real recognition that to say someone is racist is to say they're not a good person," the English professor replies. "Almost everyone, except maybe the neo-Nazis, knows you shouldn't be racist nowadays. Yet a lot of people harbor this intense arrogance around race. You know, '*I'm* not a racist; it just happens to be that where I work all the people of color are incompetent!' 'Oh, and it's not *all* people of color; it's just everyone I know!' It's self-delusional. I think that for most people, it's not that intentional, malicious kind of racism. It's just that the vast majority of people want to feel good about themselves and say, 'I'm past racism! And now I don't have to think about it or push hard against any possible complicity on my part.'"

"Why do you think so many whites claim to be color-blind?" I ask a young, white educator who works with aspiring middle and high school teachers in New York City.

"I have a lot of students, particularly whites, who say, 'I want to see all my students as the same. I don't see color. I just see people for who they are,'" she replies. "I sometimes think these people are genuinely hopeful. But on the other hand, maybe they think this way because they don't want to do the work. If you can say, 'Look, all our country's racial problems are already taken care of, so I don't have to worry anymore,' that makes life a little easier, doesn't it? It takes a lot of work to create a community that's multiracial and that has economic diversity within it. Even friendships across race and class are challenging. Personally, I'm willing to do that work. It's difficult because it has to be so conscious and intentional. But if whites can just claim we're post-racial, if it just *happens* that my friends and neighbors all look like me, then you don't have to take responsibility anymore. I think maybe that's what it is. It's just easier."

To get at the differences between communities in more depth, I talked to people of color at a variety of colleges and universities, large and small, about their experiences in this "post-racial" era. Katie is from Saipan, a 7-by 14-mile U.S. territory in the South Pacific. Her mom is Filipino and her dad, "I guess is Caucasian, white American, Irish—he's from the Midwest." It's Katie's second semester at a large research university, and her brain is fried. She's getting ready to take a semester off "to go back to the simple life on the island of Saipan just to see what I'm inclined to do when nothing and no one is *telling* me what to do." She has her parents' blessing to take a break, she says. They know how hard she worked at her private high school in order to achieve admission to a demanding university. But besides the constant studying, Katie is stressed out about what happened when she rushed a "top tier" sorority earlier this semester. This is what she wants to talk about, and it is what drew her to my call for interviewees. She is not used to being patronized, she says. In fact, just being seen as "Asian" was a shock when she arrived in the United States. People don't seem to be interested in where she's from or the interesting ethnic mix in her extended family's background, she says. They just assume she's some kind of Asian they're familiar with, like Chinese. And sometimes the "kind of Asian" she might be doesn't really matter to them. Telling me this reminds her of a disturbing incident that happened when she was hanging out one evening in the dorm room of a Mexican American friend:

"So we were just chilling, talking about this and that, when this white guy came in, took one look at me, and said in this kind of nasty, insinuating tone: '*Herrro.*' And I was *shhhhocked*. Just completely *shocked*. I couldn't even respond. I *didn't* even respond."

"How did it make you feel?"

"It really hurt my feelings, because it was so obvious that he saw me as this stereotypical Asian person who couldn't pronounce their 'L's,' or not *even* as a person, you know?"

"Did you have the impression that he thought he was being funny?"

"He was under the influence of alcohol. So I suppose he was saying what was really going through his head. He wasn't joking. In fact," Katie says softly, "it was scary because he was saying it kind of seriously. And no one laughed, you know?"

"Was that the first time you felt singled out racially?"

"No, but it was the first time it really hit me that there was something different going on in the States," says Katie. "It's not like this at home. On Saipan there are people from literally around the world, from Mongolia, to Russia, to Thailand, to the Philippines, to Canada, they're all there. And because the island is so small there's absolutely no space for segregation. So the way I grew up was that everyone could define who they were, because everyone was different. And in a way, growing up there, every culture is your culture, because you're so physically close to everyone else. You eat all kinds of ethnic food, which I think is a close connector to culture. And you hear all these languages *all the time*. And every office building is made up of different businesses: Filipino shops, and lawyers, who are mostly white, really, and restaurant owners that are Chinese; and then there are the Chamorro people, who are indigenous to the area, and they all come together, so you grow up being able to relate to any culture because you're so close to all of them. So even though there is friction sometimes, and we're not free of hierarchy between ethnic groups, we are all pretty respectful of our differences."

"So when you came to the States with that kind of critical eye about culture, what did you notice here at the university?"

"I think more than anything I notice the lack of integration of the races," says Katie. "It really hit me when I rushed for Greek life. I remember seeing, I believe, two African Americans rushing, and a handful of Indian Americans, a few more Asians or half-Asians like me, but then when I finally got into the sorority, out of 63 girls I was one of two Asians, and all the rest were white."

"How did that strike you?"

"I guess I was shocked by it," Katie says. "I suppose it's true that not that many Asians are in sororities because not many go out for Greek life. But then you have to ask, why *don't* they go out for it?"

"Do you ever talk about these issues with your friends?"

Katie pauses, looking down at her hands. "When I dropped my sorority, many people asked why I dropped."

"Oh, you dropped!" I exclaim. "How did that happen?"

"I only stayed for two months, because that was as long as I could stand it. People would say things like, 'Oh my god, you are so cute. You're so adorable.' And these were people *my age*. It was *so* condescending, I couldn't help wonder if race had something to do with it. Of course I never really clicked with them. Every conversation was so superficial—it felt like small talk that would go on and on forever. Every time I would try to say something like, 'Hey, where are you from?' —even a question like that, and that's not even that *deep!*—I could feel that they'd never had a conversation like that before. They would steer away from it as soon as they could. But on the other hand they were such nice people. It isn't their fault. I think they just grew up in that kind of environment. But there comes a point when you have to take responsibility for your life, and if you continue to be a really limited person, you *are* the one at fault. I just couldn't see them ever wanting to get away from their environment and learn more. And me being only one of two Asians, *half* Asians, really, I couldn't stop thinking about *that.* And I just hated the way they talked to me. All that time I was there I was known as 'the different one.' People would be like, 'Oh she's the *different* one.' And it was maybe because I wore things that weren't exactly like what they wore or that I talked about different things. But I also couldn't shake the fact that it must have had something to do with my race too. I remember the last thing one person said to me before I decided I was going to leave. I was saying goodbye—I'd spent the *whole* evening with her, and I was thinking, 'Hey, this is not so bad.' And the last thing she said to me was, 'You're so a*dorable.' And I'm just like—*fuck this!* Like truly, *fuck this!* Am I never going to be seen as an equal?"

I ask Katie what would help improve relationships between whites and their peers of color. After all, most white young adults believe they're not racist, that they have friends of different races, and that what's important in a friend is the "content of their character," as Martin Luther King would say, not what they look like or where they come from. Their parents or grandparents might still be holding on to a few racist attitudes, but for their generation, they believe, race is "no big deal."[4] Yet for young people of color, the experience of being "othered" by their white peers is all too common.

"I think white people have to understand that they are in the privileged group," Katie says. "They have to be conscious, and aware, and accepting of that. There are so many white people who aren't aware of that or who totally refuse to consider that and insist we're in a post-race world. They don't have to actually say 'post-race' to communicate that—they just go along as if everyone is equal, everyone has the same kinds of experiences, everyone has problems and challenges in life so why should a person's color make them any different? But if they understand that one basic thing, that being in the skin they're in *does* give them special advantages, then they can pay closer attention to how they act and speak to and treat minorities. And once they realize that, I think they can control their tendency to be condescending or arrogant or at least try their hardest to."

"And what about people of color? What do you think they can do to help change the situation?" I ask.

"My suggestion to minorities is if you know a white person who understands their privilege, try to educate them more about how you feel and how you experience life. But let's say this white person isn't aware of their privilege. That's a hard one. In that case, my advice to minorities is just—oh man!—is to try to stick around that white person who is being so condescending and arrogant and to not leave them, but stick around them so that after a certain point they see you as more than just a race. And I say that because I sometimes think about why I left that sorority and wonder if I should have stayed. That's my greatest regret, that maybe I should have stayed longer and not just left them with their prejudices. So my advice to minorities is to stick around those white people so that they finally get past your race and see you as a person."

Some of these insults ("you're so *adorable*") might appear to be small. Yet such slights exert a disproportionate effect on students of color because of our country's long history of white dominance, which is grounded, necessarily, in notions of black and brown inferiority, both socially, as in Katie's case, and intellectually, as Jawan relates:

"In my computer science classes, where I'm the one black male among two hundred or so white and Asian students, I've gotten a lot of strange looks," Jawan tells me. "Sometimes people will ask if I'm supposed to be in the class. Sometimes they even ask me, 'Are you a student? Are you sure you can handle this?' Actually, I've noticed this since high school, this assumption that when I choose higher level courses or science and math-based courses that maybe I'll not be able to do the work. I might have to get special permission from the instructor, where other students don't have to do that. And when I do get into the class, it often happens that my teachers and peers give me instructions about things that are really basic, obvious steps. Their assumption is that I'm going to need that extra explanation and that I will then follow their instructions step by step. I've noticed that happens a lot to black people. Like you don't need to be fed information! It's almost as if they see blacks as disabled. The assumption is that you're handicapped, mentally, so you need help. People simply scan you, notice your skin color or facial features, and decide you have a disability.

"Once I was just working on a little side project, not for class, just to try something interesting," Jawan continues. "I was trying to write code for a game. It was a really simple project, and because I wasn't trying to do something original, I borrowed some code from a third-party source online. And when I showed it to one of my friends, the first thing he says is, 'Well, this isn't real coding at all!' But you know, I wasn't trying to test my abilities; I was just trying to learn something more about a concept that was new to me. But he saw it as a test of the coding itself."

"So how did you react to that remark?" I ask.

"I was kind of insulted. So I asked him, 'Why would you judge this? I didn't do it to prove anything to you.' And he was like, 'Whatever, it's fine, if you say so.' That kind of immediate brush off, that discrediting of my ability, it's irritating. And it's pretty much a constant. Some people might get discouraged and maybe even decide not to go into the computer science field, but my reaction is to do the lone wolf sort of thing. I'll just go off and do it myself," Jawan, says, laughing a little. "Some people might see me as a poor team player, but I'm just trying to save myself some annoyance."

Marisa, an African American college senior who is spending her summer preparing for law school, takes the opposite tack. And even though she is extremely outgoing by nature, she says, she's not entirely comfortable reaching out all the time. "I'm that one girl that's, you know, 'The Black Friend,'" Marisa says sarcastically, making little quotation marks with her fingers. "You can *name* me. I've got a bunch of white friends and they can all name me as their one black friend. And same thing goes with some of my Asian friends. Same thing goes for my Arab friends. I'm that *one* person. I like diversity; I grew up with it. In my family we've got white, black, Filipino; we have lots of things. But it's not always easy to make those friendships because people have so many preconceived ideas about you.

"One of my friends from high school, he's Muslim, and he didn't want to be part of my study group in humanities class," Marisa continues. "And he didn't want to talk to me after I approached him. But I told him point blank, 'We're *going* to be friends. We're going to *do* this thing!' And later he said, 'After I got to know you, you were *awesome*.' And we're still best friends to this day. He's like straight Arab. He grew up in Iraq. Came to the States, learned English. And for him, I guess I can give him a little leeway because he didn't grow up in this country. But I get the same reactions, or worse, from people who did grow up here. In the classroom, you know, being a black student, it's almost a surprise to people when you participate in discussion and you say something remotely intelligent. You kinda get this silence in the room. It's an uncomfortable silence."

"Among the students?" I ask.

# 34 FRACTURED: RACE RELATIONS IN "POST-RACIAL" AMERICAN LIFE

"Among the students. And you even see it in the expressions on the professors' faces."

Marisa's friend Janine, who is listening, explodes in laughter.

"It's, it's unbelievable," says Marisa. "When you actually participate and actually say something that's *right*. It's like, 'That person's smart?' It's like, *no shit!* I got into this university; what do you think?"

Janine claps her hands in approval and recognition.

"It makes you feel uncomfortable," Marisa sighs. "You're excluded and shut out. And that sometimes turns me off from participating altogether. Which sucks, especially when participation is part of your grade. The environment is such that you're just not eager to be a part of it. And then, when you're assigned to a group for a project or something, the other people in your group think you're not going to do the work. You get this feeling—I don't know if you've ever experienced this—but you get the impression that they don't *want* you in their group. They're feeling like you're going to be the one that's slacking. I mean, I feel that *they're* going to be the one that's slacking because I know how I am, but for *them*, their judgment isn't based on my skills, it's my skin color. There's absolutely nothing else they can base their reaction on. They just *can't*. And, I don't know—you gotta move past it, you've got to be strong, you've got to overcome it. Because you can work and struggle to change people's prejudices and racial assumptions, but if they're not willing to accept it, then what? How do we overcome that?"

"You mentioned before that people looked surprised when you say something smart and then there's this silence in the room," I say.

"*Yeah!*" says Marisa, relieved I have taken her point.

"Once that moment of recognition happens, do the students change, do they get past that, or do they think, no, this can't be real?"

"I don't know about the people who aren't in my groups," replies Marisa, "but for the people who are, they do get past that. Because they have enough interaction with me. By the end of the semester we might even go out to lunch or whatever. But in most classes there aren't enough opportunities for interaction, so most people end up not moving past their prejudices. And of course when they go to their other classes, they probably don't have people like me talking to them, trying to open them up. I know I'm particularly outgoing and I'm also pretty insistent. But people of color shouldn't always have to be the initiators; whites should step up as well."

Ariana, a black, first-year student at the same university who is majoring in political science and finance, has already concluded that reaching out to

ARE WE POST-RACIAL YET? 35

her classmates is not worth the effort. "I'm not here to make friends," she says firmly. "I'm here to *work*. I'm here to get good grades and then hopefully get into grad school." Ariana came to college with a sense of excitement and what she thought was an easy familiarity with the dominant culture. She grew up "in one of those affluent suburbs that's pretty homogeneously white," she says. And for years, she participated in "multiple, competitive, intellectual summer programs" where she was the only minority, so she's kind of used to it.

But coming to this Midwestern university was a different thing altogether. In her anthropology lecture, "which is like, 300 white people and *me*, basically," Ariana has been put on the defensive. "Like when I do well on a test. Okay. So I got my first anthropology test back. I did really, really well. I was in the top of my class on it, in the top 5% of the class. And it was clear that the instructor who returned my grade was surprised. I was talking to my friend who's a black PhD candidate here, and she basically said, 'You'll get a lot of that here because your name doesn't sound distinctly African American.' So there's that element of surprise. And overall, teachers have been surprised at how well I've done here. I'm not quite sure how to interpret that."

Like the other students I've talked to, Ariana is dismissive of the idea that we have reached some sort of post-racial moment in this country. If we have, she muses, she would be getting a post-racial education—which clearly she is not. She recently made some comments in her anthropology section critiquing a book about the drug trade in Detroit, the predominantly black city that she knows well.

"We were reading an ethnographic monograph that tries to draw a dichotomy between middle-class black suburbanites and Detroiters," explains Ariana. "I don't agree with a lot of what the author says about Detroit and about people who live in the suburbs, because I do have family that still live in Detroit, so I know what it's like to live there. I went to school there for four years, and most of my life is based around that city. So I don't appreciate a lot of the things he has to say."

I ask Ariana what she disagrees with most.

"He basically makes it sound like everyone there is dealing drugs. He makes it sound like the drug trade is the most prevalent thing in the city. He tries to explain a lot of the factors that have shaped it, a lot of which I agree with. But the way he portrays the city can be semi problematic, which probably has to do with the fact that he's a rich, privileged, white guy who's never lived there. So I personally don't agree with the premise of the book at all. I was telling my class that it's an example of the 'white gaze'[5] over an African

American community that the author will never understand, no matter how much he tries to be a part of it. And they didn't get the idea of the 'white gaze' at all. You know, that's where researchers or just anyone from the dominant culture sort of gazes from a distance at the people they see as problematic and assumes the authority of their own viewpoint. It's a power thing."

"It's a pretty sophisticated concept for a first-year class," I say. "Maybe they'd never heard of it before."

"Right. But they *should*, because it's anthropology, you know?" Ariana responds.

"Good point."

"I don't think the class—I mean, they almost *couldn't* understand because they don't see the assumptions that people make about African Americans. And since they'll never have to live in that position, they think there's no point in even *trying* to understand. Like they just don't *care!* Because it will *never* matter to them." Ariana shakes her head in a gesture of resignation and disgust. "It will never matter."

I ask Ariana what a good, solid, post-racial education would look like.

"To me, a post-racial education would be where everyone has the same educational experience while in the classroom and where the topic of race is discussed, thoroughly, and understood and accepted by everyone in the room. Regardless of whether your peers agree with your points about race or not, your ideas would be valued at the same level that theirs are, and your opinions would be respected. When you have something to say, everyone would actually *listen*, rather than blowing you off because you're a minority or because they have this idea that you *shouldn't* know something. No one would make biased or stereotypical statements about your educational knowledge."

Ariana admits that not all her peers think badly of her. She is aware that because of the way she speaks and her level of knowledge, some whites see her as a "black exception" or even, best-case scenario, as an individual. But being a "model minority" isn't enough for her, she says, especially if we're going to aim at a type of education we could honestly call post-racial. *All* students, no matter what their level of knowledge and their manner of speaking, would need to be respected.

"I would like to think that I'm pretty well-spoken, so I try to convey my thoughts eloquently," she tells me. "But there may be another person in the class who can't do that yet—they haven't been exposed to that type of educational atmosphere, so they can't convey their thoughts very well, even though they *do* have valid thoughts. But the other students, white students mainly, judge them based on how they express themselves, not on what their thoughts express. So if I see that happening, I'm going to step in and say, 'You can't invalidate someone because of the way they speak, because if you'd listen, you'd know that their thoughts convey valid points.' I'm not particularly hopeful that my making that point in class will cause those students to give up their prejudices. It's just my personality. If I see something, I'm going to speak up. But I'm aware that people aren't going to be able to understand if they've never had their ideas invalidated because their race is seen as less intelligent. As I said, I'm not in college to win a racial crusade. I'm not here to make friends."

I feel disheartened as I listen to Ariana say over and over that she's not in college to make friends. To already feel, in one's first semester, that friendship is irrelevant is to give up on the opportunity to grow, to delight in shared experiences and new ideas, to make lifelong connections. Perhaps as time goes on, Ariana will find people she can bond with amid the sea of classmates who dismiss her comments as strange or unworthy of their attention. But when the number of students of color at a particular school is small, when there is no "critical mass" of students who can socialize without continually running into people who have no interest in their experience and knowledge, friendship can be a challenge. At Ariana's school, blacks make up only 4% of the student body. It's not that high-performing black students aren't attracted to the school for its intellectual challenge or that they're not qualified to be admitted. When the college experience is like Ariana's, the word gets around, and many top students choose to go elsewhere.

In an open letter to the regents of the University of Michigan, black graduate student Austin McCoy comments on the overall decline in black enrollment at that university over the last 17 years. "My experience reflects the point that as black enrollment declines, so does the racial climate," McCoy writes. So what should he tell prospective black graduate students when they come to visit? "Questions about climate, enrollment, and the lack of a critical mass of African Americans often arise in our discussions," he says. "And I would love to be able to tell them that we transformed the university into a more inclusive and just place from the bottom-up.... [But instead] I would be compelled to tell them about how life as a black graduate student could be isolating and emotionally and psychologically taxing. I would have to tell them that they would have few opportunities to engage black students in the classroom.... I would be compelled to warn them of what's to come—isolation and marginalization."[6]

Two thousand miles to the west at another research university, Mariana, a Colombian American undergraduate, is facing similar isolation and marginalization. Throughout her undergraduate years, she has developed a reputation for outspokenness on the subject of Latin American human rights issues, particularly in Colombia, where she was born. In fact, she tells me, she is known to her classmates as "the crazy one" because of her frequent corrections of her peers, and even, at times, her professors. She used to be quiet about the racial injustice she saw around her, but as her understanding of the region and its history has grown, she has developed a thicker skin.

"In this one honors seminar we were talking about a type of herbicide that's been shown to cause lower life expectancy, low fertility rates, and cancer," Mariana tells me. "It's used by agribusinesses primarily on fields—both in Colombia and the U.S.—that are tended by low-paid agricultural workers who then develop these diseases and conditions. So the professor showed a video and in one part of it there was an African American scientist who said point blank, 'This is environmental racism.' And I thought, 'Oh! Good point, man!' Because these workers, they don't have any other choice, and systemically they are being targeted. So the professor set up a debate about whether or not the U.S. should ban this particular herbicide. And I was like, 'Whoa, should this even be a debate? What are you prioritizing? Are you prioritizing profit over the cost of *life?*' And the rest of the students, you could tell from their body language how dismissive they were and how bored to hear from me—again. And I was like, 'The use of this pesticide is *racialized!* It's targeting Latino farm workers in this country!' And so one of them said, 'Well, actually, it's been proven that these groups are genetically *prone* to develop these types of cancers.' And I was like, 'I don't think they're necessarily genetically *prone* to anything. I think their cancers are caused by the environment. Because where they're spraying is where these people are *living.* These people, they don't have any other choice about where to live and where to work! If you were to get together a group of Latinos and estimate how many of us are going to get cancer, yeah, more of us are going to get it because more of us are working in the fields. More of us are exposed to these toxins whose only purpose is to ensure these corporations make a profit.' And then I was a crazy person to the class after that."

"So what was your instructor's reaction to this exchange?"

"She didn't interject. She didn't say, 'We should respect how this student feels.' She didn't say, 'We should all take a look at her argument carefully because we might learn something from it.' Instead she was like, 'Moving on!

ARE WE POST-RACIAL YET? 39

Let's just skip this. Moving on!' And well, I expected that. Because every time I raise my hand in that class, everybody sort of groans. They're like, 'Oh, no.' Every time we have a debate, they see me as the *human* advocate."

"As if that were a bad thing."

"Right. I'm the *emotional* girl."

"It sounds like human rights isn't your instructor's area of expertise."

Mariana laughs. "Not exactly."

"So how did you deal with it?"

"Actually, what I decided to do was write a paper on the issue for another class, and then I would give a copy to that professor as well. So I researched the numbers of workers who died, and the lawsuits that had been brought against these companies, and I wrote a paper on it. I stayed up all night and just *wrote* it. Because it was just *heart*breaking."

"Yes."

"But my concern now is, next semester I have to present my undergraduate thesis. And I have to present it in the Honors College, which is primarily white, and this is the college that has been resistant to some of the things I've said in the past. So that's the thing that I fear, is how people are going to react. Because I'm not going to be quiet about this."

"Try to make your argument as lawyerly as possible," I suggest. "Show that you understand the opposition's arguments and that your facts and examples are more convincing than theirs. That's the way professors were taught to debate when they were students, so that's what they'll respect, even if they disagree with you. And try not to let your emotions get the better of you."

"Thank you. That helps," Mariana says. "But you know, I'm the *emotional* girl."

"Showing your emotion isn't always a bad thing," I say, smiling. "Sometimes it can be more convincing than dry facts or unrelenting arguments. But when you're doing a high-stakes presentation that will affect your graduation, you need to be careful."

"Yeah, that's for sure. Actually I have another question," Mariana says. "This is something I've been struggling with as I do my research. The U.S. is treating illegal immigrants like they are criminals, like these are illegal beings. But at the same time, we go into *their* countries and abuse *their* people. What does that mean, in the grander scope of things, when we make it sound like they take so much from us and that we've never taken anything from them? How are we going to change that attitude?"

I have no answer.

40    FRACTURED: RACE RELATIONS IN "POST-RACIAL" AMERICAN LIFE

Reading more of the current scholarship about race, I learn a disconcerting fact: The way whites speak publicly about people of color in this "post-racial" era is not nearly as telling as what they express openly and unguardedly in private. A participant observation study of "race talk"—that is, "any talk that demeans on the basis of race or ethnicity"—in the private conversations of students, family members, employers, coworkers, professors, and strangers revealed that the most egregious racial insults are still distressingly common.[7] Old slurs are still in use: "spic," "colored," "lazy Mexican," "Chink," "gook," "dot-head," "dago," "sand nigger," and "those people" are among the demeaning terms still used by whites when they believe they are unobserved.[8] Mimicking of accents and dialects is still prevalent. One student research assistant listened to his white friend criticize his Asian professor: "Goddamn gooks. Can't speak our language; I can't understand what the hell they're saying." Another student "called a professor 'Obi-Wan Kenobe' because she spoke with a Jamaican accent and had an ethnic name with similar consonants."[9] Such slurs, which were "primarily used by dominants to degrade 'others,'"[10] both assert white authority and draw boundaries between "normal" (white) people and despised others, who were characterized as "out of control, animalistic, ignorant, dangerous, dirty, lazy, and entertaining."[11] Whites even assigned racial characteristics to objects, "including clothes, shoes, cars, animals, body parts, movies, music, and jewelry,"[12] adding to the dehumanization of people of color and marking the boundaries between "us" and "them."

Once the boundary lines are drawn, the study found, whites spend a good deal of time policing the barricades by watching and criticizing people of color, "making sense of behavior through a racist lens"[13]—the "white gaze." Whites were observed remarking on attempts by people of color to infiltrate "white space" by applying to prestigious universities, gaining access to scholarships and funding for special events and clubs, and even using public streets and crosswalks. The authors were particularly disturbed about the violent overtones in much of the white students' surveillance of people of color; research assistants' field notes were replete with remarks and "jokes" about gun violence and lynching.[14] The authors conclude that despite the fact that whites claim colorblindness and an abhorrence of racism, little has changed in the way they think and feel about race.

Curiously, the one variety of racism that is still publicly sanctioned is not about a "race" at all. "Being a Muslim after September 11th is to occupy the most despised position in American society," a Muslim American professor of rhetoric tells me. In his role as a phenotypically white American male, he has "endless access, at any time I want, to *massive* white privilege, and male privilege, and slight British accent privilege: I can get on the phone, Helen, and get *anything* done in this country!" After his many years living and teaching in multiracial settings, both in the Middle East, where he studied Arabic for many years, and at a historically black university where he taught for a decade, he accepted a position at a historically white institution in the U.S. Northwest in order to "figure out what white folks do when they're mostly alone together." There he learned "a staggering truth," he says, one that he really should have known, being white himself: "I had thought most educated whites were simply *obdurate* when they were acting on their white privilege. But what I learned when I arrived at this university is that most white folks *don't see it!* My god, no educated white person has the right to be innocently oppressive. I mean, if they're going to be oppressive, they should at least do so *consciously!*"

Because of his unique identity as a white Muslim American, a teacher and researcher who is "endlessly fascinated with the construction of conflict zones," and the sole advisor to a thousand Muslim students from 53 countries, he feels a responsibility to make that oppression visible in his classes. "Like the vast majority of any human group, white folks are good women and men who would not go out of their way to hurt people most of the time," he says. So naturally, they would want to understand their effect on people of color. During the first half of the semester, he tells students enough about his long and interesting life so that they see him simply as a "rather cool, older white guy who's lived everywhere and heard Jimi Hendrix at Woodstock." Then he gives them an article that is published by someone with a Muslim name, which, unbeknownst to the students, is part of his own. After the students read the piece in class and are ready to discuss it, he reveals that he is the Muslim who wrote the article. Their reaction, he says, is stunning. "Immediately I get reconstructed as a man of color, a despised other, and a dangerous person," he says. Yet, curiously, his students have developed enough trust in the white version of their professor during the first part of the semester that they shower *that* person, the person they *thought* they knew, with a thousand questions: "Wait, wait! Professor. So *why* did you do this? What does it mean? Why would you want to be a terrorist, professor?"

"And of course my students are smart," he tells me, smiling. "They read everything. They really want to know why I would do this to myself, and why I am revealing my Muslim identity to them now. So I answer their questions and I tell them that I'd be happy if they would just notice that I don't *have* to answer them and that it's an act of generosity on my part to do so." But it's more than that, he tells them. "I want you to see that Muslims are people."

All around this country, Muslim students, especially women who cover their hair, say that their non-Muslim peers can have difficulty seeing beyond the stereotype. A long-time writing instructor at a Midwestern school recounts a typical reaction: "One of my Muslim students came to talk to me about the social dynamics in her math class. She's very smart. Definitely, math is her thing. But she's thinking of dropping the course. Students won't make eye contact with her, she says, and they exclude her from study groups. It makes her nervous. 'Paranoid' was the word she used. She was feeling paranoid. Many of her close friends came to the university wearing the headscarf, and now, because of the way other students treat them, they've stopped wearing it, despite the fact that they chose it out of religious obligation. And that really makes her upset."

According to surveys, too, attitudes toward both Islam and Muslim Americans have turned increasingly negative in recent years. In surveys tracking American attitudes toward Muslim-Americans, Muslims in general, and Islam, most of which were conducted by the Pew Forum on Religion and Public Life, respondents gave increasingly negative answers since 2001, and even more negative ones after 2006, when the immediate danger of the attacks of September 11, 2001 had subsided. In a survey of Americans' feelings toward nine minority groups conducted by American National Election Studies between 2004 and 2012, "Muslims were rated higher only than atheists—possibly the most unpopular "religious" group in America—and illegal immigrants." This negative trend in attitudes toward Muslims "appears to be part of a growing intolerance toward all minority groups in America," concludes Charles Kurzman of *Islamic Commentary*. "In the American National Election Studies, 'thermometer' ratings for almost every group declined between 2004 and 2012—Asian-Americans, Blacks, Catholics, Christian fundamentalists, feminists, Hispanics, illegal immigrants, and Muslims—though none declined as much as feelings toward Muslims."[15]

Such attitudes help create an environment where Muslims can be targeted at will. Recently, the National Security Agency and the FBI "have covertly monitored the emails of prominent Muslim-Americans—including a political candidate and several civil rights activists, academics, and lawyers—under secretive procedures intended to target terrorists and foreign spies." FBI training materials uncovered in 2011 refer to random Muslim individuals (i.e., "John Doe") as "Mohammed Raghead" and teach agents to "treat 'mainstream'

# ARE WE POST-RACIAL YET?

Muslims as supporters of terrorism, to view charitable donations by Muslims as 'a funding mechanism for combat,' and to view Islam itself as a 'Death Star' that must be destroyed if terrorism is to be contained."[16] Although such extremist attitudes in law enforcement are not widespread, they do contribute to the general atmosphere of suspicion, not only of Muslims but of "suspected Muslims," such as President Obama. Despite the fact that Obama is a practicing Christian, one in five Americans believe that he is secretly a Muslim.[17]

Muslims and Native Americans, I learned, experience opposite kinds of exclusion. Often left off of surveys such as the Pew study of attitudes toward minorities that I mentioned earlier, Native people are invisible in many areas of the country both because of their relatively small numbers and because their cultures and histories are commonly considered relics of the past, rather than vibrant and meaningful in the present. In Massachusetts, at a small private college, I asked a professor of history who appeared quite politically progressive about the percentages of various groups of color on campus. When I came to Native Americans, he expressed surprise that I had asked at all and replied that there aren't really any Native Americans living in the state. In fact, there are over 50,000 who identify as all or part Native, according to the 2010 census.[18]

In my own classes, white students commonly say they have no friends who are Native American, or they will assert, without asking their peers, that there are no Native American students in the classroom or that they have never come across anyone who is Native American, even though there is a highly advertised powwow held annually in the sports arena that is the center of campus life come basketball season. But if Native students choose to become more visible on campus, their peers may react with incredulity and derision. A Native student told me of a friend's experience as part of a Native student organization whose members decided to dress in traditional regalia to advertise a small powwow they had organized. As she walked across campus in her ceremonial clothing, students laughed and pointed at her, mimicking Hollywood Indian stereotypes, calling out "Pocahontas" and doing "fake warrior chants and 'Native calls.'" The experience of having deeply meaningful cultural and spiritual traditions publicly mocked was so tormenting to her that she put her regalia away and resolved to never wear it again.

This sort of ridicule pales in comparison to the blatant exclusion found in some areas of the country where Native people live in greater numbers. "In the Northwest, American Indians are the most despised minority group. Just hands-down, absolutely despised," says a white teacher educator with research ties to the local reservations. In her college classroom, the predominant attitude among students is "very post-racial," she says, chuckling a bit. "Like we're going to play that we don't notice race, that we're color-blind, that we really don't need to talk about that any more, but boy, every time race comes up, and it comes up frequently in my class, I'm always surprised and a little distressed that these students are going to be teachers. The anti-Indian sentiment is really shocking. The things they say! As just one example, we were looking at high school compositions from writers at different schools to see how students learn academic writing, and out of the blue, one of my students says, 'You can tell this one was written by an Indian, because everybody knows that white people are much smarter than Indians. Indians just aren't as intelligent as white people.' And what was almost worse, this remark was met by silence from the rest of the class."

"What did you make of that?" I ask.

"I've often thought about that incident," muses the professor. "The ones who did express this view, they were clearly racist; they had strong feelings against Indians, categorically. But what about the ones who didn't speak up? Or maybe, trying to put the *best* construction on it, maybe that silence indicated that most students just didn't know, because they didn't have any contact with Indians or whatever. But that just doesn't jibe. There are Indians everywhere in this state!"

Anti-Indian sentiment is particularly blatant in towns that border on reservations, says a Nez Perce faculty member. "A lot of times the whites in those towns just *hate* Indians. I was recently at a restaurant with my cousin who is dark skinned, and we sat there waiting and waiting while white people were seated ahead of us. When we finally asked, 'What about us?' we were told, 'Oh, just wait, just wait, just wait.' They do it to make it a point: 'We don't want you here because you're Indian.' I've also had it happen when I was walking into one of those big chain stores with my kids' dad, who's also dark. The cashiers would actually refuse to check out my stuff. They'd just point to the sign that says, 'We reserve the right to refuse service,' just because I'm with a dark Indian. I look white, so I can go in to that store by myself and buy whatever I want. I can go into that same restaurant and I'll immediately get seated. But not when they know you're Indian. The border towns are *bad!*"

"So why do you think that kind of blatant racism continues in those towns?" I ask.

"I think it's intergenerational," she says. "The racism gets transferred down. So the local whites who lived here all their lives, their parents taught

ARE WE POST-RACIAL YET? 45

them to hate Indians. Nobody asks themselves, 'Well, why *should* I refuse these people's groceries just because they're brown?' The hate is not examined. And then it's on the rez, too, the parents teach their kids to hate white people. And the hate just gets passed down."

"So what are the kids taught on the rez about whites, specifically?"

"When my grandma was growing up, the signs in the stores in town used to say 'White trade only. No dogs or Indians allowed.' The only place they could go around here was the Chinese restaurants. Chinese people would let them in. Of course, that was appreciated. They made a word in our language for 'Chinese person.' But the whites never gave up on their racism. So on the rez, parents still warn their kids, 'When you go into town, this is going to happen to you and that is going to happen to you.' And when the kids *do* go into town that's *exactly* what happens to them. And then they're just kind of like, 'Why are you doing this? Why can't I buy my stuff here?' So they get mad, and then they pass it down to *their* kids. Anyone who thinks we're post-racial should just come up here and walk around with a dark Indian, and they'll see right away that nothing has changed."

African Americans, too, especially dark-skinned males, continue to be targets of blatant racism. "Yeah, racism is most definitely here on campus," says J. T., a junior who is majoring in aerospace and sociology at a prominent research university in the Midwest. "I don't want to even say it's low key. It used to bother me a lot, but now I'm used to it. I'm not *comfortable* with it, but —" he trails off, laughing a little.

"What's been your experience here, J.T.?" I ask.

"You know, people will look the other way; they'll cross the street real quick. Just coming over here for the interview some dude threw a pop can at me as he was driving down the street. I've seen ladies clutching their purse when they walk past me; that's nothing new. When you step on the elevator people get off. Stuff like that. And on the few occasions when I've tried to talk about these things, I've had people say, '*Surely*, it's not because you're black!'"

"It's because you're tall," jokes Marisa, who is listening sympathetically.

J. T. laughs. "Yeah, that's probably it. But seriously, one time I was walking down the street in broad daylight and this lady was at the intersection with her small child. And I was approaching her in order to walk past her, and I could see that she felt kind of nervous and upset, because she kept looking at me, she kept looking at me, she kept looking at traffic and then looking back at me. And right before I get up to where she's standing, she snatched her

young kid out into traffic to like, get *away* from me before I cross her path."
J. T. has become breathless and agitated as he tells this story. "I mean, cars
were coming full speed!"

"Wow. I've never had any experience like *that*," says Marisa.

"Nothing so blatant?" I ask.

"Uh, I've been called 'nigger' a few times."

"Who said that to you?"

"Random people," says Marisa. "I don't know these people."

"Do you want to describe how it happened?"

"Once I was just riding my bike, and the people who were coming the
other way just blurted out the word. And I thought, 'What? What is this?
What the heck?' And, I mean, I moved beyond it; I put it aside pretty quickly
because I had other things to do and other things to think about. But it's not
something you forget. You know, I didn't really experience anything so deliberately racist until I came to college, which is odd, because, like everyone
says, this university *on paper* is diverse, but mere physical proximity doesn't
make people respect each other. I feel like the university ought to take more
responsibility as an institution to bring us all together. Because you can't *have*
a group of people, particularly the black community, being *terrorized* by other
people on campus! It's not acceptable. It's just *not acceptable*. But there are no
repercussions for these things."

"Repercussions aren't going to change anyone's mind," says J. T. "People
might stop that stuff for a while but they're still going to think what they
think and do what they do. You have to just move on. I mean, after that
woman nearly killed her child because she wanted to get away from me so bad
I was pretty upset, but I just continued on my way. I was like—I don't know."
J. T. laughs derisively. "That kind of thing used to bother me a lot. I can still
get upset, yes, but I'm not taken aback. Like I wouldn't say, 'I can't believe a
person would do that in 2014!' Like, no no no, 2014 don't mean nothing!"

"So you don't see any progress at all, J. T.?"

"You know, I arrived at this university thinking I could talk to anyone
about any topic," he says. "Because hey, we're intellectuals now! We're supposed to be above prejudice and stereotypes! But oh boy, did I learn quick
that was not the case. It was my own ignorance, I would have to say. I'm
from Detroit, Michigan, from the southwest part of the city, which is a very
bad environment, so I knew when I came to the university that I'd have to
change my behavior. It was obvious to me that things I would do in the 'hood
wouldn't be acceptable on campus. If somebody were to say something racist

to me back home, there would be no 'let's talk about this.' I would be fighting! Of course, I don't do that here. In fact, I'm a very outgoing person. I'll talk to anybody! But I have found that people I meet here don't feel the need to modify their behavior in the same way I do. They can say anything that comes into their head about people of color, particularly African Americans, I would say, and I am forced to put up with it. But if I were to do the same to them, there would be all types of people making noise about it, saying I shouldn't do this or that. And what irritates me more than anything is these are *young* people. These are people who parade around calling themselves 'the leaders and the best.' I would understand if I was in the backwoods or the boondocks or something where people weren't claiming to be intellectual. But these are people who should know better!"

"Have you tried talking to them about this?" I ask J. T.

"I try to avoid racial topics, because sometimes people say things that make me feel a certain type of way," he says. "I engaged in racial conversation a few times with these dudes and I learned that I can't get into that subject with them because of that veil of ignorance. And especially *willful* ignorance, that just ticks me off to no end. And there's no getting through to them. It's funny, because when I've tried to talk to them about this I've stayed real calm. I don't get upset. I try to watch the volume of my voice if it's an intense subject, you know? I try to speak slowly. I try to explain things to them. But there's so much to explain, especially if they're fighting the facts I'm giving them! Because if they know what I'm saying is true, they would have to change the way they think, and they don't want to do that."

"Nope, they sure don't," agrees Janine. "But you still have to try and educate them."

"Well, no, I don't agree," says J. T. "What I've learned is, people want to feel that they're right. They want to feel that the way they understand the world is correct, so that they're okay, you know what I mean? They don't want to have to fight against what they've been taught. It's too hard. So arguing with them isn't going to change the way they've been brought up all their lives."

"But J. T., you argue with people about race all the time," objects Marissa.

"Okay, if I'm with my friends and something gets out of hand, yeah, I'll say, 'Hey, man, that's wrong and I'll tell you why that's wrong,'" J. T. concedes. "But I'm not going to keep trying to explain it to them forever. I kind of feel like these are grown men and women, you know? We're all adults here at the university. It's not my job to *re-raise* you!"

## 48 FRACTURED: RACE RELATIONS IN "POST-RACIAL" AMERICAN LIFE

"So you're resigned to the fact that this country is nowhere near post-racial?" I ask J. T.

"A post-racial America?" says J. T. "I don't think that's possible. Oh sure, the principle behind it is a good idea. It looks good on paper. But it's just not the case that people are treated the same regardless of race or that we no longer *see* race, as a lot of people like to say. I don't think that's the direction we should be going anyway. Because if I were to treat someone wrong based on race, no one would see it because race is no longer supposed to be a problem. And given the history of this country and even our experiences as this younger generation, racism is just always going to be here."

I leave this interview overwhelmed and exhausted. I am grateful for the students' candor and thrilled that they have shared so many intimate details of their lives with me. But at the same time, I am alarmed by the ways their daily experiences have been shaped by race and how hard they work to ignore or overcome them. I am forced to admit to myself that for the 20-some years I have been teaching and writing about race, I have been skeptical of the idea that people of color feel the effects of white privilege every single day and that they are forced to think about race in ways that whites do not. I knew that racism existed, of course. And like so many of the whites I interviewed for this project, I was deeply convinced that America is in no way "post-racial." But before this interview, Marisa's claim that black students are being "terrorized" on a liberal, multicultural college campus would have seemed like an exaggeration. I now realize, with a shock, that it is not.

So many of the people of color I've interviewed have felt the barbs of racism that whites refuse to acknowledge, from the tacit dismissal of their abilities, to exclusion from academic and professional opportunities, to displays of boredom at their passions, to outright ridicule, mockery, and derision. Their experiences vary, of course, depending on their gender, their religion, their geographical location, their skin tone, their forms of speech and expression, their socioeconomic class, their aspirations, their determination to be outspoken or stoic, the kinds and amount of contact they choose to have (or can't escape having) with whites, and of course, their ascribed race. What continues to surprise me is not only that we as a nation are divided, but *how* divided we are. Racial assumptions, beliefs, and denials affect everything, from the reach of the national media down to the smallest community: the street where one lives, the friends one attempts to make, the social club, the study group, the folks who gather at a pedestrian crosswalk.

A New York City art educator tells me, "The term 'post-racial' reminds me of the post-modern—the fracturing of things. And I feel like there *has* been a fracturing. Whites are threatened by increased diversity, a black president, immigration, terrorism, losing their sense of control. People of color experience the world in ways that whites deny, or minimize, or just aren't able to hear. It's not like our society has finally come together—unless we've come together as a fractured society and we're feeling the prickliness of the broken shards."

*Fractured.* I couldn't agree more.

# · 3 ·

# "SANTA JUST *IS* WHITE, KIDS."

Just before Christmas, 2013, Aisha Harris, a blogger for Slate.com, wrote a piece titled "Santa Claus Should Not Be a White Man Anymore."[1] Her proposal, that Santa be replaced by a penguin, was intended to be tongue in cheek, but it also expressed a serious concern. When she was growing up, the "real" Santa—the one who invited kids onto his lap at the mall and appeared on all of her favorite Christmas specials—was visibly white, but the Santa pictured on the holiday figurines and Christmas cards at home was African American. When the disparity began to trouble her, she asked her father whether Santa was brown like their family or if he was really a white guy. Thinking quickly, her dad reassured her that Santa is every color; in fact, he is able to magically transform himself to match each family he visits. But since small children are already astute observers of race,[2] the little girl wasn't convinced. Young as she was, she knew that brown skin wasn't considered as special—or even as "normal"—as white, so she continued to worry that her family's Santa wasn't "the real thing." Now, as an adult, she wondered whether turning Santa Claus into a loveable little animal could spare millions of kids the insecurity and shame that she remembers from childhood. As the face of America changes, with European Americans becoming a minority by 2050,[3] shouldn't we finally stop promoting the harmful idea of whiteness-as-default?[4]

Fox News picked up the story immediately. "When I saw this headline, I kind of laughed and said, this is so ridiculous, yet another person claiming it's racist to have a white Santa," said Megyn Kelly to her guests on *The Kelly File*. Hastening to assure any children who happened to be watching that Santa would not be messed with, Kelly looked directly at the camera and told them, "For all you kids watching at home, Santa just *is* white, but this person is just arguing that maybe we should also have a black Santa. Santa is what he is, and just so you know, we're debating this because someone wrote about it, kids."[5]

Of course, Harris wasn't arguing for a black Santa at all. Her suggestion was to "ditch Santa the old white man altogether, and embrace Penguin Claus."[6] So why did Kelly get it wrong? Was it because the cartoon penguin featured prominently on Harris's blog had—like all adult penguins—a black face? The whole discussion, so silly on the face of it, reflects a deep concern about race, not only for people of color whose children ask heartbreaking questions but for whites like Kelly who police the racial boundaries: Santa just *is* white, kids. You can't just magically switch his racial category.

In the three-minute debate on Kelly's program, one of her guests, Jedediah Bila, tries her best to understand the blogger's intent. Harris just wants Santa to be inclusive, she explains. "Initially I was thinking, 'Oh this is more politically correct nonsense, this is hypersensitivity in our culture,' and then you read the piece and... you realize if you were a young kid, and you were African American, and your Santa Claus was white, it *would* affect you when you went to school. Maybe you wouldn't feel that you were part of that tradition."[7]

"No. No," responds Kelly, turning serious. "Just because it makes you feel uncomfortable doesn't mean it has to *change*. I mean, *Jesus* was a white man *too*! He was a historical figure [so] how do you just revise it in the middle of the legacy of the story, and change Santa from white to black?"[8]

"Yeah, I mean, you *can't*," agrees Monica Crowley, whose title, Foreign Policy Assistant to President Nixon, adds a bizarre twist to the discussion. "You can't take facts and then try to change them to make them fit some sort of political agenda or sensitivity agenda." A familiar picture of jolly old Santa Claus drinking a glass of milk flashes on the screen. "Hey come on, how can he be alienating?" laugh the guests. "I mean, how cute is he?"[9]

Despite the efforts of the commentators to make light of Harris's complaint, the stage had been set for a fight. Harris responded on her next blog post: "That this genial, jolly man can only be seen as white—and consequently, that a Santa of any other hue is merely a 'joke' or a chance to trudge out racist stereotypes—helps perpetuate the whole 'white-as-default' notion endemic to American culture...."[10] She linked her post to a news story about an incident at Indiana University, where in a bumbling attempt to get students talking about race, a bulletin board in a dormitory hallway invited passersby to comment on the question, "Can Santa be a black man?" Three paper stockings had been hung below, each topped with another question: "If Santa Claus is a black man, wouldn't all the presents be stolen?" "If Santa Claus is a black man, would you let him come down your chimney?" "If Santa Claus is a black man, would he only visit the ghetto?"[11]

Like much of the "national conversation" about race that takes place online, in the news media, on anonymous bulletin boards, in chat rooms and online comments, and occasionally, face-to-face, the Harris-Kelly exchange tapped into a painful core of American culture. As Harris pointed out, Santa Claus exists as an incredibly powerful image in the imaginations of many children across the country, a mythical being whose appearance every year assures kids that someone who (presumably) looks like their grandpa finds them deserving and lovable. The entry of Jesus into the conversation signals how serious the issue is for many adults as well. The emotional attachment to the presumed race of both of these cultural icons, the anger generated by attempts to laugh off the incident as trivial nonsense, the challenge to the idea of "white as default," all affirm the enduring power of race to normalize, elevate, demean, or exclude, according to a hierarchy of presumed worth.

Kelly and her guests seem to believe that Santa's whiteness cannot be challenged because race "just *is*." But ever since race was invented, racial categories have been challenged and reconstructed according to the needs of the dominant group and the beliefs of the times. As historian Juan Cole points out,[12] Kelly has an Irish name, and if she is Irish American, she herself would have been considered non-white by many in 19th century America, when the Irish were derided as "low-browed, savage, groveling, bestial, lazy, wild, simian, and sensual," terms almost identical to those describing blacks.[13] When Irish immigrants arrived in this country, they were despised for their poverty, their "foreignness," and their tendency to enter into egalitarian relationships with people of African descent. Despite their skin color, which made them "eligible for membership in the white race,"[14] the Irish were consigned to an intermediate race located socially between black and white and could only "become white" by turning against their black neighbors and coworkers, upholding slavery rather than joining the abolitionists, and driving free blacks out of jobs, thus establishing their claims to full citizenship in a white-dominated country.

Irish immigrants were not the only group whose racial status changed from "not quite white" to the privileged "white" position they enjoy today. Jews, Poles, Italians, Sicilians, Hungarians, Russians, Ukrainians, Czechs, Slovaks, Greeks, Finns—in fact, every European group that was not of "pure Anglo Saxon stock" was considered suspect when they arrived in America in the early 20th century. It was true that these "new immigrants" were always considered fully white by the courts, while blacks, Native Americans, and Asians almost always were not. And it is also true that the framers of the U.S. Constitution had accorded "free white persons" privileged status back in 1790 when the first Congress determined who could seek naturalized citizenship. But who, exactly, did the founders mean by "white"? As the Supreme Court commented in 1923, they must have been thinking of people who looked and acted most like themselves. "The immigration of that day was almost exclusively from the British Isles and Northwestern Europe, whence [the founders] and their forbears had come," the Court declared. "When they extended the privilege of American citizenship to 'any alien, being a free white person,' it was these immigrants—bone of their bone and flesh of their flesh—and their kind whom they must have had affirmatively in mind."[15]

So when Southern and Eastern Europeans began arriving in the late 19th and early 20th centuries, immigrants who had already established themselves as "white" saw the newcomers as different. Horribly different. Civic leaders and intellectuals of the day called them "scum," "trash," "dregs," and "filth," "peculiarly unable to be assimilated into the 'American race.'"[16] A professor of education wrote the following of the new immigrants in 1909: "Illiterate, docile, lacking in self-reliance and initiative and not possessing Anglo-Teutonic conceptions of law, order, and government, their coming served to dilute tremendously our national stock and to corrupt our civic life."[17] The new immigrants were "repeatedly scrutinized, tried, examined, and ranked"[18] against the white establishment. As the distinguished American sociologist Henry Pratt Fairchild wrote of Southern and Eastern Europeans in 1911, "If he proves himself a man, and... acquires wealth and cleans himself up—very well, we might receive him in a generation or two. But at present he is far beneath us, and the burden of proof rests with him."[19]

Great effort was expended by progressive reformers to remake the new immigrants into assimilated, "respectable" Americans who might eventually be considered "fully white." Industrialists like Henry Ford, who reaped grand profits from the influx of cheap labor, joined the effort with enthusiasm. Free language and culture classes were organized in factories and settlement houses where new arrivals were shamed and cajoled into giving up the trappings of the old country: their amusingly unfashionable clothes, their unintelligible languages, their bizarre foods (pasta and rice, they learned, were "uncivilized and un-American"[20]). Many new immigrants jumped at the chance to remake themselves. Says Italian American poet Diane Di Prima, "This pseudo 'white' identity... was not something that just fell on us out of the blue, but something that many Italian Americans grabbed at with both hands. Many felt that their culture, language, food, songs, music, identity, was a small price to pay for entering the American mainstream."[21]

Discarding their "old country" identity in exchange for the opportunity to survive and thrive in their new country was one thing. But becoming American—white American—also required immigrant children and their parents to learn to enact the racial hierarchy of their new country. This, too, came easily to them. As Malcolm X said as he watched immigrant children disembark in the United States in the early 1960s, "By tomorrow night they'll know how to say their first English word: 'Nigger.'"[22] Long before Malcolm X made this observation, new immigrants were being taught to look down on blacks, "Orientals," "Mexicans," and "Indians." Demeaning songs and playground rhymes, movie house cartoons, comic books, and the colorful "Sunday funnies" that could easily be read by people with limited English skills taught the new immigrants who they were supposed to consider beneath them. Amusement parks featured "Hit the Nigger" ball games. Advertisers used belittling "Aunt Jemima" and "pickaninny" images to hawk their products. Soap manufacturers used "endlessly repeated... sight gags... showing a black child being washed white."[23] World's fairs, circuses, museums, travelling shows, and even zoos displayed captive, conquered, and exoticized people from imperial conquests all over the globe.[24] While the new immigrants were learning which groups to humiliate and exclude, employers and unions were reinforcing the racial hierarchy by keeping labor divided by race and national origin, as they had found that pitting their workers against each other kept wages low, discouraged union organizing, and spurred productivity.[25] But regardless of the suspicion and ill will incited among white and "not fully white" immigrants on the job, when it came to defending their neighborhoods, old and new immigrants banded together to exclude blacks by signing restrictive covenants that limited the sale of their homes to whites only. This campaign to keep the neighborhood white offered the new immigrants some protection from the racialization they had been suffering themselves. As historian David Roediger explains, "At the very moment when millions of Klan members decried [the new immigrants'] presence, when educational experts quantified the 'retardation' of their children, when trade unions retreated from inclusive organizing campaigns, when progressive reformers insisted on '100 percent Americanism,' and, above all, when a racist Congress decimated legal immigration from southern and eastern Europe on the grounds of the immigrants' unfitness as citizen workers, new immigrants were warmly welcomed as 'white' and as fit neighbors in the grassroots campaigns to blanket whole urban areas with covenants."[26]

Thus, the assimilation of new immigrants included both Americanizing— through English language classes and the jettisoning of cultural baggage from the old country—and "whitening"—doing whatever was necessary to become accepted as full members in the most powerful racial group in the United States.[27] Their struggle for inclusion in mainstream American life underscores both the rigidity and the mutability of race. The whole notion of race depends on strict boundary lines that keep people "in their place" and make racial categories seem obvious, a fact of life ("Santa Claus is white, folks. He just is."). But at the same time, the "white" racial category can relax, on occasion, to include people who manage to remake themselves to look, act, and sound like the powerful majority. Racial boundaries freeze and thaw in response to the opinions and prejudices of intellectual leaders, the decisions of the courts, the interests of elected officials and captains of industry, and the squabbling of immigrants trying to get ahead in a highly competitive society.

Even the number of races into which humanity has been divided has changed dramatically over the years. According to one of the earliest categorists of race, German anatomist Johann Freidrich Blumenbach, mankind was divided into five races: Caucasian, Mongolian, Ethiopian, Malay, and American Indian, which he linked, simplistically, to five skin colors: white, yellow, black, brown, and red.[28] By 1888, experts in the United States recognized anywhere between 2 and 63 races. In 1924, "an exasperated U.S. Supreme Court hearing a case on race and naturalized citizenship complained that various scientific authorities placed the number of races at between four and twenty-nine"[29] By the end of World War II, anthropologists had reduced the number of races to three: Caucasian, Negroid, and Mongolian, with liberals like anthropologist Ashley Montagu arguing that the idea of race should be discarded altogether in favor of a more neutral term like "ethnic group."[30]

# "SANTA JUST *IS* WHITE, KIDS."

But the trend toward reducing the number of racial categories was reversed in the 1960s, as immigration quotas were lifted and people who had formerly been denied entry into the United States began arriving from all over the world. As they sought out their compatriots for comfort and security as well as help in finding jobs and communicating with authorities in a new language, immigrants of color formed ethnic communities and identities that complicated white-designated racial categories. By 2000, the U.S. Census was asking the following, for example: "Is Person 1 Spanish/Hispanic/Latino?" If so, are they Mexican, Mexican American, or Chicano? Or are they Puerto Rican, Cuban, or other Spanish/Hispanic/Latino?" In 2010, in response to grassroots pressure, respondents were instructed that, "for this census, Hispanic origins are not races." Household members were to choose among the various "Spanish/Hispanic/Latino" ethnicities and then among 15 racial categories. The Chamorro and Guamanian people, who hail from tiny U.S. possessions in the South Pacific and had never before been mentioned by the census, were accorded their own "race," as were people from Samoa, Fiji, Tonga, and other Pacific Islands.[31]

But despite the ever-shifting racial categories and the liberalizing attitudes toward race since the civil rights era, people who are considered "lower" in the U.S. racial hierarchy still cannot just decide to change the racial order— or even be taken seriously when they make a polite suggestion. Fox News commentator Megyn Kelly and her guests understood this implicitly. They knew that Aisha Harris, a black woman, is not supposed to "take facts and then try to change them to make them fit some kind of a political agenda or sensitivity agenda" just because a white Santa Claus makes her feel uncomfortable—or even because as a child, she felt demeaned and excluded from mainstream American life. This is not to claim that Kelly and her guests were deliberately or even consciously saying that Harris should not challenge the white category because she is black. But in their ignorance of how America became racialized and how their own ancestors figured into that process, the three commentators could not have understood how their comments on the immutability of race were fighting words to people of color.

While the immigrant ancestors of the three women on the Fox News panel—Kelly (Irish), Bila (Czech or Slovak), and Crowley (Irish)—were proving themselves "fit" to be white, other Americans—blacks, Asians, Latinos, Native peoples—were being firmly blocked from dominant group advantages or "white privileges," as feminist scholar Peggy Mackintosh[32] has called them: guaranteed rights to full citizenship, access to a solid education and decent

## 58 FRACTURED: RACE RELATIONS IN "POST-RACIAL" AMERICAN LIFE

jobs, financial relief when in difficulty, low-cost home loans, preferential access to land, fairness in the criminal justice system, protection from being used as experimental subjects in medical science, immunity from racial bullying and outright violence, and so on.

How were whole groups of people, defined by race, denied the privileges that are central to America's conception of itself as a free and equal society? A look at how laws were constructed and interpreted to keep America white, or, euphemistically, how the country would be preserved for "those of us who are interested in keeping American stock up to the highest standard"[33] suggests how this was done. After the Civil War, black rights might have seemed reasonably secure when the 14th Amendment was passed to mark the end of slavery, grant citizenship to former slaves, and guarantee voting rights to black males. Yet by the 1890s, "specially designed race-conscious laws, discriminatory punishments, and new forms of everyday racial surveillance had been institutionalized as a way to suppress black freedom."[34] In 1898, when Homer Plessy, a "seven-eighths white" person with a black great-grandparent had the temerity to challenge the racial rules that kept him from sitting in a "white" railroad car, the Supreme Court ruled that no, he wouldn't be allowed to ride with fully recognized whites, and furthermore, the whole country could keep such individuals separate from whites as long as their facilities were "equal." Of course, the facilities in question—schools, hospitals, bathrooms, drinking fountains, swimming pools, beaches, buses and trains, hotels and restaurants, seats at concerts and the theater, and so on—were never equal to those of whites. But the Supreme Court's decision had even more damaging effects than simply upholding segregation as it was practiced in the Deep South: *Plessy v. Ferguson* extended outright white supremacy to the rest of the United States. The court's rationale was that the 14th Amendment never intended for blacks and whites to mix. "The object of the amendment," the court declared, "was undoubtedly to enforce the absolute equality of the two races before the law, but, in the nature of things, it could not have been intended to abolish distinctions based upon color, or to enforce social, as distinguished from political, equality, or a commingling of the two races upon terms unsatisfactory to either."[35] In other words, as an American black, you might be technically free to make your own destiny, but the people who had constructed themselves as superior to you would always be able to block your progress.

Asians in early 20th-century America fared little better than blacks. In a manual for English teachers of European immigrants in 1912, the author warns that "Hindus," Chinese, and Japanese suffered from "a heritage of inefficiency and sloth." Trade unions objected to the Chinese, whose "slave-like subservience" and willingness to be accepted as "cheap men" made them not only undesirable but unassimilable. A diet of rice and, it was alleged, rats rather than meat, "symbolized Chinese failure to seek the 'American standard of living'"[36] Chinese immigrants to California in the late 19th century were depicted in a magazine cartoon as "a bloodsucking vampire with slanted eyes, a pigtail, dark skin, and thick lips. Like blacks, the Chinese were described as heathen, morally inferior, savage, childlike, and lustful. Chinese women were considered as a 'depraved class,' and their depravity was associated with their physical appearance, which seemed to show 'but a slight removal from the African race.'"[37]

Like Homer Plessy before them, several bold Asian individuals attempted to challenge their racial status before the country's highest court. In 1922, Takao Ozawa, an immigrant from Japan, argued he should be allowed to become a U.S. citizen not only because he was the right color but because he had *acted* in ways that signaled he was white. First of all, he told the court, his skin was as white or even whiter than some of his American acquaintances who enjoyed the privileges of dominant racial category. But he had also taken great care to act like a proper white American and raise his children accordingly. His children spoke only English. He maintained no contact with Japan. He made sure his family regularly attended a Christian church. Didn't that make him fully American, he asked? His plea was denied. The court argued that the original intention of the founding fathers was "to confer the privilege of citizenship upon that class of persons whom the fathers knew as white, and to deny it to all who could not be so classified." No matter what he did to prove his fitness for citizenship, the court declared, Ozawa "is clearly of a race which is not Caucasian." Astonishingly, the court hastened to add that its decision was not racist: "Of course there is not implied—either in the legislation or in our interpretation of it—any suggestion of individual unworthiness or racial inferiority. These considerations are in no manner involved."[38]

The following year, the Supreme Court rejected a plea for citizenship by Mr. Bhagat Singh Thind, an immigrant from India, who had attempted to argue that his Aryan origins made him fully white in America. Reversing its logic from the Ozawa case, the court declared that even though it could be argued that Thind was of Aryan stock, and that the terms "Aryan," "Caucasian," and "white" had similar meanings and origins, anyone would know from looking at Mr. Thind that he was not the kind of white person the founding fathers intended to enjoy the full rights and privileges of naturalized citizenship. "It may be true that the blond Scandinavian and the brown Hindu have a common ancestor in the dim reaches of antiquity," the Supreme Court declared, "but the average man knows perfectly well that there are unmistakable and profound differences between them today."[39] In an attempt to shore up its case, the court added that although the term "Aryan" had to do with the connection between the European and Indian languages, that common linguistic root was buried so far in the past that it is "altogether inadequate to prove common racial origin." Who knows which groups of people spoke the Aryan language in ancient times, the court mused. "Our own history has witnessed the adoption of the English tongue by millions of Negroes, whose descendants can never be classified racially with the descendants of white persons notwithstanding both may speak a common root language."[40]

The Supreme Court concluded its arguments with the same sort of absurd claim it made in the Ozawa case: "It is very far from our thought to suggest the slightest question of racial superiority or inferiority. What we suggest is merely racial difference, and it is of such character and extent that the great body of our people instinctively recognize it and reject the thought of assimilation."[41] Long before our own "post-racial" era, whites were careful to insist that their exclusionary judgments were not racist at all.

Native Americans, too, had been excluded from the privileges of the white racial category since America's founding. In a series of challenges throughout the early 1800s, the Supreme Court declared that the European "discoverers" of America had established their right to Indian territories, which "effectively made the tribes only inhabitants, not owners, of their lands."[42] By the early 20th century, the desire of the dominant race for living space, their generalized fear of "savages," and the taken-for-granted atmosphere of white superiority had divested the Native people of their lives, their cultures, their languages, their livelihoods, and almost all of their traditional lands. Surviving Indians were exhibited, along with other conquered peoples, at white-organized world's fairs.

Over a hundred years later, the memory of racial and cultural extermination continues to fracture Native-white relations. At a small reservation in the Midwest, I interviewed three tribal members who explained how the tragedy resonates across the generations. We had gathered at a restaurant in the beautiful tribal casino resort—the first such enterprise in the United States— where my host had made reservations for us for lunch. As we looked out over the expanse of lakes and forests, now almost exclusively federal or state property, the three women explained how their ancestors had lived under the most

## "SANTA JUST *IS* WHITE, KIDS." 61

extreme conditions for most of the 20th century. Families existed in tarpaper shacks without health care, sanitation, adequate clothing, or nourishment. Their rights to fish and hunt on their former territories had been trampled when state game wardens arrested tribal members who attempted to feed their families in traditional ways. Relying on each other was the only way they had stayed alive through the frigid winters. One hundred and sixty years of broken treaties, mismanagement, trickery, and stalling by the federal government had deprived the tribe of the promised compensation for their vast tracts of land. Only a few decades ago, unemployment had peaked at 59%. And casual racism by whites blamed Native people for their predicament.

"When I was growing up we were called dirty little Indian kids," says the tribal historian, a cheerful middle-aged woman whose sudden flashes of anger had already caught me off guard. "Even my own grandmother, a white woman who actually ended up marrying a Native guy, don't ask me why—we weren't allowed to be around her. We had to *tiptoe* around her because we were the 'dirty little Indians.' That was my first memory of race. And then later, in high school, one of the teachers, a white guy, naturally, asked the class a question, though why he asked I have no clue: 'Who wants to get rid of all the Indians?' That was the question. And then when you saw all your so-called friends raise their hands, it totally pissed us Indian kids off. That really hurt and I'll never forget that."

"Sounds crazy," I agree. "But would anyone ask such a question nowadays?"

"The question might change," replies the historian, "but the meaning behind it is pretty much the same. Just a few years ago there was a debate at the high school and the topic was, 'Who's tired of the Indians getting free stuff?' And I mean, that set off a *war* between the whites and the Indians all over again. Why should our kids have to go through that? What was the purpose of that debate? And if they had to have a question like that why couldn't it be, 'Who's tired of the white man here?'"

The two other women laugh quietly.

"So the debate was set up so that kids had to take sides?" I ask.

"Yeah!" responds the historian. "And then, you know, 'the Indians get *free stuff*.' It *isn't* free. Our ancestors *fought* for these rights that we have. *Nothing* was free!"

"Still ain't free," says an older woman emphatically. As the education director for the tribe and a matriarch in her large extended family, she had started the interview claiming that she never in her life had any problems with non-Indians.

62 FRACTURED: RACE RELATIONS IN "POST-RACIAL" AMERICAN LIFE

"What's the tribe's relationship with the outside world today?" I ask.

"Well, I mean, we're still fighting the United States," replies the matriarch. "We're in court right now, trying to get the federal government to release the rest of the money they've owed the tribes in this state since the 1800s."

"The government owes the tribe money?" I ask.

"Yeah, from selling this entire state back in the day," says the tribal historian. "The land for the casino was purchased with money that we were supposed to get back in the 1800s. And we finally got it. We always refer to it as our 'Indian money.' And we purchased land. And then it became Indian land again. But now the state is trying to take some of it back."[43]

"I think we'll always be fighting for the land," says the matriarch.

"Of course the outside world was fit to be tied when we started the casino," adds the historian. "Even though visitors come here by the busload for the blackjack and that. Can you imagine? *Finally*, we have something they can't take away from us. *Finally*, we've been able to build decent houses for everyone. And with our gaming revenues, we've built a tribal health center, some pretty good schools, and of course we provide funds for any tribal member who wants to go to college, which is a lot of us these days! We have a sense of pride in our community now. And the best thing is our kids; they don't have to move away now that they're grown. Before it was like"—the historian groans like a terminally bored teenager—"*Nothin'* to look forward to. Maybe I'm going to have to *leave.*' But now, it's like, this community is home! And I just *love* it here!"

"And you get your Indian money," adds the matriarch. "I don't care if I only get 10 dollars. I don't care *what* it is. We finally got it."

"What about the language?" I ask. "I understand that the tribe is trying to revive it. How important is it to you that the language doesn't die?"

"I don't let it affect me," says the matriarch. "I never did learn to speak it, and what's more, I never will." She turns to a younger woman, her assistant in the education office. "Can you speak it?"

"I've taken some classes. They have immersion weekends up at the tribal college. But if you don't hear it that often you lose it."

"When I was growing up I never even knew a word," says the historian, settling in for another story. "When I was young, I had the opportunity to move in with my grandmother—not the racist one, the one from my mom's side. I adored her. And I had the opportunity to take care of her before she passed. One day, a couple of her friends were over and they were speaking Ojibwe. And I was like, 'Grandma, how come you understand what they're

# "SANTA JUST *IS* WHITE, KIDS." 63

saying and that?' And she says, 'Well I can understand it. But I won't speak it anymore.' And I go, 'Why didn't you teach mom, and why didn't you teach us?' And she says, 'Because I didn't want my children to go through what I had to go through.' She was taken from her home at 5 years of age and put in a boarding school run by whites. She was beaten and locked in a closet for five days because she spoke only Ojibwe. And she says, 'I didn't want you guys to go through that.' So the language was lost in our family because of that."

The younger woman is sitting silently, listening. She has just moved back to the reservation so her children can grow up with their extended family. "My grandma used to tell us stories like they used to rub gasoline on their skin to make it white," she ventures.

"Who did that to her?" I ask.

"At the boarding schools," she says, almost inaudibly.

"The teachers did that?"

Silence. The hurt and shame on the women's faces is almost palpable.

"Her grandma was born in the 1800s," says the historian quietly. "So she was one of the earlier ones."

"There is a lot of pain from the past," I say finally.

"Ooh," sighs the historian. "It's still here. It's the trickle effect. You had all these children who had a strong sense of community, who were taught to hunt, take care of the children, live off the land. Then they went to the boarding school and they lost all that. We have historical documentation from the parents who were writing to the boarding school in those days, saying, 'You made our children useless. They come back here and they don't know how to hunt, they don't know how to take care of the children. They don't know how to do *anything*. You ruined our children.'"

"I'm not really concerned with any of that now though," says the younger woman. "It didn't affect me that much as a kid growing up. I'm sure our parents had to deal with it more than we did. And they sheltered us so we didn't have to go through it."

"But there *is* a trickle effect," insists the historian. "None of us can fluently speak the language. It's *gone*. Because of the boarding schools."

"I think it's always going to be gone," says the matriarch. "Even when people go up there and take those classes. And when they get all done, they don't have no one to talk to! You can't carry on like that if you don't have someone to have a conversation with you!"

The women nod pensively.

"I don't speak it either but I know some words and things," offers the historian.

"I know some bad ones," says the matriarch, her eyes twinkling. We all laugh together in a moment of camaraderie.

"Here's another thing," says the historian. "I could go on forever but...."

"No, go on!" I encourage her.

"As part of my job as a tribal historic preservation officer, I go to universities and bring back our ancestors that are on shelves."

My mind flashes back to a white graduate student I'd known who was categorizing human bones at the university museum to ready them for repatriation to Native communities. He was a nice guy, thoughtful, intelligent. He thought the idea of repatriating the Indian remains was ridiculous, but hey, he told me, it was a summer job.

"Back in the 1800s they took Native American remains from gravesites around here because they didn't think they were human," says the historian. "They thought they had to be animal. Reading that documentation makes you want to cringe. How could they not...." The historian falters a moment. "I don't understand how they could think we were not human, you know, that we're some kind of animal."

I nod, thinking that was a cruel affront, but surely, that was a long time ago.

"I don't think they acknowledge us as human even now," says the tribal historian.

"How so?" I ask.

"Well, why are we sending all this money over to foreign countries when they don't put any of it back into the reservations?" asks the historian. "I mean, I think our tribe is blessed, I really do. But if you go out West, well, there are other reservations that are not so blessed. They're *so* remote and *so* poor. They have almost no contact with the rest of the country so there's no jobs, no source of income. Why doesn't the government put some of that foreign aid back into *those* communities? They took everything away from them. How about giving a little back?"

The other women nod gravely.

"But to this day, we're still fighting back," says the historian. "We're in the courts, fighting the broken treaties. We're getting back little bits of our land. We're getting back our fishing rights. And we're getting our ancestors' remains off the shelves and putting them back in the ground."

"Did you have to fight for that, too?" I ask.

"You know, it wasn't so easy to get the museums to give up what they claimed was their property," says the historian. "They made all kinds of arguments: 'Oh, you don't even know if these are really your ancestors.' 'Oh, you know, we can learn stuff from these bones that will benefit all humanity.' But would they say that if it was *their* people's remains?"

The youngest woman sighs deeply. "I don't think it's right," she says softly. "I just don't think it's right."

"And who labeled us 'minorities'?" the matriarch breaks in suddenly.

Startled, I grope for an answer.

"And how are we even going to know who labeled us like that?" she asks hotly.

"Well, I don't feel like I'm a minority," says the historian.

"I don't either!" say the two other women. "Never did and never will."

"Technically though, what's meant by 'minority' is just a matter of numbers...." I begin hesitantly.

"What makes me lesser than you?" the historian says suddenly, flashing her eyes at me across the table.

"Right. Okay, so you're thinking of minority as...."

"You're sitting here asking us questions and here we're labeled minorities, but *you're* not labeled the minority—*we* are. So if you're so—why are you questioning us? You should know it all!"

The three women start to chuckle, cutting through the tension.

"I don't see us as minorities," says the matriarch finally. "I see us all sitting at a round table here in this restaurant. We're all equal."

"So minority to you means—what does it mean?" I persist stupidly, my nerves finally getting the better of me.

"It doesn't mean a heck of a lot of anything," says the matriarch with finality. "I haven't ever felt and I never *will* think I'm a minority. I have the same emotions as other humans and I'm just as good as anybody else. That's my strong feeling."

"Minority," sniffs the historian. "That's a racist word."

"And it's always been *us* who are the minority," adds the matriarch. "Or it has been since the Europeans came over here and started calling themselves white and everybody else a minority. *We* never thought of ourselves as minorities."

"I'm hungry," says the historian, picking up the menu. "Let's have lunch."

"Can we get rid of 'white' as a category, please?" asks historian Juan Cole. He is blogging about the racial origin of St. Nicholas[44]—he was Turkish, it turns out. Cole's "Photo of the Day" shows the Russian icon depicting the original St. Nick.[45] The saint looks worried, maybe prophetically. His raised right hand appears to be blessing us, the confused and contentious viewers far in the future. His color is dark, like the skin of a raw almond. His eyes are a deep brown. Cole tells us that Eastern Orthodox icons of St. Nicholas often depicted him as dark skinned, to show his Mediterranean origins. So Santa Claus didn't start out "white" after all. Or maybe not "fully white." In fact, he looked more like the black Santa in Aisha Harris's household than the jolly old man most American kids know today. "Likewise, a Jew from Nazareth would not have been considered 'white' by many Protestant Americans in the early twentieth century," adds Cole. "There would have been social clubs he couldn't have gotten into." So why not ditch our present-day, snow-white Santa Claus and while we're at it, get rid of "white" as a racial category? Both seem ridiculous—or they would if they hadn't caused so much suffering. "The very use of the term 'white' is a form of constructed racism designed to exclude rather than include," argues Cole. "Can't we just be Americans?" But even when proposed by "whites," ridding the world of its most destructive racial category is not so easy. As sociologist Milton Gordon said back in 1964, "Race is the category from which one may not voluntarily resign."[46]

What is the meaning of race in "post-racial" America? Anthropologists, social scientists, biologists, and in fact, most educated Americans now understand that race is not so much a biological category as a political one, created by dominant human groups for their own social and economic benefit. We know that race has absolutely nothing do to with a person's cultural, behavioral, or moral capabilities, as it has been so confidently asserted by influential "whites" over the last 500 years. We are finally recognizing what should be obvious to any world traveler: no genetic boundary lines mark off discrete "racial" groups; skin color, hair texture, body type, and facial features change gradually across geographical regions and can be very diverse even within them. We now know that the visual differences that seem to mark a person's race are extremely superficial, genetically speaking. Scientists using new technologies have found there is no way—biologically, chemically, or visually—to determine a person's race from his or her DNA. As President Clinton remarked in 2000, the Human Genome Project revealed a great truth: In genetic terms, "all human beings, regardless of race, are more than 99.9% the same."[47] Craig Ventner, the director of the project, had achieved the capability to sequence the entire genetic code of five individuals who identified as Hispanic, Asian, Caucasian, or African American. Although there were plenty of genetic differences among the samples, his team of scientists found no way to tell the race of one sample from another.[48]

Not only is there no clue to a person's "race" at the molecular level, we now know that most of the physical variation that exists between humans lies *within* conventional geographic "racial" groupings rather than between them. So, for example, people who identify as "black" differ biologically among themselves more than they do from "whites." In fact, since humans arose on the African continent and lived there for 200,000 years before they ventured into the rest of the world, the greatest amount of genetic diversity is found in sub-Saharan Africa. "A person from the Congo, a person from South Africa, and a person from Ethiopia are more genetically different from each other than [they are] from a person from France," explains legal scholar Dorothy Roberts. "This seems astonishing because we are so used to focusing on a tiny set of physical features, especially skin color, to assign people to racial categories."[49] Black Americans are arguably even more diverse than Africans, given the amount of mixing over the years with the immigrant and indigenous populations of our country. African Americans look racially similar only because Americans of all backgrounds have learned to recognize the thing called "race" by scanning people's bodies for minute cues that signal some degree of African ancestry. And once we find those cues, our brains organize them into the categories that seem to be so natural and meaningful that "race just *is*."

So not only is race an enduring way of marking social and political divisions between people that is unbecoming to a democratic society, it is a completely bogus way of assigning biological characteristics to human populations. And since that is the case, shouldn't we be trying to do away with the idea of race altogether? Shouldn't we be working to change the post-racial lie—that race no longer has any social, historical, psychological, economic, or political meaning—into a demonstrable truth?

Let's consider this idea for a minute. Suppose we simply declare that from now on, "race" will have no meaning. No longer will college applicants or census respondents have to check boxes to indicate their racial identity. Sociologists will stop studying racialized hiring practices and the racial composition of neighborhoods. Human rights activists will no longer mention racial disparities in education or the criminal justice system. Pollsters will stop collecting information from "racial" groups about anything, from their political opinions to their economic situation to their experience with racism. If the best-equipped schools are majority white and the most dilapidated are majority black, or Hispanic, or Native American, depending on the region of

68 FRACTURED: RACE RELATIONS IN "POST-RACIAL" AMERICAN LIFE

the country, no one will notice, since we will now be officially color-blind. As Roberts points out, "race is very real as a political grouping of human beings and has actual consequences for people's health, wealth, social status, reputation, and opportunities in life."[50] Ignoring these consequences doesn't seem to get us any closer to the goal of equality. In fact, abolishing the idea of race would institutionalize racial disparities even more firmly.

But strangely, even if we do continue to acknowledge the existence of race, we could be heading toward the same unwanted result, especially if we hold on to the belief that our current racial divisions are natural and normal—that is, if we decide we do "see" race (since it's so obvious to us) but declare it doesn't matter anymore, that we're "over" all of its negative implications about people's relative worth. If we continue to believe that race is about natural, biological divisions in human populations, says Roberts, "it [would be] easy to dismiss the glaring differences in people's welfare as fair and even insurmountable; even liberals could feel comfortable with the pace of racial progress, which leaves huge gaps between white and nonwhite well-being."[51]

What if we replaced "race" with ethnicity? If race is a category that has been ascribed by others, ethnicity implies more choice. A combination of nationality, ancestral origins, language, cultural identification, and to some extent, how the community sees and accepts us, ethnicity might allow us to note our interesting differences in a more egalitarian way. Of course, ethnicity can be complicated. I interviewed a student whose mother is Korean and father is white but who identifies with and is fully accepted by his African American neighborhood, as that was where he grew up, learned to speak the vernacular, absorbed the culture, and made lifelong friends. Another interviewee told me he is technically Afro-Cuban, but since people in his community expect a person to "look mixed" if they say they're part Hispanic, he identifies solely as African American. A women who identifies as half black, half Iranian, asked, "But in the end, how can you be half anything? You're double!" A young man who looks white but has Chinese and Latino roots in addition to his European ancestry tells me he would prefer to call himself a person of color, but that doesn't fly with his peers. Looking at my own ancestry, I would say I'm ethnically German with perhaps some Irish and Scottish mixed in. Since I have some choice in the matter, I might go with German alone. But I don't really have any ties to Germany. I know little of the language and not much about the culture except what I read. So can I choose American? That would be fine, except that if every American did so, we'd run into the same problem I mentioned earlier: By disregarding people's backgrounds and racialized life experiences over many generations, we ignore the very real effects on their health, wealth, social status, reputation, and opportunities in life. Not to mention their pride in their history of struggle and the experiences, both positive and negative, that bring them together in community today. So it seems that for the moment at least, we are stuck with race.

Even though there is no such thing as race.

# · 4 ·

# RACISM BY ANY OTHER NAME

Given the tenacity of the idea of race, we might wonder if prejudice based on the "look" of a person might somehow be endemic to the human condition. Haven't human groups always othered, feared, and fought with people who looked different from themselves? Haven't people always found some reason to create hierarchies, with the most powerful group benefitting from its dominant position? And isn't it sort of logical to group people according to their most obvious visual features: skin color, hair type, the shape of their eyes, nose, and lips? Even though we know that a person's "race" cannot be accurately detected in his or her genetic code, maybe racism itself is somehow embedded in human nature. If so, would it be our fault if we haven't erased every bit of prejudice from our psyches? If we err, maybe we are simply being human.

Such questions are often on the minds of students in courses I've taught about race. The answers are not easy to come by. We know that the cultural systems that humans devise are powerful determinants of behavior and that these systems can be harsh or kind, discriminatory or fair, depending on the people who create them—the flexibility or rigidity of their thinking, their political and religious convictions, their life experiences, their economic motives, their inner demons, their collective histories. We know that once a system is in place, especially if it rewards powerful groups at the expense of others, it is very hard to dislodge. Racism as a system of power, exploitation, and exclusion seems to be particularly devious, appearing and reappearing in different communities at different points in time. And what's even more concerning, racism is picked up remarkably quickly by children—even very young children.

This might surprise us because of the common belief that young children are free of racial bias, that they, more than the rest of us, really don't "see" race, or if they do, they don't let it get in the way of having fun together. But researchers have found that very young children do have sophisticated knowledge of the racial hierarchy and are capable of using it to dominate others in their play.[1] Even at the liberal preschool that the authors studied, white children were observed experimenting with how to handle the privileges and behaviors associated with the white position, while children of color were learning to cope with the reality of their status as ethnic "minorities." In one of the study's many vignettes, the authors watch a 4-year-old white child, Renee, trying to pull a 4-year-old white girl and a 3-year-old Asian girl, Lingmai, across the playground in a wagon. Although Renee tugs enthusiastically at the handle, she cannot budge the wagon, which is sitting on uneven ground. Eventually she drops the handle, and Lingmai, eager to continue the game, jumps from the wagon and begins to pull. "No, No. You can't pull this wagon," Renee scolds her. "Only *white Americans* can pull this wagon." Lingmai tries to ignore her but again, Renee admonishes her, frowning, her hands on her hips, making it clear that only "white Americans" are permitted this task. Lingmai runs to the teacher, sobbing that Renee has hurt her feelings. The teacher comforts her and gently insists that Renee apologize. Renee does so reluctantly, not looking at Lingmai, who then runs off somewhere else to play.[2]

This startling example might suggest that a tendency toward race prejudice is endemic in human nature simply because the children are so young. The researchers point out that already, at age 4, little Renee has considerable knowledge about the U.S. racial hierarchy. She is not merely repeating racial epithets or copying stereotypical behavior she's seen on television. Her understanding of race is more sophisticated than that. She knows she is a "white American" and that Lingmai, the child of Asian international students, is not. She knows the white identity can give her power and authority over others, and she can enact the "white American" role with some skill. If racism is this easy for youngsters to pick up, even in a school environment that encourages positive multiracial interaction, maybe the idea that humans are programmed to learn to demean and control others who are "different" is not so far-fetched.

But as much as these examples could let humans off the hook, at least somewhat, for our exclusionary tendencies, I am not convinced that Renee's early knowledge of how to enact the American idea of race means that racism is engrained in our nature. As the researchers point out, 4-year-olds are more sophisticated observers of the world around them than most adults realize; they are adept at picking up both overt and subtle messages about language, culture, and human psychology without being consciously taught. Children's fascination with the alluring sounds and visual effects of film makes them particularly susceptible to subtle cues about race and class that creep into even the most fair-minded of productions.[3] But even before television and video were invented, children were quick learners of the racial hierarchy. I learned I was superior to blacks and Native people from nonsense rhymes that were passed from one child to another on the sidewalks of Chicago in the 1950s. I picked up anti-Mexican bias from offhand comments my mother made about a "dirty" tamale cart selling lunch on the street. Even though I had Asian friends, I learned to regard their parents with suspicion after hearing about "Chinese water torture" from a white playmate. I was careful to treat others nicely—I picked up those messages too—but before I went to kindergarten, before I had ever heard the words "race" or "white," I knew that I was part of a superior group, although why that was, and how that would affect my life chances, I did not know.

In the same way, children of color learn about their inferior racial status by picking up cues, sometimes very subtle cues, from the world around them. A young adult who immigrated to the United States from Haiti as a 5-year-old tells me that her first memory of race was walking to a candy machine in a laundromat where she had gone to help her mother. As she passed a white woman who was loading wet clothes into the dryer, the woman took one look at her and grabbed her purse out of her laundry cart. No words were exchanged. Yet this searing memory stayed with the child, initiating her into the racial hierarchy of her new country. She had learned that she is black, she says, and that black is seen by the white world as a bad thing. "That was such a blatant experience for me, and such an early one," she says. "I remember feeling really, really upset. I just wanted a candy, you know? But I knew then that the world was different for me." There is no question that racism is learned and that it is learned much earlier and from more subtle and transient encounters than adults might think. Yet whether it is picked up so quickly because humans are programmed to fear and hate people who seem "different" is still unclear.

## 74 FRACTURED: RACE RELATIONS IN "POST-RACIAL" AMERICAN LIFE

But if we knew of a complex, hierarchically organized society that did not demean and exclude people from neighboring cultures on the basis of color or other easily identifiable features, we might have evidence that the propensity toward race prejudice isn't hardwired in our biology after all. Furthermore, if we knew of "white" people—that is, people who would be seen as white in America today—whose society was completely free of prejudice against people of color, we might be convinced even further. Interestingly, such societies did exist in the Mediterranean world thousands of years ago in the very civilizations we consider foundational to our own. According to professor of classics Frank Snowden, in the ancient world Egyptians, Greeks, and Romans treated their dark-skinned neighbors, the Nubians (who they called Ethiopians), with clear-cut respect.[4] They traded with them on fair terms. They saw each other as military and diplomatic equals. They fought and conquered one another. They learned each other's languages. They intermarried. Homer spoke of "the blameless Ethiopians, the most distant of men, favorites of the gods." Greek and Roman artists carved figures of Ethiopian adults and children in exquisite detail. These favorable impressions of blacks "were explained and amplified, generation after generation, by poets, historians, and philosophers."[5] It's not that the people of the ancient world "didn't see color," as "colorblind" folks would have it today. In fact, "from the Greek and Roman point of view," says Snowden, "the most arresting characteristic of Ethiopians was their blackness."[6] Skin color and hair type were remarked on, but they were never seen as inferior. Above all, the ancients did not stereotype all blacks as primitives who were defective in religion and culture. "Nothing comparable to the virulent color prejudice of modern times existed in the ancient world," says Snowden.[7] That was to come later, with the advent of race-based slavery.

It is true that slavery was practiced in many ancient societies, from Rome, Greece, and Egypt to Ancient China, Ancient India, the Islamic Caliphate, and the pre-Colombian civilizations of the Americas. But in those days, African peoples were no more likely to be captured or sold into slavery than any other group. "By far, the vast majority of the thousands of slaves [in the ancient world] was white, not black," says Snowden.[8] In fact, the English word "slave" comes from "Slav," since so many conquered Slavic people were sold into slavery. Since blackness was not yet equated with slavery, no ideas were developed that black skin was God's punishment, or that the slavery of Africans was "natural," or that Africans were "radically defective in religion, libidinous, bestial, a source of slaves."[9]

## RACISM BY ANY OTHER NAME

Why did the European adventurers have such a different view of dark-skinned people than the Egyptians, Greeks, and Romans? Snowden suggests that it was the distance, the lack of everyday contact, the suddenness of the first encounters between sailors on their "voyages of discovery" and the people who had long inhabited the rest of the world. The shock of visual difference combined, perhaps, with the missions of exploration on which they were sent, the assumption that any "discovered" bodies, land, and resources existed for their—or their sovereign's—benefit, and their belief that the beings they encountered had no preexisting religion, no intellectual or creative life, no social, military, or political system of any import, all gave Europeans the idea that they were far superior to black and brown-skinned "natives." These encounters and the exploitation that followed were totally at odds with the experiences of people in the ancient Mediterranean world, where "the black man was seldom a strange, unknown being" and where the civilizations of blacks were never seen as defective or in fact, radically different from their own.[10]

But over the last 500 years, philosopher Charles Mills explains, "an opposition of us against them with multiple overlapping dimensions" began to develop: "Europeans versus non-Europeans (geography), civilized versus wild/savage/barbarians (culture), Christians versus heathens (religion)" that eventually coalesced into the basic opposition of "white" versus "nonwhite."[11] This worldview, formulated at a time when Europeans were consolidating their economic and cultural power around the world, served as the foundation for both the invention of race and the white supremacist laws, beliefs, and practices that held the oppressive system in place. Once the economic benefits of the exploitation of lands and bodies became apparent to the "lords of all the world," as they called themselves, slaves were no longer seen as human beings who had the misfortune of being captured in war as they were in ancient times; they, and all colonized and conquered people, slaves or not, were relegated to a new category: "*humanoid* but not fully *human*."[12] Theories concocted by European philosophers and so-called race scientists gave this nefarious idea added weight: The minds of non-whites were childlike, they claimed; the "uncivilized" were incapable of logical thought or analysis; their brain capacity was limited by the size and structure of their skull; they were unable to govern themselves by any other system but tyranny; their cultures, their histories, their languages, and their literature, if they had any at all, were worthless, and so on.

These beliefs, taken together, made up what Mills calls "the Racial Contract," a set of agreements between one set of humans who classify themselves as full persons ("making due allowances for gender differentiation") and another set of persons, or rather, subpersons, with a different and inferior moral status.[13] The purpose of the contract "is always the differential privileging of the whites as a group with respect to the nonwhites as a group, the exploitation of their bodies, land, and resources, and the denial of equal socioeconomic opportunities to them."[14] The Racial Contract is not an actual written document that can be read and agreed upon by equals who genuinely consent to its terms, Mills explains. Like the more familiar "social contract" of European philosophers—Hobbes, Locke, and Rousseau, among others—the Racial Contract is "a purely hypothetical exercise, a thought experiment"[15] that establishes relationships between people and society, explains how the state was created to organize and mediate human affairs, and lays out what counts as a "correct, moral, and objective" interpretation of the world. But unlike the social contract, which describes theoretically "how a just society would be formed, ruled by a moral government, and regulated by a defensible moral code,"[16] the Racial Contract describes what actually happened to "non-whites" as Europeans came to dominate the world. "Non-whites" were never signatories to the Racial Contract, of course. And they never would have accepted that the freedom and equality so extolled by white European thinkers and moral leaders did not apply to them had these terms not been enforced through terror, ideological conditioning, and all means of physical and psychological torture.

The ideas, assumptions, and practices of the Racial Contract were so well established by the 18th century that we shouldn't be surprised at the claim that it was white supremacy rather than freedom and justice for all that laid the ideological foundation of the United States. As historian Manning Marable argues, race was used at the founding of our country to deliberately restrict the democratic process. "The American state was constructed first and foremost on a racial foundation," Marable says. "Its major laws and its framework were originally designed to preserve the institution of slavery and to give permanent structural advantages to propertied classes."[17] Even after slavery was abolished, economic, political, and social benefits continued to accrue to whites of all social classes through racially biased laws and practices that lifted up whites at the expense of racial "others": the near-extermination of the Native American tribes and the granting of their lands to white settlers; the abrogation of Native treaties, especially when valuable resources were at stake; the reinvention of slavery through the practices of tenant farming, debt peonage, and convict labor; the quotas on "non-white" immigration that preserved jobs, schools, and neighborhoods for "white Americans"; the material and social assistance that was preferentially given to impoverished European immigrants to help them become "white"; the ethnic cleansing of Mexican Americans during hard economic times; the denial of loans and mortgages on equal terms to "non-whites"; the construction of Social Security so as to deny benefits to racial "others," and so on.[18] As the white majority thrived from these exploitative practices, America rose in stature and wealth to become the world's greatest super-power. But as black social critic Ta-Nehisi Coates points out, "Everything we are, everything we have, is built on past sins."[19]

Why do most white Americans (and some "non-whites" as well) balk at this interpretation of our history? Curiously, Mills says, the Racial Contract is not so much about how one should interpret the world as it actually exists but an unspoken agreement among its signatories, whites, that is, to *mis*interpret the system they set up. This produces "the ironic outcome that whites will in general be unable to understand the world they themselves have created."[20] "One could say then, as a general rule, that white misunderstanding, misrepresentation, evasion, and self-deception on matters related to race are among the most pervasive mental phenomena of the past few hundred years, a cognitive and moral economy psychically required for conquest, colonization, and enslavement."[21] In other words, in order for whites to champion the ideals of freedom and equality, they had to deny, minimize, or be utterly blind to what they were actually doing, saying, and believing about human beings they had designated as inferior.

Regardless of whether one accepts that the sum total of America's greatness was built on past sins, it's pretty clear that for the past 500 years, "racism" has meant a lot more than simply calling people names, or preferring to keep company with one's own "racial" group, or even denying "non-whites" equal opportunity to survive and thrive. Racism was designed as an all-encompassing system of social and economic domination by people who called themselves "white" and who believed themselves to be biologically, culturally, socially, and intellectually superior to the people they designated as "non-white." There's no question that these beliefs and practices are changing. As Martin Luther King said on many occasions, "the arc of the moral universe is long, but it bends toward justice." It does not bend on its own, of course. Active resistance to white domination by both people of color and progressive whites has been—and continues to be—essential in bringing some of the worst excesses of that system down. The overt behavior that demeans and excludes "non-whites" is no longer fashionable, or even tolerated, at least in public.

78 FRACTURED: RACE RELATIONS IN "POST-RACIAL" AMERICAN LIFE

As white social critic Jonathan Chait writes about black progress, life is not perfect, but it's improving: "Since the abolition of de jure segregation, most social metrics relevant to black prosperity have turned sharply upward. The achievement gap has shrunk, the black poverty rate has fallen, the rates at which African-Americans are victims of homicide has collapsed, while the proportion of black police officers has exploded."[22] But after all that, has the Racial Contract finally expired? No, says Mills. It has merely taken a different form.

While it is true that much of the blatant, obvious racism has become an embarrassment, the economic, social, and psychological privileges that have accrued to whites at the expense of their imagined "racial inferiors" are hard for whites to give up—or even consciously notice, if one accepts what Mills says about the invisibility—to whites, at least—of the racial order. Ta-Nehisi Coates, among many other critics, explains how white supremacy still pervades our everyday interactions and institutions. It is obvious, he says, "when the rising number of arrests for marijuana are mostly borne by African-Americans; when segregation drives a foreclosure crisis that helped expand the wealth gap; when big banks busy themselves baiting black people with 'wealth-building seminars' and instead offering 'ghetto loans' for 'mud people'; when studies find that black low-wage job applicants with no criminal record 'fared no better than a white applicant just released from prison'; when, even after controlling for neighborhoods and crime rates, my [black] son finds himself more likely to be stopped and frisked."[23]

Why do these and so many other variations on the Racial Contract—the racial profiling of Muslim Americans at airports; the immigration "detention centers" that imprison random people of color, sometimes for years, without charge or trial; the dumping of hazardous refuse on Native American lands, the resegregation of schools and neighborhoods all across America—continue, if we have actually made great strides toward equality? The answer is complicated. It has to do with the tendency for whites and white-dominated media to deny and minimize the Racial Contract, a misunderstanding of what counts as "racism," and the devious nature of white supremacy itself. Let's look at how that system works.

Most whites play down the extent of white supremacy today. Even the term seems antiquated, as if it referred to some obscure racist skinhead group or a few crazies who shout epithets at immigrants of color. Of course, whites do recognize the remnants of overt or "old-fashioned" racism. They might notice a string of blatantly racist comments on the Internet in response to a news report or a video that went viral. They might overhear the drunken ranting of some white college students emerging from a bar as they demean and challenge their African American or Latino or Asian or Native American peers. They might hear from friends of color about the "micro-aggressions" they suffer on a daily basis: the questioning of their abilities and knowledge, the insults on the street, the assumption that everything they worked so hard for was given to them by affirmative action. They might even, like one person I interviewed, know of a professor who still believes in the innate inferiority of languages other than English, telling his students that "the level of excellence a language can achieve is built into the structure of the language itself, so that no piece of Spanish poetry could possibly come up to the level of the best poetry in English." But mostly, they believe, individuals who hold these views are throwbacks, "bad apples" who are in no way representative of the majority of whites today. As for the biases against people of color in the judicial process, in housing and health, in education, in all those areas where "non-whites" were barricaded from equal treatment in the past, so much of that is gone now, they say, or at least it is so changed that it is barely recognizable.

Even whites who roll their eyes at the term "post-racial," as literally everyone I talked to did, still act as though—and *live* as though—the American system can work for everyone as long as they work hard, dream big, and ignore the idiots who stand in their way. People of color are astonished to learn the extent to which whites are blind to their own privilege. How can white people *not* know that they live in an unequal world when their advantages are so obvious, they ask. It just doesn't make sense. So could it be that they really *do* know and act as if they don't? But why would they do that? Most likely, they conclude, whites aren't blind to reality. They just don't care.

Yet as a white person who has always cared, I know that it is quite possible to be blind to the ways I benefit from the racialized system that I abhor. Whether the Racial Contract gives me preferential access to pleasant, well-equipped schools for my children and the opportunity to buy or rent in a clean, safe neighborhood (the garbage truck arrives on schedule; the police and fire fighters are there in a jiffy); whether it's the help I have received through the modest assets of my parents, who were given a fair shot at their first mortgage back in the 1930s when racist laws and procedures were still on the books; whether it's my networks of family, friends, and colleagues, almost exclusively white, who, over generations of white privilege have developed the connections and the means to advise me on applying to college, help me in a job search, or bail me out in a financial emergency; whether it's the credibility

I have with authorities because of the language I speak or the acceptability of my home dialect; whether it's my trust that the medical establishment is looking out for my best interests instead of ignoring my child's pain[24] or using me as a guinea pig for some experiment never before performed on humans;[25] whether it's the feeling of anonymity and safety I feel at ordinary vacation spots—campgrounds, beaches, small-town restaurants, a fishing excursion to a local pier; whether it's the certainty that the history of people who look like me will be celebrated at monuments and museums and in the schoolbooks of my children; whether it's the knowledge that if my children speak Spanish fluently, their bilingualism will be seen as an asset rather than a liability; whether it's my understanding, learned as a child, that police officers are my friends rather than potential assailants; whether it's the relaxed feeling I get when I sit on my front steps drinking a beer on a hot summer day, knowing that passersby will not gaze at me with barely disguised scorn; whether it's the certainty that when the next "crazed gunman" shoots up a movie theater or a classroom full of schoolchildren, no one will say that white people need to get their act together; all of these privileges and expectations of daily life, so ordinary to most whites, are legacies of white-sponsored abuse and disenfranchisement of their so-called racial "inferiors." Whites may not pay much attention to their race privilege; it is likely that they take it for granted. But these everyday, ordinary decencies cannot always be counted on by people of color.

Young whites are especially likely to minimize or deny the current iteration of the Racial Contract. As one teacher I interviewed told me, "White students have this automatic defense: 'We don't live in unjust, inequitable, unequal, racist times! Like, *no*, we *don't*! Barack Obama is president!'" In a poll sponsored by MTV of 14- to 24-year-olds, young Millennials believe themselves to be more tolerant and diverse and profess a deeper commitment to equality and fairness than previous generations. A majority say that their generation, at least, is post-racial. Most think that their generation is more egalitarian than their elders. About two-thirds say that the election of a black president shows that there are no longer barriers to minority achievement. They believe so firmly that we have now reached an ideal state of equality that 88% say that racial preferences are unfair as a matter of course and 70% believe they are unfair regardless of historical inequalities. Sixty-eight percent of these young people believe that focusing on race prevents society from becoming color-blind. Seventy-three percent "believe that never considering race would improve society." And a huge majority—90%—believe that "everyone should be treated the same regardless of race."[26] This all might sound like good news; it will only be a matter of time, it seems, before the Racial Contract will expire.

But sadly, young whites' attempts at racelessness tend to fracture our society even more. Since we are all supposed to be equal now, the very mention of race can be seen as racist. "Like if you're describing someone to a friend," a white undergraduate tells me, "you might say they have curly hair, or they're tall, or they have a beard or whatever. What you don't say is that they're dark skinned, or black, or anything about their color. That would make it seem like you're noticing when you're supposed to be color-blind."

"I'm worried that if I notice race, people will think I'm racist," says another white teen. "I mean, wouldn't that look like I care what race someone is?"

Young people of color find this attitude amusing. First of all, the behavior of their white peers makes it obvious that they do, in fact, notice color; otherwise, why would they hang out with mostly white people? And if they do have friends of color, why do they seem so proud of it? Furthermore, why do so many young whites feel uncomfortable when they have to engage with the actual cultures of their "multicultural" friends?

"We let minorities into our sorority now," says a white undergraduate to her African American roommate. "We have Asians. Oh, they're not *Asian* Asians," she hastens to explain, as her roommate stands there, speechless. "They're like *white* Asians. They talk like us, they walk like us, they don't eat any of that Asian food or speak any Asian language."

"Um, that's not good," ventures the roommate. "Aren't they losing their culture, their language, their identity?"

"We don't think about it like that," replies the white teen.

"That's assimilation," counters the roommate, clearly frustrated. "How can you not see that?"

"What's wrong with assimilation? It makes things nicer for everybody. It's not like we're racist. I mean, my mom, she's always racist, but I'm not. I even have a black friend at home."

Even young, progressive whites who have worked to create totally seamless friendships with people of color can say and do things that add to the sense of separation and fracture.

"I feel there's a lot of ignorance in my generation," says Sandra, a biracial African American and white undergraduate. "I think some things should be obvious to people and they're not. Like my friend Jeremy, he's white, but he's actually a really good rapper. Last night, the three of us were in the car, me, Jeremy, and another friend, Steve, who's African American. We're all really good friends, and we're on our way to a party. And then Jeremy drops the N-word."

"While he was doing a rap?"

"Right. And then he says, using that word, he says that he's 'with one and a half.' One and a half N's. So that would be me being the half, because I'm biracial, plus Steve, who's black. So finally Jeremy realizes that something is wrong because Steve isn't laughing, and Steve laughs at *everything*. So then Jeremy is like, 'Wait, is that all right?' And then Steve says, in this very serious voice, 'I think you're kind of taking it a little too far.' And then I think Jeremy felt really bad. But that just shows the complete ignorance of some people in my generation. Did he not pay attention to the things we learned in grade school about black history? Did he not know how degrading that word was at the time? Not that I think black people should use the word either, but I feel like it should be obvious to white people that whatever black people choose to say or not say, whites should never use the N-word!"[27]

I think Jeremy, like so many other white young adults, is so caught up in the idea of the post-racial—though he might not put it that way—that he truly believes that young people of his generation have put all that history behind them, that racial slurs have lost their power, that the old degrading insults are just words that anyone can use to joke around among friends without causing offense. He probably hasn't studied much black history, and he isn't old enough to remember the ways racial slurs were so deliberately used to dehumanize people of color in the past. His gaffe with his friends may be the beginnings of a deeper understanding of what it means to be a person of color in this country today. That would be an excellent result, even if it meant that Jeremy had to feel a little hurt and embarrassed for the rest of the trip.

But I predict it will be difficult for Jeremy to see that what is okay for black people to say may not be okay for whites. For to be nonracist in this "post-racial" era is to appear absolutely egalitarian. Not only are we not supposed to notice race, we're supposed to avoid thinking about how our racist history has imparted meanings and consequences that are strikingly different for groups of color than they are for whites. If a black student union forms on campus, there should also be a white student union. If there is black history month, there should also be a white history month. Anything else would be racist because it gives preference to one group over another—never mind that "white history" is taught in standard history courses every day of the year and that student unions, even though they're not called "white student unions," still represent almost exclusively the concerns and perspectives of the white majority on campus.

Many young whites believe, even if they do not say it, that black students who sit together in class are racist because for some unfathomable reason they are more comfortable with blacks than they are with whites. If students speak Spanish with each other in the halls they're being racist, since their conversation excludes non-Spanish speakers. A class on Chicano history and culture, open to all, is seen as a threat to "American" history that focuses on the achievements and positive contributions of white people. The idea of equal treatment is taken to even more ridiculous lengths by conservative politicians: Florida Representative Ted Yoho, in an attempt to discredit "Obamacare," claimed that a provision that taxes tanning beds is racist because it places an unfair burden on white people.[28] Media advertising, perhaps in an honest attempt to be unbiased, shows happy, middle-class families of color enjoying the same activities that happy, middle-class white families do. And of course, that is sometimes true. But the message that everyone not only deserves to be equal but has actually achieved equality adds to the illusion of a benign, post-racial order.

It is easy to see how a belief in fairness and equality can lead young whites to the conclusion that racism is nothing more than prejudice by any racial group against any other. Since white racists of the sneering, nasty sort are not so visible these days, and since, as most young whites imagine, the doors to achievement are now open to all, *any* discrimination on the basis of race would be noxious, regardless of whether it impacts blacks, browns, or whites. If equality has now been established throughout America, either by the election of a black president, or by the gains of the civil rights era, or by the liberalism and fair-mindedness of the Millennial generation, then it would be logical to assume that racism goes both ways.

This idea that anything that privileges one race over another should be called "racism" is new. It would have been ludicrous for someone, in say, 1850, before the Civil War, or even in 1950, when I was a child, to claim that it was equally wrong for blacks to discriminate against whites as for whites to discriminate against blacks. In those days, it was obvious to everyone that blacks had no possible opportunity to discriminate against whites even if they wanted to; it would have taken a complete reversal of the racial order for any "non-white" group to impose its authority on white people's freedom, life chances, education, employment, and personal dignity the way whites did to blacks. Of course, blacks resented and often hated whites in those days, both for their acts of racism and for their convictions about white supremacy.[29] But interpersonal hatred and resentment are vastly different from an entire system of authority, privilege, and domination constructed to keep "non-whites" in their place.

True, the world has changed since 1950. Yet whites continue to reap the economic, social, and psychological "wages of whiteness," as one scholar of race puts it.[30] If you appear to be white, no one will refuse to check out your groceries or neglect to show you housing in a pleasant part of town. Cars generally stop for you when you push the button at a crosswalk.[31] No one questions your citizenship or your right to vote. No one will report you to airport security if you speak another language, wear a beard, or sit silently and pray. No one seems unduly surprised when you do well on the job or at school. If you chronically oversleep or turn in a few poorly written assignments, your teachers may think you're not up to the level of the class, but they won't harbor a suspicion that your behavior represents something all too common about the white race.

Even though the world has changed so much that a black man can occupy the most powerful position in the nation, people who are seen as "white" still call most of the shots. So as long as the Racial Contract continues to hold true, "racism" cannot be defined by a simple equation: What A does to B equals what B does to A. Racism, now as in the past, must be defined as any speech or act that perpetuates white control, white norms, white privileges, and white assumptions about the inferiority of whoever fails to meet white standards, regardless of the motives, the intent, the character, the lifestyle, or the number of friends of color of the perpetrator. As some say in shorthand, "Racism equals prejudice plus power." But this "power" isn't simply the authority of one individual over another. In a face-off between, say, a white man and a black man, if the black succeeds in knocking the white off his pedestal, the black has demonstrated a certain degree of power. But when he walks away from the fight, victorious, he is still living in a society that by law, custom, and historical precedent denies blacks equal justice, equal rights, and equal opportunity with whites. The black individual's power in the altercation may be considerable, but it cannot, by itself, give him control over his own life. As long as the system as a whole is dominated by the ideology of white supremacy, a person of color cannot—by definition—be racist against whites. As long as "non-whites" lack the power to keep whites from voting, restrict their neighborhoods, lock them up for life for minor crimes, deport them to countries they've never lived in, ignore the intellectual potential of

RACISM BY ANY OTHER NAME 85

their children, ban their languages, erase their history from school curricula, and then tell them that they just haven't worked hard enough to earn their respect, "non-whites" cannot be racist against whites.

This definition of racism—prejudice plus the power of whiteness—is hard for many whites to hear, even when they agree that America is far from "post-racial." The accusation of racism is one of the worst moral insults that can be flung at white people today. Since whites commonly equate racism with crude stereotypes or individual acts of meanness that they would never engage in, they are put off by the idea that something they might do, think, or say could be considered racist, which would seem to put them on the same level as the Klan. As a result, we now have what sociologist Eduardo Bonilla-Silva calls "racism without racists."[32] And in such a society, white denial can go to ridiculous lengths:

A popular cooking show host defends herself against a racial bias lawsuit, saying her plans for a nostalgic, southern, plantation-style wedding "weren't racist in themselves, although some people might take them the wrong way." When asked by an employee what uniforms the servers should wear she allegedly replied, "Well, what I would really like is a bunch of little niggers to wear long-sleeve white shirts, black shorts and black bow ties, you know in the Shirley Temple days, they used to tap dance around. Now that would be a true southern wedding, wouldn't it? But we can't do that because the media would be on me about that."[33]

The mother of a white teen accused of murdering a Latino immigrant declares that her son cannot have committed a hate crime because their family allows his black friend to sleep on their couch and eat off their dinnerware.[34]

The wealthy, white owner of a sports team implores his biracial companion to stop appearing in public with black people, and when challenged, declares his remarks can't be construed as racist because he enjoys the company of black prostitutes.

Racism today is generally enacted under conditions of "plausible deniability," where the comments or the actions are not so blatant that they can immediately be identified as racist. If someone objects to a joke where Mexicans are characterized as gardeners and servants to white people, the person who told the joke can put on an incredulous look and ask why anyone would imagine she's racist since she dated a Hispanic guy in high school. If a white fraternity throws a "thug" theme party, encouraging members to come in blackface and dress in baggy pants and do-rags, it can plausibly deny that the party idea is racist because "black people portray themselves that way on TV all the time."

# 86 FRACTURED: RACE RELATIONS IN "POST-RACIAL" AMERICAN LIFE

If the university police issue a crime alert describing the perpetrator as a black man between five and a half and six and a half feet tall, a description that would cover all of the black men on campus except for the basketball team, they could justify it by saying this was the description given by the victim and that they were only doing their job. Even if a white defendant is accused of a racially motivated attack against a black, he can bring witnesses to the trial to say that he couldn't possibly be accused of racism because he has black friends.

This strange situation, where whites refuse to take responsibility for their racism, or even admit that *somebody's* racism continues to cause massive social and economic disparities, leads Bonilla-Silva to ask, "How is it possible to have this tremendous degree of racial inequality in a country where most whites claim that race is no longer relevant? More important, how do whites explain the apparent contradiction between their professed color blindness and the United States' color-coded inequality?"[35] The answer, he says, is color-blind racism, or, as others have called it, "cultural racism," where whites assume that racial inequality is the result of the cultural deficiencies and self-defeating behavior of people of color themselves.

These assumptions are not new, Bonilla-Silva explains. In fact, whites have been blaming people of color for failing to thrive since the end of the civil rights era.[36] But over the next several decades, activists of color and their allies began to push back, providing evidence that "cultural inferiority" and personal irresponsibility were inadequate explanations for the poverty, joblessness, educational failure, and disproportionate incarceration that remained after de jure segregation ended and that racism in white-dominated institutions could account for much of the economic and social gap. Yet many whites continue to believe that poverty and inequality must be caused by individual and cultural failure. "Shielded by color blindness," Bonilla-Silva says, "whites can express resentment toward minorities; criticize their morality, values, and work ethic; and even claim to be the victims of 'reverse racism.'"[37]

Here are some examples I've come across recently: A white suburban newscaster defends the decision of an inner-city public utility to shut off water in midsummer to residents, mostly black, who owe more than two months in bills, which have increased 119% over the last decade. Breaking from his role as objective reporter, he informs his audience that "some people" are choosing to ignore their water bills and buy expensive entertainment instead. He presents no evidence to back up his claim, expecting the audience to agree that poor blacks are irresponsible.

A white adult volunteer at an afterschool program expresses her sense of satisfaction in helping African American kids with their homework. "Of course, it's an uphill battle," she confides in a half-whisper, as we are in a public place. "When you have parents that don't care about their children's education, and then on top of that, you have other kids telling them they're not really black if they read a book, you can't expect to make a lot of progress." When I ask whether she thinks the school, which is desperately underfunded, is part of the problem, she tells me the story of her European grandparents, who came to this country with nothing, yet made a small fortune through hard work and responsibility.

A white professor attempts to block a person of color from tenure, telling the review committee bluntly, "Whenever you diversify your faculty you *always* lower your standards. That's not racist," he adds. "That's just true." His white colleague, shocked by this statement, says nothing. "We have to live with these people," the colleague explains to me later. "Now that we're supposed to be post-racial, faculty think they no longer have to watch what they say. But I've been department chair, and I know for a fact that we simply *can't hire* somebody who's not qualified! If it's clear from a candidate's file that they're not qualified, we're not allowed to bring them to campus to interview. It doesn't work that way. But still there are faculty who will argue that if you hire for diversity you're threatening standards. And they insist they're unbiased! I think that attitude is there with a fair number of our faculty."[38]

Such attitudes are not reserved for groups of color that continue to struggle for economic inclusion. Even "model minorities" are targets:

I am visiting a small, liberal, East Coast college, where a history professor is telling me why the school has such a hard time retaining faculty of color despite its earnest attempts at diversity. "When I first came here there was an Asian woman in the Philosophy Department who was engaged in research on Chinese views of science," the professor tells me. "I knew her quite well. The department had told her they had hired her to 'harmonize' them—they were divided into factions, and they believed an Asian woman could bring harmony to them. So that was her first indication that things would not go well for her. And soon it became clear that not only did they see her as a stereotype, they didn't respect her research either. She was trying to show the importance of looking at philosophy from a non-Western point of view, and that just wasn't done in that department! The prevailing view, of course, is that 'West is best,' that sort of thing. So the faculty didn't give her the respect of arguing with her ideas on equal terms. They just dismissed her work as inconsequential, something they didn't need to engage with seriously. And on top of that, some of her colleagues thought they could joke with her using the most outrageous Asian stereotypes. Once someone suggested to her at a faculty meeting that they go to a department Halloween party together as Shakespearian characters: 'I'll be the wall and you be the "Chink" in the wall.'"

"And the colleague thought that was funny?" I ask.

"Yes. And what's worse, no one said anything to the guy. Finally the whole atmosphere at the college got so bad that she left. I'll never forget it. She told me she'd had two miscarriages and that she felt she had become so poisonous that she couldn't carry a baby to term."

"My god, that is so extreme!"

"Yes, it is. Oh, I can tell you story after story about what happens here."

"But I don't suppose her colleagues thought they'd done anything to upset her," I remark.

"Right. Their position was that she should have been able to deal with criticism of her research, and that she was being way too sensitive about their light-hearted jokes. They even argued that there's always some truth in a stereotype, that in fact, Asian women *are* known for bringing harmony; it's part of the culture!"

"Do you think they were saying these things to get her to leave?"

"I don't think so. I mean, they were kind of stunned when she handed in her resignation. The racism in these kinds of comments has always been unconscious at our institution. It's like they don't hear themselves saying these things, and even when it's pointed out to them, they are unable to see how they made her feel dehumanized. Even after all the attempts the college has made at diversity, it's still really hard to get most faculty to take these things seriously."

Elegant racism, Ta-Nehesi Coates calls it—in contrast to the "oafish racism" of blatant, unrepentant racists. "Elegant racism is invisible, supple, and enduring. It disguises itself in the national vocabulary, avoids epithets and didacticism."[39]

This is racism without racists, color-blind racism, no-fault racism, "I-didn't-mean-to-offend" racism, "you-couldn't-possibly-think-I'm-racist" racism—racism by any other name.

# · 5 ·

# DUMPING ON THE POOR

I am standing in line at a gift shop in an upscale mall in a Seattle suburb, considering whether the Christmas ornaments I'm about to buy will fit into my suitcase for the trip home from my interviewing jaunt out west. The mall looks gorgeous for the holidays: A huge evergreen tree, decked out in red velvet and glittering crystal, soars upward toward the vaulted ceiling. Crowds of shoppers cram the toy stores and check out the newest electronic gadgets. Children dash about, oblivious of their parents' attempts to keep track of them. Espresso machines hiss and purr. Grandparents balancing lavish plates of sweets make their way to café tables in the center of all the confusion.

Just ahead of me in the check-out line, two young white women are planning a holiday party. One of them is explaining to her friend that the decorations will include a ghetto Christmas tree.

"What's that?" asks the friend, raising an eyebrow.

"That's where you hang the trashiest ornaments on the ugliest tree you can find."

The friends laugh quietly, glancing at me, as if they sense I am listening.

"You have to look for a scrawny one with hardly any branches," adds the first.

"They don't even sell those kinds of trees around here!" objects the other.

"Yeah, so I was thinking, we'll get an artificial tree and a scissors...."

"Art project!" laughs the friend. "I'm in."

Earlier in the week I had been talking with a white professor of education at a university in the Northwest, and I had asked her, as I had asked other people across the country, "Which do you think divides our country more, race or class?"

"That's hard to say, since race and class are so intertwined," the professor replies, echoing what so many others had told me. "But I do think that people who have been impoverished for generations are the most despised group in this country," she adds. "I've been startled to see how blatant people are in their hatred of anyone who's poor. The lower class is even more despised than ax murderers!"

"Unbelievable, right?" she says, chuckling at my alarmed expression. "But I'm serious. My education majors this semester were actually more sympathetic to serial killers than they were to poor people. We had started out talking about mental illness and how delusional thinking can contribute to violent crime. The whole class was really interested in that idea and the implications it could have for sentencing. 'What would be a fair punishment for a murderer who was hearing voices or driven by paranoia?' they wondered. And I was thinking, isn't it great that future teachers can imagine what motivates people who are so different from themselves? That's such an essential skill in education! But later, when the discussion turned to poor people, all that empathy evaporated."

"What were they saying?" I ask.

"Basically, they believe the poor are an irresponsible bunch of whiners."

"Your students are middle class?"

"Yep, middle or upper middle, mostly, with one exception. Krystal is the only African American in this class of white education majors. I don't know if the rest of the class realizes this, but she's a high-profile figure on campus among the students of color, a clear leader. She grew up in poverty. Her mom worked as a secretary and was frequently unemployed. She knows next to nothing about her dad. She was a self-described 'bad ass' in junior high but got turned around by a few caring teachers, which is what inspired her to go into education. So when it came time for my students to do their class presentations, Krystal chose to do hers on the difficulties people face when they try to escape from poverty, even though she knew her classmates wouldn't be very receptive."

"How did it go?" I ask.

DUMPING ON THE POOR

The professor sighs. "As badly as she expected. Worse, actually. I think she was as shocked as I was by their response. She had sent the class an article about fast food workers who were demanding a raise in the minimum wage. The idea had gotten a lot of press—mostly negative, by the way. And along with it, she sent around an op-ed piece written by a guy who was working two jobs, one of them at a burger joint, the other as a janitor, and he still couldn't support his kids with the wages he was getting. And just as Krystal predicted, the class had no sympathy for his situation. Their reaction was, 'What's *his* problem? Those fast food jobs are supposed to be for high school students, not adults! They're meant to be steps up to the next level so kids can buy a car.'"[1]

"They're really out of touch, aren't they?"

"Yeah. But it gets worse," replies the professor. "They also read a letter to the editor in response to that op-ed that basically argued if you can't afford kids you shouldn't have had them in the first place. And the entire class agreed with that more radical voice in the conversation—except Krystal, who was just stunned."

"How did she deal with their reaction?"

"Well, it's interesting. This is how class and race get folded together. Krystal had put some statistics up on the screen saying that the number of poor children in this country had increased by 4.5 million since 2000.[2] And at that point, a few really loud voices interrupted her and argued that all that shows is that poor people are having more children. And the rest of the class chimed in about how irresponsible that is. Nothing Krystal could say would dissuade them from that idea. They were so blinded by their notions of individual failure that they couldn't even get their heads around the possibility of reading that stat in a different way. They'd never thought about why the poverty rate would go up as the politics and economics of our state changes."

"So Krystal couldn't convince them with stats. Did she talk about anyone's personal experience? Tell any stories?"

"Even better—or so I thought—she gave the class a poverty exercise. The scenario is this: You're a single mom with two kids, and you're living just above the poverty line so you don't receive any public assistance. Here's your monthly income, and here's a list of things you've got to work into your monthly budget: rent, utilities, phone, food, transportation, medical expenses, child care, and so on. Students work in groups to see if they can manage it. The point of the exercise is that it's darn near impossible. It's supposed to get them to see why families get behind on their water bill and face a shutoff or why they might be evicted from their apartment and become homeless.

But the students were quite flippant about it. They said, 'That's the same as *my* budget on campus! I have to pay for this and that with the same amount of money!' And I just had the sense the whole time that the students saw poverty as code for race. So I'm waiting for Krystal to kick in and counter their arguments. But they were bent on drowning her out, and she was pretty overwhelmed."

"How did the students bring race into it?" I ask.

"They didn't, at least not openly," she replies. "But race was definitely the subtext for them. They kept referring to the woman in the scenario as a black woman who had babies out of wedlock. And there was nothing in the script that suggested her race or even her marital status at the time she'd had her kids!"

"I wonder why they immediately assumed she was black. It's not like your students have much contact with African Americans of any class background, right?"

"Right," says the professor. "Most whites in this state live in majority white communities, and as you've probably noticed, there aren't very many African Americans on campus. And basically none live in town."

"So why would your students immediately think of a black woman?"

"It's not only my students, of course," the professor replies. "The whole discourse in this country is saturated with assumptions about who is poor and how their own bad behavior justifies their poverty.[3] It's true that a lot of the stats Krystal had found were about African Americans. But also, the class was looking at Krystal standing right there in front of them. And it was so obvious to me that these white students thought that her presentation was a defense of poor blacks or even blacks in general. Their position was that if people choose to ruin their lives by having out-of-wedlock children it's their own fault. If they're so poor, why did they go and have kids? But then Krystal stumbled a bit when she said that one in three women of color has been raped, so maybe these were children of rape. It was a weak explanation, but it was all Krystal could think of at the moment. And then the class just went for blood. One of the male students says, 'Well that's a horrible statistic, and rape is a sad, tragic thing, and not for a minute am I *justifying* it, but at the same time, only a tiny portion of rapes result in pregnancy. So that's not necessarily the reason people are poor.' And Krystal was just speechless."

"Oh boy. So did you help her out?"

"No, I let it play out as long as I possibly could, thinking that Krystal would recover. She's got great charisma in the classroom and wonderful group management skills. But the situation was just too personal. The class was basically telling her that she should never have been born—or at least that's how she read it."

"So no one in the class could come up with another explanation for how the woman in the scenario might have gotten those two kids?"

"None of my students has an understanding of how that happens," replies the instructor. "They never even questioned how this hypothetical mom might have become single. Maybe she was divorced. Maybe her husband walked out on her. Maybe he died! Maybe he lost his job and health care benefits and couldn't afford proper treatment for a terminal illness. On the other hand, maybe this single mother had been a middle-class homeowner whose property was repossessed when the economy crashed. Or maybe she lost her job and had to take a significant pay cut with her next one. Maybe she had no transportation to anyplace that was hiring at her skill level. There are so many variations on this theme. People don't realize how close the middle class is to falling into poverty, given a few bad breaks.[4] But whatever her backstory, it's quite likely that the woman in the scenario didn't see her way out of her situation but thought her kids would do better if they got an education. None of those possibilities came out in the discussion. The class could only understand the situation in terms of, 'If you're poor you shouldn't have children,' and 'I live on $19,000 a year. I pay *my* bills. *I'm* not on public assistance. *I* can do it.'"

"So it sounds like your students are all pretty right wing, politically."

"Actually, they run the gamut from left to right," replies the instructor. "We have some very right-wing people and some very left-wing people in there. But they were united in their opinions about the poor. And what I find really strange is the way the old arguments about poor women keep reappearing through the generations. You hear things like, 'They're poppin' out babies.' I overheard one of my students the other day talking with her friend about a book she was reading for her Native American literature class, and she was like, 'Could you believe that? Why didn't she just leave the guy? But no, she just stayed there, poppin' out babies.' And this is one of my left-leaning students!"

"I remember that expression from the 1950s."

The instructor laughs. "I hadn't heard it for a while either. Maybe since I left the South. I can hear my old Arkansas grandmother 50, 60 years ago: 'They just poppin' out babies. Can't feed 'em, gonna have more kids on welfare so they can get a bigger check.' And now we hear that same phrase from the Millennial generation, which is supposed to be the most progressive in history!"[5]

Why do these young adults, who as a generation are reputed to be so egalitarian, dump on the poor so readily? "Students here think that being liberal is cool," a graduate student instructor tells me. "They all watch The Daily Show with Jon Stewart, and they support smoking weed, and gay marriage is all right, and they're totally fine with interracial dating—even if they don't engage in it—but at the same time, they're very reliant on individualistic narratives, which is a rather conservative trait. They have that bootstraps mentality, white students in particular. The majority of white students here think they're in college because they worked really hard to get here and that their success so far has nothing to do with the neighborhood where they grew up, or the jobs their parents have, or the perks their schools and communities had to offer. So according to them, anyone can pull themselves out of poverty on their own, and certainly without relying on government support."[6]

Are these attitudes unique to the Northwest, I wondered? Or are they more widespread? Checking a recent Pew Research Center survey, I found that all over the country, the majority of young liberals blame "a lack of effort" rather than "circumstances" for the poverty in America today, and in fact, they are much more likely to do so than their politically liberal elders.[7] And when race is brought into it, and they are asked to choose between racial discrimination and personal responsibility for the reasons why some blacks can't get ahead, 68% of the younger respondents say that blacks "are mostly responsible for their own condition," while older liberals "blame discrimination by an 80 to 10 percent margin."[8] So young people across the country do seem to have become conservative on this issue and more unsympathetic toward the struggles of the poor, particularly poor people of color.

An African American professor of education on the East Coast offers some insight as to why this shift has occurred and how attitudes about poverty are tied up with feelings about race. "A lot of white folks want the racism thing to go away," he tells me. "And they want it to go away in a way that doesn't cause them to have to give up anything or do anything dramatic. The 'post-racial' mindset offers young people that opportunity, and the bootstraps mentality is the perfect foil."

Interesting, I thought. If you want the racism thing to go away, you simply claim you're color-blind and treat everyone as an individual. And since everyone is now equal, in your eyes, it would be only logical to see all people as equally able to do well for themselves, no matter what their income, or social

DUMPING ON THE POOR 95

standing, or life circumstances. And that would mean that with enough hard work, anyone should be able to pull themselves out of poverty.

"Barack Obama's election is a case in point," continues the professor. "A black man made it to the top. That's pretty dramatic in itself. It seems to say to these young people that race can't hold you back anymore, because if he can do it, anyone can. And at the same time, Obama's election didn't really cost anybody anything. It didn't affect anything. The system has been left intact."

"But didn't you think Obama's 2008 win was a game-changer?" I ask him. I still get goose bumps when I think of the *New York Times* headline: "OBAMA: Racial Barrier Falls in Decisive Victory." In fact, I've got that front page framed at home in my study.

"Initially we were all so hopeful," agrees the professor. "You know, it's interesting; the night he won the presidency everything felt surreal to me. For the first time in my life I thought, 'Maybe I actually belong here! Maybe this *is* my country!' And this after 60-plus years of life. But then, almost immediately, I saw how it was going to go. How he would be blocked at every turn. Oh yes, we're going after the black man. And we don't want anything of his to last that's seen as good. Particularly if it has his name on it or has him associated with it."[9]

"So when you say the system has been left intact after Obama's election, do you mean the racial hierarchy?"

"Of course. And the economic system. And the judicial system. And the political system. All these intertwining systems that keep people of color and poor people down. None of these systems have been touched in any meaningful way by Obama's election. None of these folks are substantially better off economically, or politically, or in the courts, or anywhere else. In fact, for many, their situation has gotten worse. And now these privileged young whites are beginning to repeat the old conservative line: 'It's their own fault.'"

Yes, I thought; I can see it. Blaming the victim is an effective way to avoid having to make any dramatic changes to a system that privileges whites, especially wealthy whites, at the expense of the rest of the population. But, I wondered, how can these young people blame poor people of color and still believe they're color-blind? If young people are "so over race," how can we account for the race consciousness so obvious to the white instructor when her students piled on the African American student presenter? It must take some twisted logic for people to believe that they don't see race, yet at the same time, see a hypothetical poor, single mother as black when her race hasn't even been mentioned.

Scholars of race explain this contradiction as a psychological struggle, largely unconscious, between what well-meaning whites want to believe about people of color and what they actually feel about them. Their egalitarian mind-set causes many young whites to reject overt racism, but their negative stereotypes about people of color persist, reinforced by popular and social media. So instead of declaring outright that poor blacks are lazy and irresponsible, which would be racist and therefore objectionable, young whites assert that it's the poor who haven't gotten their act together. Because of their unconscious or semiconscious racist attitudes, they express their feelings about race in subtle, coded ways. Like Krystal's fellow students, they might simply make the assumption that a random impoverished single mother is black. Or, like the two young women who were planning their Christmas party, they might use code words like "trashy" or "ugly" or "ghetto" to signify that they are making fun of poor people of color. The word "ghetto," by the way, used to mean something more dignified than it does today. Black ghettos in the United States, like Jewish ghettos throughout Europe, used to be seen—by liberals, at least—as segregated spaces where human beings were trapped by powerful societal forces beyond their control. But these days, when being poor is widely viewed as avoidable, the "ghetto" has come to mean a trashy, no-account place. A dark-skinned place. A place where someone would put up a ridiculous-looking Christmas tree decorated with cheap, flashy ornaments because they're too ignorant to know any better and too shamefully poor to buy anything decent.

To be fair, it's not just white people who indulge in blaming poor people of color for their own condition. Even Barack Obama can imply that blacks are responsible for their failure through his humorous comments, often directed toward an audience of the black elite, about a fictitious character named "Cousin Pookie," or "Ray-Ray," or "Uncle Jethro"—all cultural references to poor blacks, who, he implies, need to get off the couch, quit blaming "the man," stop watching Sports Central all day, and find a job.[10] I have been struck by how often my own students of color, particularly upper middle class or upper class blacks, toss around the term "ghetto" these days. A few use the term affectionately, especially if they grew up in a poor black neighborhood where they still maintain friendships and family ties. But most use the term to distance themselves from lower class blacks. One of my undergraduate interviewees, who describes herself as "biracial or black, depending," explains what she tells her white peers who come to college with stereotypes about blacks: "It's not every African American female whose hair's not real, because that's

DUMPING ON THE POOR                                    97

all me up there," she says, gesturing toward her long, wavy locks. "I'm not going to be loud and in your face like the ghetto blacks you see on TV. I can run organizations and have intelligent conversations and speak proper English. And my earrings aren't going to be the size of an apple; I prefer studs."[11]

The word "ghetto" doesn't even need to be mentioned to communicate the speaker's contempt of poor blacks. A smart, young, black professional, a former student of mine, posts a video on social media featuring two black women having an uncouth, screaming argument over an item of clothing at a holiday sale. "OMG," he comments. "Y'all know that's why I support voter ID."[12]

Social critic Charles Blow has some thoughts about why this country is so fractured along lines of race and class. "We are self-sorting," he says, "not only along racial lines but also along educational and income ones, particularly in our big cities. Our cities are increasingly becoming vast outposts of homogeneity and advantage, arcing ever upward, interspersed by deserts of despair, all of which produces in them some of the highest levels of income inequality ever seen in this country."[13] Indeed, a Pew Research Center report shows that over the past three decades, residential segregation by income has increased in 27 out of 30 of the nation's largest cities. Residential segregation by race—regardless of income—is even more pervasive.[14] "It's easy to demonize, or simply dismiss, people you don't know or see," says Blow. "It's in this context that we can keep having inane conversations about the 'habits' and 'culture' of the poor and 'inner city' citizens. It's nearly impossible to commiserate with the unseen and unknown."[15]

It does seem logical that geographical fracturing along lines of class and race would promote psychological distancing as well. But living as neighbors with the poor doesn't always lead to empathy with their struggles. Blacks and whites have always lived side by side in the U.S. South; since slavery, blacks have worked in white homes, raised white people's children, cooked their meals, and tended them in old age. Yet until recently, most whites saw black subordination and attendant poverty as natural, and few whites expressed outrage at the racist system. Likewise, the old Arkansas grandmother who went on about "poppin' out babies" surely lived near poor people. No doubt she was poor herself. Yet she was quick to criticize women she considered a peg beneath her. Psychologists call this mental quirk the "fundamental attribution error": Humans are more likely to blame others' failings on their bad habits or poor character than on their life circumstances. Yet when they're accounting for their own failures, people tend to blame situational factors rather than their own personal shortcomings. In other words, the old Arkansas grandmother blames her poor neighbors for their poverty and even insinuates that they're having more children just to increase the amount of help they get from the government, but when it comes to her own family's poverty, she's apt to explain it by misfortune beyond her control: her husband's sudden illness, the poor growing season, the tractor that broke down just before the harvest, and so on.

Another explanation for people's lack of empathy for the poor comes from recent experiments in psychology and neuroscience that show that people who are in positions of power, even temporarily, are less able to take on the perspective of people who are relatively powerless. Some researchers explain this result by noting that powerful people or people from a higher social class pay scant attention to those they see as socially beneath them because they don't need their resources—they already have plenty for themselves. Other scientists prefer a physiological explanation: Regions of the brain that allow people to take the perspective of others show less electrical activity when the subject feels powerful.[16] It's important to note that this tendency is not irreversible; people can develop more empathy for others when their own circumstances change or when they think more deeply about the reasons for other people's misfortune. With facts, analysis, and practice applying theory to real-life situations, it appears that anyone, even the heartless, can learn to overcome their bias against the poor.

"But no one asks young people to think critically, if at all, about the reasons for poverty anymore," a graduate student instructor tells me. "They have never really heard the perspectives of people who are poor.[17] And few people point out to them that their acceptance of 'difference,' which they're so proud of, doesn't include the poor—the people they see as not working as hard as they are."

Krystal's professor was determined that her students would not leave her class without questioning their beliefs and feelings about the poor. After some time had passed and the class had a chance to settle down, the professor returned to the minimum wage issue. "This is the way I handle disruptions over race or class," she tells me. "I let it die down. But then we're coming back to it. Once I can make sure we have enough time to very carefully unpack the arguments and learn more information, we'll reopen that discussion. Because I believe that students can change. You know, one of my students remarked— and she wasn't being flip; it was her honest opinion: 'Well, poor people will always be despised. It's just in our culture. There's no way you'll ever turn people around about poor people.' She was quite certain about that. But amazingly

DUMPING ON THE POOR

enough, my class *has* turned around. Even Max, the student who had been the most obnoxious with his glib remarks all semester, even he began to see things differently."

"What kind of things was he saying?"

"This was a young man who had bragged to the class about getting a full ride scholarship to a university in Florida where he had played on the beach for three years and had a big time with his buddies and never did a lick of schoolwork. Max had told Krystal, rather arrogantly, I thought, that he had $300 left over from the poverty exercise, which proved it wasn't impossible after all. He hadn't considered child care, which Krystal pointed out to him, but that didn't seem to deter him from claiming it could be done. Well, later in the semester, Max started working for a big chain store to cover his educational expenses, and wouldn't you know it, the store cut back on his hours to avoid paying health benefits. And at that point, Max started listening seriously to my arguments in class. I was so tickled—I overheard him telling his friends what I'd said about how the taxpayers end up paying for workers' health expenses through emergency room care, which is reimbursed to hospitals by the government when patients don't have the resources to pay for it. So even Max could take a different perspective when he began to understand other people's struggles in terms of his own experience."

Later, when I talked with Krystal about the incident, it was clear that she was not nearly as optimistic as her professor about how much her peers had learned about race and class by the end of the semester. Sure, Max had understood that he was being exploited by his new employer, and maybe he would be able to extend his new sensibility to other low-wage workers. But she had not forgotten the insinuating remarks of her white classmates about the race of the woman in the poverty exercise and especially their belief that poor people should just give up the idea of having children.

"We need to start shedding some of the assumptions we make about race and class," Krystal tells me. "You know, things like, 'If people of color tried harder they would make it.' Or, 'The reason people are the way they are is because of their own personal choice.' And, 'America is great because you can do anything you want with hard work.' All these are myths. There are so many reasons that people get stuck in poverty, sometimes for generations—reasons that are not their fault at all![18] It's so frustrating to have to explain that over and over."

"Do you ever feel you get through to people?" I ask Krystal.

"Well, I try to leave them with something to think about at least. When I tell white people what people of color face in terms of both race and class, they say, real sarcastically, 'Oh, do I have to start feeling guilty now?' 'No,' I tell them. 'You need to take responsibility.'"

"Class is the hidden log we keep tripping over," says a white professor at an elite eastern school. "That whole overlap of race and class, I wish we could be more forthright in discussing it. We have wonderful, sweet kids at this school, but there's a huge divide, economically, between the very wealthy students and the very poor. Yet they don't seem to talk about it. There's a kind of self-perception that 'we're all middle class,' even though we don't have very many middle-class students at all. They wouldn't be able to come here if they were, because our tuition is one of the highest in the nation. Our students are, if anything, polite. So they don't mention it. Whether they see it or not, I don't know."

"Sure, you can see who's wealthy!" exclaims a group of students of color when I mention the professor's comment. "Class is so apparent here; you can't ignore it."

"How can you tell what class someone is?" I ask.

"Their dress! Their watches! Their gadgets!" exclaims Patricia, a biracial student who is here on scholarship. "We'll be sitting in the dining hall, and one of my friends will say, 'Oh wow, did you see that girl, her dad is so-and-so.' I actually wish I were never told those kinds of things, because it makes me look at the person differently. One of my close friends, his dad is the CEO of some construction company. I didn't know that until the end of last year. And I then started thinking, 'Well no wonder you want to invite me to your lake house *all the time.*' So even though the class thing is not talked about, it's so obvious! You can just walk through the dining hall and you'll see it."

"But at certain times, class can be very subtle," another student breaks in. "Like someone is wearing a bracelet that costs $10,000 that's screwed onto their wrist and is very hard to get off."

"That's being subtle?" I ask, smiling.

"Yeah it is," says Patricia, "compared to the ones who are driving Daddy's Range Rover. But the funny thing is, these very wealthy kids don't imagine that anyone's life might be different from theirs. Say we're in a study group together; they'll just casually plan for the whole group to go to this Asian bistro where you can easily run up a bill of $500. Mind you, there's five of us. But I don't have a hundred dollar bill lying around for dinner. So at times, it seems as though class is this huge elephant in the room and other times it's in your face. But we never openly talk about it because professors try to steer clear of it, and in social activities it becomes this ambiguous place where people assume things about each other, which makes it uncomfortable for anyone who has to kind of deviate from those assumptions."

"Class is the last frontier for Americans," comments an African American staff member who is listening to the students' conversation. "Even though we're supposed to be a classless society, class runs deep. Young people care about how they're perceived, especially when as a society we're all so focused on material things. So what I notice, especially listening to the students, is that a lot of them fake it. They can easily buy knockoffs, so they can dress like their family is successful monetarily. On the other hand, I see students of color, especially black males, who play down their class. If their family is wealthy, they're seen as 'bougie'—'bourgeois' snobs who tend to live in their own world. So other blacks might tell these guys they're 'not black enough'—especially if their class status is obvious. Even though wealthy blacks experience plenty of racism and social exclusion from whites, the rest of the black community doesn't necessarily see them as the 'real' people, the people with the black creds, the ones who take the brunt of this country's racism and classism, the tough guys."

"Yeah, I've seen that happen," says David, an African American student. "But that's not the main challenge I face at this school in terms of class."

"What's the most difficult thing for you?" I ask.

"A lot of people come here from the nation's top prep schools, so they're prepared to be extremely competitive," David says. "And unfortunately, they're under the impression that people who didn't go to those schools—which is most students of color—are not going to be as smart as they are. So there's this belief that black and Latino students are not up to their level of intellect. Students of color, students of Latino descent, everyone who falls under the cloud of affirmative action, we're all in a position of having to prove ourselves to people who think we're not up to it. I mean, I like these guys, and I'm friends with a lot of them. But I have to show them I'm not only capable of interacting with them socially, I'm just as smart as they are."

"That's kind of annoying, don't you think?"

"Well, yes," David replies. "Though I can understand why they would think that way since they've never been around us much. And our school puts so much emphasis on diversity that when they come here, all of a sudden they're in contact with people they've only heard about through the media. But I'll have to say, their attitude is more than annoying—it eats away at your self-esteem."

"How do you experience that?"

"Well, for me, it started in the very first class I went to at this school, 'Intro to Political Philosophy.' I remember it like the back of my hand. The professor was asking questions on the first day, and I was totally lost. I felt like the other students had done some reading over the summer that I missed, which was weird. And I remember turning to the person next to me and asking, 'Did we have homework to read?' And he was like, 'No, I just knew this in high school.' And mind you, I went to an exam school in Boston—a public school where you have to take an exam to get in. It's the third best school in the city, and I graduated near the top of my class, so I was confident that I was prepared. But when I got here, I felt like I was behind even before there was any homework assigned! And because of that, I felt like I had to take the reading ten times more seriously than the others did."

"So did you?"

"Oh yes. After that class I decided that the next time we met, I had to be the one raising my hand. Even if my answers might be wrong, I would have to prove to the others that hey, I know some of this material also. Of course that made me study really hard, which was a good thing. But it was also a bad thing, since it made me doubt myself. Even though I knew from high school that I had the background to do well here, I would ask myself, 'Wow, is this the school for me? Can I do this?' It wasn't until I did well on my first paper that I felt I could fit in here, which was pretty sad."

"So it was just the first few weeks that you were feeling that way?" I ask.

"Well actually, the feeling lasts longer than that," David replies. "I mean, nobody ever says to your face—thank god—that you're just here to diversify the student body. But you feel it. It's in the air. So you need a lot of support from your family back home in order to stop second-guessing yourself. Fortunately I have a brother who went here, and he gives me a lot of advice on how to deal with it."

Despite these students' frustrations, they feel they've been pretty successful at negotiating the interlocking divide of race and class that separates them from their wealthy, white classmates, and so far, they have been willing to work at it, even if it means distancing themselves from the communities they came from.

"I get the phrase, 'Hey, you're different,'" says David.

"Ooh! All the time!" agrees Patricia.

"And half of me sees that as a good thing," David muses. "But the other half sees it as a bad thing. Being told I'm not like the others reminds me that I'm doing well for myself, which is good, I guess. Yeah. It even takes away

# DUMPING ON THE POOR

for a moment that feeling of self-doubt. But at the same time, that constant mantra, 'You're different,' is so full of negative assumptions about the black community in general, I don't know how to take it."

Patricia nods. "Some people come from very privileged neighborhoods where they haven't been exposed to different ways of life. They don't know what it means to have to decide between paying a light bill and buying books, because their biggest struggle is whether they should get the J.Crew top or the Polo Ralph Lauren jacket. So people like me and David end up trying to educate them about the realities of the world, which students here unfortunately haven't been exposed to."

Patricia sighs deeply and lapses into uncharacteristic silence as David, always optimistic, picks up the thread. "I feel like there's more students of color like me and Patricia coming up in the world," he says brightly. "There's this new generation of students of color that actually are doing quite well. I see it in my own family, and I think throughout the country there's probably more of that happening. That's why I feel like a pioneer at this school. Even though there were brothers before me who set the path for us, I feel like we're still doing the same thing as they did when this school was first integrated back in the '60s. I feel like we're leaving a legacy for the next generation of students of color."

"That must feel good."

"Yes, but it puts us under a spotlight. We're under a lot of pressure to do well. I have to be extra vigilant in what I do and extra vigilant in *how* I do, so as not to mess it up for the people coming in after me."

Patricia and David are strivers—smart, energetic go-getters who are willing to accept the cultural norms and standards of their white, upper-class peers that have been formed through centuries of race and class privilege and whose history and meaning are now obscured. I have no doubt these students will realize their professional dreams. They are doing exactly what most Americans think students of color and working-class students should be doing: working hard, making friends with people of all races, and trying not to blame others for any setbacks they might encounter. As they go through life, they will continue to try to integrate themselves into a society that at best, considers them exceptions. And because of their superior education, their positive attitude, their language, their manners, and their willingness to keep their race and class-based struggles to themselves, they will be seen as "acceptable."[19] But they will not be seen as equal. Because equality implies more than grudging acceptance against a backdrop of disdain and ridicule of the people they come from.[20]

*Acceptable so long as you are 'like us' is not diversity!*

Perhaps David and Patricia find their path relatively smooth because their parents and older siblings paved the way for them. But for students who are the first to come to elite schools from working-class and immigrant families, the race/class divide is wider, the culture shock more extreme, and the road to adulthood fraught with a good deal more frustration and resistance. I talked to Andrea, a senior at another private college that until very recently had been a haven for the sons and daughters of the white elite. Under a new president, the school had admitted so many students of color and lower-income students that it was now one of the most diverse in the nation.

"I'll be the first in my family to graduate from college," Andrea tells me proudly. "That's first-generation blood. My parents have been in this country for about 25 years. My father is Egyptian and my mother is Peruvian, so technically, I'm not considered a person of color even though I'm brown-skinned, because according to the census I'm 'white' in both categories—Middle Eastern and Hispanic. Northern New Jersey, where I'm from, is so unbelievably diverse that I hadn't thought about my racial identity until I came to college, but now, it's become really clear that I'm a person of color even though, weirdly, I'm white. Before I came here I didn't know anyone who came from money, either, so I wasn't aware of what it meant to be upper class. But from the moment I moved into my dorm room I could tell that something was different."

"What was the first thing you noticed?"

Andrea laughs. "Well, I came to college with one suitcase. When my mom put me on the bus she was telling me that my big suitcase would make me look like I was putting on airs. 'The kids will make fun of you,' she says. 'You'll seem like a princess.' But of course when I arrived, I found that kids had TVs and couches and all sorts of fancy treats that their parents had brought for them. And I took the *bus* to come here! I'm telling you, coming to this school was the biggest culture shock of my life—there's no other way to describe it. And I've lived abroad! I lived in Cuba for a year, but I never experienced anything like this. So for me it was extremely traumatic."

"Tell me more about the differences. What else did you notice?"

"Well at first, it was the emphasis on sports, especially sports I had never heard of like lacrosse and squash, which are very big here. There's not even a football team in Newark, so I didn't know why the game is considered such a big deal, or how everybody knew about it except me, apparently, or how central it is to American culture. Another difference that really freaked me out was the drugs. Oh, my gosh, I had never been in close contact with hard

DUMPING ON THE POOR

105

drugs before. I mean, I know some crackheads because they live on the street in my neighborhood, but here at school, the people involved in drugs are the privileged kids, the upper class! And their attitude toward drugs was totally different from anything I had ever encountered."

"What was their attitude?"

"They were totally nonchalant. I mean, you'd think that if people were going to do something illegal they'd be hiding it? But I remember the first time I went to my economics study group, there was a bowl of cocaine right there—right in the room! And my group mates were all like, 'Oh, do you want some?' And I said, 'No!' Probably way too loudly. I was *so* nervous. I thought I had such a strong character that I could deal with anything. But how am I supposed to fit in with these people?"[21]

"Mmm, right."

"So coming to a wealthy, privileged school was extremely traumatic for me," Andrea continues. "And that feeling of shock is shared pretty widely amongst all the minorities on campus, because while there's a big push to get us here, there's no mentorship offered once we're here. I mean, when I came, the college had no dean of students, no first-generation advisor, no multicultural student center, no discussion of race or class."[22] Andrea is stumbling over her words, breathless, passionate, laughing one moment and serious the next. "Sorry," she exclaims. "There's so much I want to tell you!"

"Take your time."

"I came to college when I was 17. I had gone to a charter high school in Princeton, New Jersey, that was created especially for first-generation students. I loved it there, and I did extremely well. I never would have been able to come here if it wasn't for the education I got at that school. Everyone there had the same struggles. All of our parents worked crazy hours. A lot of my friends filled out invoices for their parents because they didn't speak English. But when I got to college, I was just thrown into the mix without any thought as to what we were about to encounter. I know there's supposed to be benefits for everyone when there's a mix of cultures and perspectives, but here, you aren't even supposed to talk about those differences. And you're definitely not supposed to talk about being working class."

"How did you find that out?"

"Oh gosh. The first week I went around asking people, 'Hey, are you going to go to the financial aid meeting? Where is it? Do you happen to know?' But everyone seemed really embarrassed that I even asked that question. One girl even told me, 'Don't say that.' She was like, 'You'll see it in the email. Just read the email more carefully. Don't tell people.' And that made me really uncomfortable."

"So it's considered shameful here to admit you're not wealthy?"

"Of course. I know that now. But I still don't understand *why* it should be such a shame. I'm proud of where I come from!"

"What's been your experience here with faculty?'

"Not so great," sighs Andrea. "Because of the way I was raised and the neighborhood I come from, when I'm genuinely confused or have urgent concerns I can come off as aggressive or rhetorical. You know, the loud female. Or the loud female of color. Or the loud, *working-class* female of color. And that hasn't been received well. I've tried to change my style. But it's not working. There are two professors on campus who, when they see me, will actually walk the other way."

"Goodness."

"The faculty reaction is not always that extreme, but still, it's never easy for me to form the relationships that everyone says are so important. You know, when you're looking for letters of recommendation or just when you want to talk about your work in office hours, it's going to be a lot easier when the professor can relate to you. So for me, most of the time, there's just this uncomfortable distance that makes it hard to have a conversation. I don't have the same sort of casual banter with my professors that other students have. Like when they joke about what's going on at the Cape, where I guess a lot of rich people go, or even when they make jokes about bat mitzvahs and Judaism or whatever, I'm lost. That's not a culture I identify with."

"But you could learn about different cultures, just like you did when you were in Cuba."

"Sure, I guess. But sometimes you feel so targeted you don't want to identify with people in any way, shape, or form. I'm actually taking a class now, there's 42 students, and I'm the only woman; I'm the only woman of color. And there are jokes made about abortion that I can't find funny, or you know, make me uncomfortable. And I feel like there's an expectation among both students and faculty that I won't say anything in class. And not just because I'm a woman. I'm seen as this alien being, this woman of color who comes from some poor neighborhood. I'm not 'one of them.' In fact, there's an assumption that the only reason I deserve to be at this school is that I work *really* hard. Not because I have any endowed intelligence."

"*Endowed* intelligence?"

"There's this idea that if you are at an elite school it's because you're quote naturally smart," Andrea says.

"What does that mean?"

"Well, it means that all your classes are easy for you. You just get it, so you don't have to work very hard at anything. But since I was so obviously studying and trying to write papers—which would take forever—I must be lacking something that everyone else had."[23]

"Were your classes harder than you'd expected?"

"Not really, if they were at the right level. But somehow, in my first semester, I enrolled in a political science class that turned out to be an advanced seminar. It had only 10 students, and 9 of those students were the thesis advisees of the professor. So I was drowning, and I was drowning fast. But I refused to drop the class. I had been raised with an immigrant mentality that believes this country is a meritocracy, so if you fail, it's due to your lack of merit. And when I couldn't keep up I thought, yeah, maybe I *do* lack intelligence. Maybe I *don't* belong here. And that made me very depressed. But I couldn't talk to my parents about it."

"Why not?"

"Well, according to the immigrant mentality, depression is not a thing. Like when I was in high school and my mom would hear about girls who had committed suicide because of cyberbullying, she'd say, 'I don't understand. If you have food and a roof over your head, you shouldn't be depressed.' Because both my parents had very real, *tangible* struggles, first in their home countries, and then, coming to America and providing for three children. So depression is not a thing for them. Like, it *can't* be a thing. So of course I couldn't let my parents know that I was feeling down all the time and falling behind in my work."

"Did you try psychological services?"

"Yeah, but here's the thing. I went to the health center, and I told them, 'I don't know what's wrong, but I don't feel right. Something's not right.' And the counselor said, 'I can't help you if you're not suicidal.' And I said, 'I'm not suicidal. I just feel really uncomfortable here.' And then she says, right out of the blue, 'You know it could just be because you're a student of color and this is not really a place that was meant for you.'"

"Goodness. What's her ethnicity?"

"She's white."

"What was she thinking, telling you that!"

"Yeah. I felt so shunned, I never went back. And you know, I was only seventeen! I had no experience with depression, and absolutely no idea what was going on in terms of race and class. And the counselor had no cultural competency to deal with me, so there was no basis for communication. I would go back to my dorm room and think, 'How am I going to get through this?' And I was realizing that it's not just about being an immigrant, and not just about being a woman of color. At no point in your life will you ever again live in the same room with a person who has an income that is *so* exponentially greater than yours. It will never happen!"

"So the class divide was right there with you every day."

"Every day. And I felt I should be able to deal with it. Because so many of my friends come from much more difficult circumstances than I do. I have a very loving home; my parents are always so welcoming and eager for me to succeed. But my friends here all seem so broken. I've got one friend who doesn't know her father, her mother and two uncles are crackheads, and her grandmother suffers from dementia. Another friend's mother is schizophrenic, and her father is verbally and emotionally abusive. She comes from a rural area in the South. She became legally emancipated from her parents during her freshman year, and she worked three jobs, one in town and two for the college, to support herself. Hearing their stories made me terrified, because I couldn't imagine why I was doing so poorly, yet it seemed I had everything I needed."

"So you had to struggle with your feelings alone."

"Well finally, I took a sociology course. I had absolutely no interest in sociology, but I needed to put language to my feelings. And nobody else was offering that. It was the first time I really thought about what it meant to be a person of color, what it meant to be from a low socioeconomic class, and especially, the barriers that I would have to face from now on. And that scared me even more."

"Why did it scare you?"

"Well, it suggested that the immigrant mentality wasn't going to be enough. I kind of knew it by that time anyway. You know, class mobility is supposed to rise with each immigrant generation. It sounds so easy, so smooth. The first generation struggles to make it easier for the kids. The kids are supposed to do better than their parents. But they often do it by discarding their language and their values. Then, *their* kids can't even talk to their grandparents, because they're now totally alienated from the immigrant culture. They've become assimilated, which is supposed to be the goal. But what if you *like* your values? What if you *care* about your language, or languages, in my case? And even if you *do* want to assimilate, which a lot of people do, what happens when you hit barriers of race and class like I've encountered here? How will you handle that?"

DUMPING ON THE POOR                    109

Andrea tells me that one of the more dispiriting meetings she'd had with faculty was with a well-meaning writing instructor who was devoted to the idea that college should be a delightful exploration of the intellect, a smorgasbord of options and opportunities. Frustrated that she received only a B on her first paper, Andrea went to see the professor in conference and asked how she could improve. "Through exploration!" he told her. "Just have fun with your writing. Let your mind go free, and then write what comes to you." "But what exactly are you looking for?" Andrea asked him, near tears. The professor sighed. "Look, maybe this will help you," he told her gently. "Don't think about the grade. That's not the important thing. Just think about what you want to say and how you want to say it." And Andrea replied, "With all due respect, Professor, grades are what got me here, and grades are what will take me to what I want to do next. They *are* all-important. In fact, they're all I have."

"It sounds like you're saying you couldn't afford to express yourself," I tell Andrea in response to her story.

"Exactly. And the professor looked so disappointed and frustrated. I guess he had no way to understand where I was coming from. So he just closed his computer and said, 'Well, I don't know how I can help you.'"

"Oh! So then you were left with nothing!"

"I was dismissed—just like that."

As Andrea struggled through her first two years, an unusual number of bias incidents were reported on campus. Hanukkah arrived, and a large Menorah statue that stood in the center of the quadrangle was vandalized. That same night, swastikas were painted all over the health center. Then someone lit the Pride flag on fire. A comic strip was found in the biology department that joked about Native people being gifted with smallpox-infected blankets. And on the night of the Black Student Union's biggest gala of the year, the black students' dorm was defaced with eggs and toilet paper, and the word "nigger" was written in the snow. All this had the effect of energizing students like Andrea to demand changes from the college. As she began to write outraged letters to the newspaper and meet with administrators and faculty about her concerns, the word got around among the students that she was the go-to person for people of color and first-generation students like herself. But Andrea was in no position to give advice, as she was still in the midst of her own crisis.

"I remember talking with one girl who had dreams of going to law school," Andrea says. "She was juggling a lot of different issues, academically, socially, emotionally, you name it. So as I was thinking about how to help her, I noticed the brochure for the college that was lying there on the table. On the cover were the words, 'Challenge yourself.' And I thought, wow, are you kidding? That's privilege for you! So I said to the girl, 'My advice to you is *don't challenge yourself*.' And she got this scared look on her face and she said, 'Why not?' And I said, 'Just find out what you're good at and *hold on*. All you have to do is get a 3.8 grade-point average and graduate, and you'll have the name of this school on your resume and then you'll be able to go anywhere you want. Or so they tell us. And that's what I want to believe. In fact, that's what I *have* to believe to get through this ordeal. But no matter what, *don't challenge yourself*. Because that brochure was not written for you. It was written for the people who can afford the school and who actually paid for you to be here.' And she was just standing there in shock. I felt really bad afterwards, but at that moment I felt like I was saying something I'd been thinking for three years that I'd never quite been able to express. So I told her, 'One of the biggest mistakes of my life was to challenge myself. Somebody should have told me there are two different brochures for this school. *But they're not writing yours.*'"

"What would help change the culture of the college?" I ask Andrea. "If you were in charge, what would you do?"

"Mmm, if I were in charge," says Andrea. "Interesting thought. Actually, I have a lot of ideas."

First of all, she tells me, the college shouldn't be accepting diversity if it's not going to accommodate diversity. And right now, the administration is just reacting to each crisis as it happens, rather than thinking strategically. Yes, the president's office has a vision, of sorts, about multiculturalism and inclusion, and yes, the school has put a lot of faculty committees to work on these issues. But they're either talking very abstractly or they're coming up with Band-Aid solutions to problems as they arise. They're not asking themselves, "*Why* do we have these issues?" Instead, there's the assumption that we all agree that diversity is a good thing, that nobody's racist here, and that students don't notice class differences. "But that's not true!" Andrea says, her voice rising in exasperation. "Class and race are stigmatized here! That was clear to me from day one. Why don't the administrators see it?"

If this campus is ever going to change, Andrea says, everyone needs to find ways to make marginalized students feel welcome and valued. First-generation students, working-class students, students of color, and students from immigrant families now make up almost half of the student body. But if the wealthy white students, the "traditional students" at this school, don't recognize the ways their peers are battling discrimination and exclusion, how can they change their behavior? Even the well intentioned won't know what to do if they don't understand how race and class work together as a system of oppression. So in order to get everyone on the same page, Andrea says, why not require all students to take an introductory seminar where they would have open, honest conversations about race and class—not just batting around the half-formed ideas that people come to college with, but deep, thoughtful discussions based on readings, solid information, scholarly analysis, and the experiences of people of color and people who are struggling economically that the so-called traditional students have never heard or imagined?

If everyone had a better understanding of race and class, Andrea says, students of color might not feel as though they had to major in sociology in order to find classes where the material makes sense. "We all have so many other dreams for ourselves," she tells me. "We want to be neuroscientists, and mathematicians, and doctors, and art historians, and literature majors. But many of us end up in the social sciences, even if we didn't intend to, because that's the only field that has the vocabulary and the analysis to help us understand our experience. There's nothing wrong with sociology, far from it, but if *everyone* were required to learn how systems of exploitation operate, we would feel as if we had more choice. And if professors in other departments started integrating concepts of race and class into their courses, it would be even better. For example, there's so much interest in human rights and development in other countries. But what about here at home? In economics, professors could use poverty data from rural Vermont or Kentucky as well as impoverished countries abroad. Political science could include the ways people of color are kept from voting, both historically and today. Statistics courses, language courses, writing courses, all could easily deal with these topics. Not that race and class have to dominate everything; they just shouldn't be ignored, or denied, or swept under the rug."

Once the college has a working vision of a more socially and academically inclusive campus, Andrea continues, the administration would need to back it up with solid academic support—tutoring, study groups, introductory courses, mentorship—not just for the "underprivileged" but for anyone who felt they needed it. Then, of course, faculty and staff would need to look and sound more like the student body. "Hiring and retaining more faculty of color is essential, as everyone knows," Andrea says, "but nobody is thinking about how the *staff* needs to be representative of the student population as well. For example, if everyone working in the financial aid office is a white woman who speaks only English, they aren't going to be able to communicate with immigrant parents very well. Why not make skill in another language part of the job description? And why isn't the counseling office staffed with psychologists who have the cultural competency to understand students' frustrations and anxieties as they interact with their privileged peers?" Even the way the college communicates with families should be rethought, Andrea says. It's hard to keep working-class parents involved when everything is digitized. "Newsletters, grades, and even financial aid forms may be cheaper and faster to send electronically, but a lot of low-income families lack Internet access. If you were really thinking about how to be inclusive, why would you send information that people need through a network they can't afford?"

Andrea is so full of good ideas that I encourage her to write them down and deliver them to the administration as a sort of good-bye present when she graduates. But later, as I thought about the impact of elite college reforms like these, I realized that such measures will barely touch the great divide of race and class in this country. So few people from poor communities make it to college at all. The divide between the wealthy and the struggling is widening, cities have fallen into bankruptcy, mass incarceration has devastated communities of color, and the traditional institutions that educate people in a democracy—public schools and neighborhood libraries—are deteriorating or closing altogether. Supporting the talented young adults who have managed to beat the odds is a start, but it's not nearly enough. As long as we continue to think of the chronically poor as an "irresponsible bunch of whiners," as long as we continue to treat them as if their ordinary human failings justify their own marginalization, poor people will remain trapped in communities where racism, classism, and destitution conspire to keep them down.

*Challenge yourself*—that's the refrain of the American dream. As an advertisement for America, it calls out to the rich and poor alike: the eager, suburban, white kid, the professor's daughter, the immigrant, the impoverished person of color. It's the headline on the cover of the full-color, glossy brochure that cheers this country on: "Take risks, dream big, work hard, thrust yourself into opportunity, and you will achieve everything you desire."

But as Andrea reminds us, the American dream has always denied the reality of racialized poverty. And "challenge yourself" is a cruel thing to say to people who are drowning. The trouble is, she tells us, "There are two different brochures. And what if they're not writing yours?"

# · 6 ·

# RACISM AS A COMPLEX SYSTEM

On August 9, 2014, two African American teenagers, Michael Brown and his friend Dorian Johnson, were stopped by police for walking down the middle of a quiet street in the working-class community of Ferguson, Missouri. According to Johnson,[1] the white officer, Darren Wilson, cruised slowly by the teens, telling them to "get the fuck on the sidewalk." Annoyed at the officer's contempt, Johnson countered that they were only a minute away from their destination, and Brown, who was walking a few steps behind him, may have uttered a profanity. Suddenly, they heard the screech of tires as the officer backed up at an angle to confront the teens, causing them to jump aside to keep clear of the car. "*What* did you say?" the officer demanded. As he attempted to get out of the car, the door bumped hard against Brown's legs and abruptly closed again. Enraged, the officer grabbed Brown by the shirt and pulled his head into the police car. A scuffle ensued, with both the officer and Michael Brown "yelling and cussing." "I'm gonna shoot you," the officer threatened Brown. One shot, maybe two, rang out from inside the cruiser. Brown broke free from the officer's grip and dashed away down the street, followed by a terrified Dorian Johnson, who took cover behind a parked car. The officer got out of his vehicle, gun drawn, and strode down the street, firing at least ten shots in Brown's direction, first six shots, then a pause, then at least four more.[2] After the shooting started, according to other eyewitnesses, the unarmed teen stopped running and turned around to face the officer, his hands in the air in a gesture of surrender, yelling "OK! OK! OK! OK! OK!"[3] The officer continued to fire as Brown stumbled forward. Six of the ten shots hit Brown, two of them in the head, killing him.[4]

In a display of gross disrespect to the community, Ferguson police left Michael Brown's body face down on the blistering pavement for more than four hours, a river of blood streaming from his wounds. Relatives and friends frantically tried to push through the yellow tape barrier but were not allowed to approach the body, which at first was not even covered by a sheet. "Neighbors were horrified by the gruesome scene," reported *The Boston Globe*. "They ushered their children into rooms that faced away from Canfield Drive. They called friends and local news stations to tell them what had happened. They posted on Twitter and Facebook, and recorded cellphone videos." It took more than 40 minutes for police officers to call homicide detectives, and by that time, the neighborhood was "in sheer chaos." That evening, after a candlelight vigil, angry and terrified residents took to the streets in protest. According to a Ferguson committeewoman, the treatment of Michael Brown's body "sent the message from law enforcement that, 'We can do this to you any day, any time, in broad daylight, and there's nothing you can do about it.'"[5]

Over the next 11 days,[6] hundreds of Ferguson residents of all ages marched in protest, chanting, "Hands up, don't shoot!" a slogan that soon became a universal sign of resistance to police violence among black youth across the nation. The demonstrations were angry but nonviolent, according to reporters at the scene. Community peacekeepers came out on the streets, keeping people calm and organizing youth to stand in front of stores to prevent looting. Several small groups broke off from the march and began to destroy property, torching neighborhood businesses, smashing windows, and grabbing food and other household goods. Armored vehicles appeared, and police began firing rubber bullets and tear gas into the crowd. At one point, according to Purvi Shah, a human rights lawyer from the Center for Constitutional Rights who was marching with the Ferguson residents, police suddenly turned on the demonstrators for no apparent reason. "Just got tear gassed," she tweeted. "Eyes burning. No warnings. People running with someone in wheelchair. This is lawlessness. Police fired on peaceful protestors." In the melee that followed, a tear gas canister hit an 8-year-old child. Police pointed assault rifles at the crowd and one officer threated to shoot a reporter in the face. Purvi

Shah tweeted, "To the police: you just organized a bunch of freedom fighters. Thanks."[7]

By August 12, African American youth across the nation had called their own protests, and photos of black college students with their hands up began circulating on the Internet, making it clear that all black youth, no matter how educated or "respectable," are potential targets of unwarranted police violence. Hundreds of Howard University students rallied when a 2012 alumna, Mya Aatan-White, posted a photo of herself in an ambulance, bloody and bandaged, after being shot in the head by police at a Ferguson protest.[8] When the Missouri Highway Patrol finally were called in to relieve local police of their law enforcement authority, the mood of the crowd became calmer—even festive, according to *The Wall Street Journal*.[9] But emotions shot up again on August 15, when the Ferguson police released a convenience store videotape filmed shortly before the teens were stopped for jaywalking, which showed a young man resembling Michael Brown swiping a handful of cigarillos and pushing a clerk rudely out of the way. Since the shoplifting incident—described in the media as a "strong-arm robbery"—was apparently unknown to Officer Wilson when he stopped the teens, the release of the videotape to the media suggested to many in the neighborhood that police were attempting to link the two incidents in viewers' minds or even that they were planting the idea that Brown's behavior at the corner store justified his murder.

As the protests in the streets of Ferguson grew louder, police responded with a show of force that shocked even Missouri Governor Jay Nixon. "I, all of us were thunderstruck by the pictures we saw [of the police response to the demonstrations]," Nixon told ABC News in an interview in Ferguson. "I mean, the over-militarization, the MRAPs[10] rolling in, the guns pointed at kids in the street. All of that I think instead of ratcheting down brought emotion up."[11]

A former Marine explained in detail what the police weaponry on the streets of Ferguson looked like. Commenting on an AP photograph he remarked, "What we're seeing here is a gaggle of cops wearing more elite killing gear than your average squad leader leading a foot patrol through the most hostile sands or hills of Afghanistan. They are equipped with Kevlar helmets, assault-friendly gas masks, combat gloves and knee pads (all four of them), woodland Marine Pattern utility trousers, tactical body armor vests, about 120 to 180 rounds for each shooter, semiautomatic pistols attached to their thighs, disposable handcuff restraints hanging from their vests, close-quarter-battle receivers for their M4 carbine rifles and Advanced Combat Optical Gunsights. In other words, they're itching for a fight. A big one."[12]

Nationally, people's reaction to the police behavior in Ferguson split neatly down black and white racial lines. "African Americans are very concerned about what's happening in Ferguson," warned a *Washington Post* headline. "Whites are not."[13] A Pew Research Center poll taken days after Brown was killed carried the headline, "Stark racial divisions in reactions to Ferguson police shooting." Eighty percent of blacks said that the Michael Brown shooting raises important issues about race, while only 37% of whites felt the same. Sixty-seven percent of blacks and 33% of whites said they thought the police response to the shooting had gone too far. Perhaps most telling was the fact that 76% of blacks but only 33% of whites declared they had "no or little confidence in the investigation into the shooting."[14]

Although some whites were alarmed, even outraged, about the events in Ferguson, most white reactions that I encountered that August, both in conversations and in the media, varied from unequivocal support of the police to wariness about judging Officer Wilson until all of the facts were known.[15] "There are some things we will never know for sure," a white social worker remarked to me after the protests had died down. "Eyewitnesses are notoriously unreliable, so you have to take their version of events with a grain of salt. I can easily believe the police officer overstepped his authority and that the shooting was unjustified. But knowing adolescents as I do, I can just as easily imagine that Michael Brown took some risks that put his life in danger. How will we ever know what happened inside that police car? Maybe Michael grabbed at the officer's gun, causing it to go off accidentally. That would be a wildly dangerous thing for an 18-year-old to do, especially if he's black and the officer is white. But teens can be impulsive and unaware of their own reactions. Even if the officer started shooting at him for no reason, who knows, Michael might have come back to confront the guy. For a teen, he was very large, 6 foot 4, I believe, which is rather intimidating. We need to look at all the plausible ways these events might have played out. It's not impossible that the officer shot the kid because he feared for his own life."

African Americans, on the other hand, tended to find such a scenario highly unrealistic. First of all, they said, look at the disproportionate number of people of color who have been killed by white police in this country. In fact, according to historian Isabelle Wilkerson, "the rate of police killings of black Americans [today] is nearly the same as the rate of lynchings in the early decades of the 20th century," one every three or four days. "That number is incomplete and likely an undercount," Wilkerson adds, "as only a fraction of local police jurisdictions even report such deaths—and those reported are the ones deemed somehow 'justifiable.' The injustice is so banal that we hardly notice it."[16] A week after the shooting, MSNBC's Melissa Harris-Perry solemnly read the names of some of the unarmed black men who have been killed by police over the past decade, from Sean Bell, shot by white undercover police the morning before his wedding, to Oscar Grant, who was shot point blank while lying face down on a rapid transit platform after celebrating New Year's Eve with his friends, to Eric Garner, who was put in a lethal chokehold while selling unlicensed cigarettes, to 18-year-old Michael Brown. All of these men and hundreds more were unarmed at the time of their death.[17] Black women and girls, too, are victims of unprovoked police violence: Tarika Wilson, shot and killed in her home while holding her 1-year-old baby in her arms; 7-year-old Aiyana Stanley-Jones, who fell asleep on the couch while watching TV and was shot in the head as officers stormed into her house in a midnight SWAT-style operation—filmed on reality TV; Marlene Pinnock, a great-grandmother who was beaten within an inch of her life by white police for walking in and out of traffic lanes on a freeway;[18] Miriam Carey, a young woman distraught by postpartum depression, shot as she surrendered peacefully to police after running her car into a barricade near the White House.[19]

But African Americans' anger at the Michael Brown episode was not just about the alarming number of unarmed blacks shot by law enforcement. In their long experience with profiling, disrespect, and gratuitous violence at the hands of the police, many blacks saw what happened in Ferguson in the context of a much larger problem: widespread racial profiling of blacks and Latinos, hyper-criminalization of black and brown youth, a criminal justice system skewed against them, and everyday racist attitudes and actions by white officers that are denied, covered up, and masqueraded as the victim's fault. What happened in Ferguson, many blacks said, is part of a pattern of systemic racism that pervades American society. As Dennis Parker, director of the American Civil Liberties Union's Racial Justice Program explains, when blacks see on the nightly news a SWAT team invading the home of an innocent family of color with battering rams and flash grenades, when they see the town of Ferguson turned into a war zone, when they remember the not too distant footage of black people desperately awaiting assistance in the wake of Hurricane Katrina—all of these images and events have accumulated in the memories and souls of people of color, making it obvious that the significance of Michael Brown's tragic death is not limited to the criminal actions of one racist cop.[20]

This point was brought home to me by blogger Anand Jahi, whose cousin had recently been killed by an off-duty police officer. "Cops just shot my cousin dead," he writes. "[But] if I told you the details, I'm afraid you would focus on his individual story when you should really focus on an institutional crisis." He could tell us that his cousin was a college graduate, a professional who had worked in information technology for decades, but he won't do that, he says, because that would humanize him for us, and then we might think that other unarmed, nonthreatening blacks who die at the hands of white police are less human than he is or even that they deserved their fate. He could provide us with details about the police officer who killed his cousin, but he won't, because then we might think that particular officer is the problem. ("He is a problem, but he is not *the* problem," Jahi adds pointedly.) He could tell us that the media ignored his cousin's killing, but that might suggest that the media usually pay attention to black death, which they do not. He could tell us about the pain his cousin's family is feeling, but he won't, because that might make us think his family's pain is uncommon, when it is not. If we are led to believe that people who commit acts of racial violence are just a few bad apples, the system will be left intact: "If a tree keeps producing bad apples," Jahi writes, "something is wrong with the tree." Too often we get caught up in the individual tragedy and not the environment that created it. "I don't want to tell you my cousin's story because I want you to fight, but I want you to fight the right battle."[21]

Jahi is saying, I think, that if he described his cousin as the college graduate, the computer programmer, the solid citizen, and the husband and father that he was, then white, liberal, middle-class readers of his blog post—for that's who reads stories about race written in a friendly, sympathetic tone—would identify with his cousin and be appalled that he was so randomly executed by an officer of the law. They would realize that he could be their coworker, their neighbor, their teacher, or the father of their child's best friend. And because they could see how much his cousin is like them, they would see him as an exception to the way they believe, perhaps unconsciously, that blacks generally are, and they would see his white, deputized killer as a bad apple—an exception to the way they believe whites generally are. In other words, Jahi worries that if middle-class, liberal whites identify too closely with his cousin's tragedy, they will too easily ignore or explain away the black victims that are not so much like them: Tarika Wilson, the ex-girlfriend of a suspected drug

RACISM AS A COMPLEX SYSTEM

dealer; Oscar Grant, the high school dropout who got into a brawl on the subway; Eric Garner, the unemployed street-seller of loose cigarettes. If they are encouraged to think in terms of just a few humanized exceptions who they can easily identify with, they will be less likely to notice the striking numbers of unarmed blacks, many of them lower class, who have been harassed, roughed up, shot, or killed by white police, and less likely to deduce from those numbers that we, as a society, have a larger problem on our hands than what a few bad apples can explain.

If we want to understand the larger problem, many people of color say, we need to view it as more than a series of horrible incidents where someone has died when they should have lived. We need to look at the way societal systems work against the people who are most likely to suffer in those encounters and the power dynamics that drive the ways they become targets. Focusing on individual unjust events like what happened in Ferguson, or disciplining individuals, like out-of-control police officers, divert us from tackling the underlying problem, or rather, *the* problem, as Jahi puts it: institutional racism. It is often said that institutional racism doesn't actually require anyone to be racist to produce a racially biased outcome; the system has developed a life of its own—"business as usual." Standard policies, procedures, and practices, all perfectly legal, often seemingly fair, polite, reasonable, and objective, somehow produce an outcome that safeguards white advantages and causes people of color to end up dead.

I can see why people of color would want whites to "fight the right battle," as Jahi says, to focus their anger and activism on systems and institutions, rather than on the actions and attitudes of individuals. But at the same time, I don't think it's useful to limit our view of racism to its institutionalized forms, because in the end, it is interpersonal racism, both blatant and subtle, conscious and unconscious, that drives the institutions that are so impervious to change. Racism is a complex system with multiple components that interact, like a living organism, in multifarious ways. The Michael Brown affair provides us with an opportunity to untangle that system and see how the personal and the institutional work together.

One of the lessons from the shooting of Michael Brown, at least for me, is that there are a lot more blatant racists out there than most whites realize—or would like to admit. Since most people keep their attitudes about race in check these days, it might seem that the "old-fashioned" form of racism, the kind that was displayed so cavalierly by white folks 50 years ago, is mostly gone. But in the aftermath of the Michael Brown affair, a startling amount of vicious interpersonal racism was on display; one only had to read the anonymous online comments in response to news articles about the shooting and the demonstrations that followed. In one of the most painful examples I came across, when Michael Brown's mother, Lesley McSpadden, appeared on MSNBC nine days after her son's death in a pretty white blouse that contrasted vividly with her grief-stricken face, an online commenter sneered, "Someone should tell ghetto Mama an interview is not an excuse to wear a wedding dress."

One might hope that such individuals are rare. But McSpadden's brief interview provoked hundreds of brutal comments. Asked by ABC News[22] how peace could be restored to the streets of Ferguson, Michael Brown's mother responded quietly, "With justice."

"And what is justice to you?" she was asked.

"Being fair. Arresting this man and making him accountable for his actions," she responded.

But of the 236 comments that followed the posting of this interview, the overwhelming majority blamed the mother, black people in general, or Michael Brown himself for his death at the hands of the police. The woman raised her son badly and now she wants sympathy, commenters wrote. She thinks she can sell her story for cash. Her son was a thug; he deserved to die:

"Justice? It has been served already. Your criminal thug is dead. Maybe if you were a better mother he would still be alive."

"Mommy's little boy got exactly what he deserved."

"She should have raised a human boy instead of a chimpanzee."

"Best way to stop this from occurring. Ship all blacks back to dark continent. Either that or put on island."

"Sorry Mom but your son being dead does all of hard-working, tax-paying society a favor."

Interpersonal racism was again all too clear when the South Carolina-based New Empire Knights of the Ku Klux Klan boasted that its Missouri chapter was raising money for Officer Wilson: "We are setting up a reward fund for the police officer who shot this thug," said the Klan group in an email to the Southern Poverty Law Center. "He is a hero!"[23] A Facebook group called "Support Darren Wilson" that had no apparent connection to any established hate organization received more than 77,000 "likes" just days after the shooting. The site offered $7 T-shirts imprinted with a police-style badge that read, "Officer Darren Wilson—I stand by you." The shirts sold out quickly and were soon replaced by other versions at three and four times

RACISM AS A COMPLEX SYSTEM

the price. "Officer Darren Wilson is my hero," read one shirt. "Warning: I shoot first and ask questions later," said another. One fundraising site for the officer was apparently the work of a teenage girl from the St. Louis area who "thought she would raise a few hundred dollars and ended up raising a few hundred thousand dollars."[24] Several crowd-sourced sites together pulled in over $400,000 to help Officer Wilson with any court costs and legal fees he might face, even though it seemed unlikely that he would ever go to trial.[25]

In addition to the blatant racism that appeared in the days and weeks after the shooting were the much more widespread insinuations about the black teenage victim that permeated the mainstream liberal media—"the shaming of the victim rather than an investigation into the actions of the shooter," as Wilkerson puts it.[26] For instance, why did newscasters pay so much attention to Michael Brown's apparent petty theft at the convenience store when the event had no connection to his run-in with the police for jaywalking? African American actor Jesse Williams spoke of his frustration with the assumption among whites that black teens are, as a class of human beings, uniquely prone to antisocial behavior: "I've lived in white suburbs of this country for a long time; I know plenty of white kids who steal stuff from a convenience store," Williams told CNN. "We're not the only ones who sell and do drugs all the time. We're not the only ones that steal and talk crazy to cops. There's a complete double standard and a complete different experience that a certain element of this country has the privilege of being treated like human beings, and the rest of us are not treated like human beings—period."[27]

Williams goes on to ask why the mainstream media don't tell the story of a crime from its logical beginning, the point at which the story is the most intriguing. "You'll find that the people doing the oppressing always want to start the narrative at a convenient part," he says, referring to the shoplifting incident. The truly newsworthy story about Michael Brown "started with a kid getting shot and killed and left in the street for four hours. I've never seen a white body left in the street for four hours in the sweltering heat. The cop doesn't call in the shooting, the body isn't put in an ambulance, it's shuttled away in some shady unmarked SUV. There's a lot of bizarre behavior going on and *that* is the story; that's where we need journalism. That's where we need that element of society to kick into gear and not just keep playing a loop of what the kid may have done in a convenience store."[28]

Other insinuations and assumptions about Michael Brown appeared in the press, including the nation's most respected newspapers. Many African Americans and their allies questioned, for example, why it was that the victim

## 122 FRACTURED: RACE RELATIONS IN "POST-RACIAL" AMERICAN LIFE

of the shooting was described in a *New York Times* piece as "no angel." Why were his teenage faults so prominently displayed in a story that ostensibly was written to humanize him to readers on the day of his funeral? In a piece titled "Michael Brown spent last weeks grappling with problems and promise," *New York Times* reporter John Eligon wrote the following:

> Michael Brown, 18, due to be buried on Monday, was no angel, with public records and interviews with friends and family revealing both problems and promise in his young life. Shortly before his encounter with Officer Wilson, the police say he was caught on a security camera stealing a box of cigars, pushing the clerk of a convenience store into a display case. He lived in a community that had rough patches, and he dabbled in drugs and alcohol. He had taken to rapping in recent months, producing lyrics that were by turns contemplative and vulgar. He got into at least one scuffle with a neighbor.[29]

The article went on to mention other trivial character traits that suggested Michael Brown had been unruly all his life. He was "a handful" as a youngster. When his parents put up a "security gate," a device parents often use to keep their toddlers from falling downstairs, little Michael would try to climb over it. When they left pens and pencils lying around the house, he would use them to write on the wall. As a ninth grader, he was accused of stealing an iPod that turned out to be his own. There were times when he would talk back to his parents.

This absurd characterization of Michael Brown as a troublemaker from the get-go was quickly picked up by African American bloggers, and soon, more than 1,700 sarcastic tweets flooded the Internet:

"If I get killed by a racist cop, please tell the @nytimes I drank booze underage in college and used to argue with my mother #ideservedit."

"Lived in what @nytimes would call 'a rough patch,' smoked weed and even, once, attempted to make a hip-hop beat. #ideservedit."

"@nytimes I shoplifted as a teen. Got in fights. Kicked out of school. But being white, if a cop shot me, no one would say #ideservedit."[30]

Reporter Kia Makarechi at *Vanity Fair* researched *The New York Times'* use of the phrase "no angel" to describe people of note. "A pattern emerges," she writes. "'No angel' seems to most commonly describe either hardened white criminals, or men of color." Mafia crime boss Al Capone was "no angel" as a teen. So was Whitey Bulger, the most notorious mobster to terrorize the Boston area; so was Nazi Field Marshal Erwin Rommel, a war hero in Hitler's Third Reich; so was Donald Manuel Paradis, the leader of a motorcycle gang

RACISM AS A COMPLEX SYSTEM 123

who spent years on death row; and so was one of the mass murderers of school-children at Columbine High School. Men of color who have been described with this phrase include Magic Johnson, Michael Jackson, and a young black victim of a killing by four white men. In other words, "[a] sample of the white folks the *Times* has called 'no angel' includes infamous mobsters, murderers, a pornographer, and a Nazi," writes Makarechi. "Black Americans described similarly by the paper include a basketball player, a singer, criminal suspects, and unarmed men killed by white people."[31]

Despite the outraged reaction to the double standard in *The New York Times* "no angel" piece, the paper defended its reporter's characterization of Michael Brown, calling the story a "sensitive, nuanced account" in which there was "certainly no hint that this poor young man should have been shot."[32] No overt hint, perhaps, but the subtle suggestions that Michael Brown could be unruly (attempting to climb over his security gate as a toddler), was prone to disobey authority (all of those pencil marks on the wall), and that he "got into at least one scuffle with a neighbor" made the idea that he intention-ally provoked the officer plausible to readers who already suspect that black males are potential criminals.

Liberal journalists who slant their stories against people of color do not do so intentionally. They merely follow and perpetrate mainstream assump-tions about blacks and browns, often without consciously realizing it. This "implicit racial bias," as psychologists call it, "influences the way that we see and treat others, even when we are determined to be fair and objective."[33] But the effect of these unintentional practices can be highly discriminatory, even deadly. According to professor of African American Studies Clarence Lang, only when African Americans "exemplify moral virtue, thrift, sobriety, proper speech and appearance, upright comportment, and respectability," are they seen as worthy of the rights other Americans take for granted. Where white victims of police violence are seen as individuals, "... black people bear the burden of proving their humanity before a disbelieving white majority."[34] And since the facts of the actual altercation between Michael Brown and the police officer are murky, as they often are in such cases, the reporter's mention of the "difficult" aspects of Michael Brown's young life smoothly and subtly normalized the officer's actions through the power of suggestion.

Implicit bias is a central aspect of racism's complex system because it af-fects everyone, regardless of race, ethnicity, or good intentions. Hidden so deeply within ourselves that it is inaccessible to reflection, implicit bias has been brought to light by psychologists and neuroscientists through a wide

## 124 FRACTURED: RACE RELATIONS IN "POST-RACIAL" AMERICAN LIFE

variety of experiments. These studies run the gamut from the physiological, where electrical activity in response to various stimuli is recorded in the amygdala, the region of the brain associated with hatred and fear, to the psychological, where, for example, participants playing video game simulations are instructed to "shoot" black, white, Latino, or Asian individuals holding weapons but not those holding innocuous objects like cell phones.[35] Through hundreds of such studies conducted over the past 30 years, researchers have come to the astonishing conclusion that pro-white/anti-black implicit bias can be found in most Americans, regardless of their own racial group.[36] Implicit racial bias can be found in people from every occupation and walk of life: doctors, teachers, bankers, judges, police officers, babysitters, real estate agents, hiring committees, and the cashier at the corner store. The fact that one can harbor unconscious anti-black bias even if one is black helps make sense of the fact that the reporter who wrote the controversial minibiography of Michael Brown depicting him as troubled and unruly was African American.[37]

Implicit bias against blacks is fed by casual talk among friends and family, opinions of influential people in the community, and especially, media focus on black criminals, welfare recipients, school dropouts, drug addicts, irresponsible parents, and the use of innocuous-sounding phrases like "no angel" that resonate in the background as accurate descriptors of black life. Newscasters, reporters, and screenwriters may choose such depictions because of their own implicit racial biases, and they may defend the way they tell their stories for the same reason. When implicit bias is compounded by lack of meaningful, sustained contact with the black community, even people of good will may avoid questioning media depictions too deeply and lose interest once a story about a black victim has been eclipsed by other headlines. This indifference to black suffering plus a nagging, guilty, half-belief that blacks are chronically irresponsible help racism's complex system maintain its stability. For not only does the denial and apathy of good people leave remedies to racism unpursued, they enable the consciously racist folks to discriminate with impunity.

After the Michael Brown shooting began to fade from the headlines that fall, several African American bloggers tried to bridge the gap between their own perceptions and those of their white friends and coworkers through heart-rending personal appeals. Shortly after the shooting, Keesha Beckford, a young black mom, wrote an open letter to a white woman she has been friends with since childhood. "I love you, girl, you know I do," Beckford writes. "But now I need something. I don't ask for much—you know I hate asking for anything, but now I need help, desperately, and so I'm going to put myself out there." She reminds her white friend how similar their 6-year-olds are and how her own son is goofy and silly and loves to do "all those stereotypical boy things." He likes to tussle, she says. Sometimes he can't control his temper. Right now he's like a puppy to most people—cute and non-threatening. But "what happens when he's grown up and not so cute and non-threatening?" she asks. "When he's walking through the world alone? No more the floppy-eared, playful youngster—he's now the feral stray dog, worthy of extermination." She pleads with her white friend to talk to her friends and neighbors about how "the news makes it seem as though only African-Americans commit crimes." She asks her friend to call people out on their racism when she sees it. She tells her to stop saying she doesn't want to offend people on Facebook by being political. "It kills me when I see posts about kittens and new shoes and not one share about boys left to die in the street," Beckford writes. She can't educate the whole world alone. She needs her white friend to step up.[38]

But African American moms may not have the luxury of waiting until their children are grown before they are targeted. "My son has been suspended five times," writes Tunette Powell in a *Washington Post* op-ed piece. "He's 3."[39] She describes how she had been called by the school to come and pick up her little boy who had hit a staff member on the arm. "After that incident," she writes, "they deemed him a 'danger to the staff.'" Her older son, too, had been suspended by the preschool for behavior that she and her husband had found inappropriate but hardly dangerous. As a child, Powell herself had been suspended from school more times than she could remember and had suffered for a long time from her teachers' humiliating words. So Powell asked herself again and again what she might have done to cause her child to be so disruptive. She was sure it was her fault. But why? The family was living a comfortable life. Her husband was an amazing father to his sons. The children gave them very few problems at home; even babysitters reported no particular trouble.

Powell would have kept on blaming herself had she not happened to bring up her 3-year-old's five suspensions with a group of white parents she was chatting with at a child's birthday party. The other parents were shocked. Their own kids had done much worse things at school, they told Powell, and very little had happened to them. "My son threw something at a kid on purpose and the kid had to be rushed to the hospital," one white parent told her. "All I got was a phone call." Parent after parent related things their children had done at school, some similar to her son's behavior, some much worse. None of the white children had been suspended.

Powell's friends and relatives encouraged her to find another preschool for her son. But after doing a little research on the suspensions and expulsions of black children, Powell decided to do the more difficult thing: keep her child in the program and pursue the issue of racial bias with the preschool staff. She knew her son's teachers and administrators were not intentionally biased against black children, nor did she believe that to be true at most preschools. Yet her son's school followed the national trend in its singling out of black children. African American youngsters, Powell found, "represent 18 percent of preschool enrollment but make up 48 percent of preschool children receiving more than one out-of-school suspension."[40] The trend continues throughout elementary school, junior high, and high school, where, according to the U.S. Department of Education, black students are three and a half times as likely to be suspended or expelled as their white peers. Over 70% of the students involved in school-related arrests or referred to law enforcement are black or Hispanic. African American children with disabilities are disproportionately subject to seclusion or mechanical restraint, such as being strapped down. Of students who were restrained, 44% were black, despite the fact that blacks made up only 21% of the total. "These numbers are extremely dramatic," says Deborah J. Vagins, senior legislative counsel at the American Civil Liberties Union's Washington legislative office. "The harsh punishments, especially expulsion under zero tolerance and referrals to law enforcement, show that students of color and students with disabilities are increasingly being pushed out of schools, oftentimes into the criminal justice system."[41]

It's not that black children, on average, are any more unruly or aggressive than white children from the time they are tots. The difference between black and white children's behavior, these studies suggest, is more likely to be in the eye of the beholder. This idea of observer bias might seem plausible, especially to people who are unfamiliar with the black community, as long as the children in question are young. But as they grow up, black children, especially boys, are no longer perceived as "cute and non-threatening," as Beckford puts it in her letter to her white friend. In fact, an extensive study by psychologist Phillip Atiba Goff shows that "black boys can be seen as responsible for their actions at an age when white boys still benefit from the assumption that children are essentially innocent."[42] Goff's research found that black children and teens age 10 to 17 were likely to be perceived as older—by four and a half years—than they actually are. Black youth also were more likely than whites or Latinos to be seen by the college-age study participants—mostly white

RACISM AS A COMPLEX SYSTEM 127

females—as guilty, especially when they were experimentally matched with a serious crime. A particularly shocking study tested 176 police officers, mostly white males working in large urban areas, to determine two types of bias: prejudice—such as the likelihood that blacks moving to nonblack neighborhoods will bring violence into the community—and "unconscious dehumanization of black people by comparing them to apes." Officers whose implicit bias included the dehumanizing of blacks were more likely to have used force against a black child in custody, that is, "takedown or wrist lock; kicking or punching; striking with a blunt object; using a police dog, restraints or hobbling; or using tear gas, electric shock, or killing."[43]

Fast forward to the Michael Brown affair. Ferguson police officers are bound by 12 pages of police department regulations that govern their use of force in any charged encounter. But all of these rules are preempted by a single imperative: "If an officer believes he or someone else is in imminent danger of grievous injury or death, he is allowed to shoot first, and ask questions later."[44] If implicit racial bias can cause police officers to see black teens as fully grown adults and to perceive them as criminal and threatening, then the officer who shot Michael Brown need not even be consciously racist to have carried out a racially biased killing. This might give us insight into why so many unarmed blacks are killed by police. Since unconscious racial bias affects everyone, it stands to reason that in highly charged encounters, bias against blacks is very likely to affect officers' split-second decisions. Yet in Ferguson, as elsewhere, department regulations on the use of deadly force have rarely been changed to reflect the findings of 30 years of implicit bias research.

When the Grand Jury convened in Ferguson to establish whether Officer Wilson should be brought to trial for the killing of Michael Brown, an even more bizarre form of racial bias emerged. According to Wilson's testimony, as he was struggling with the 18-year-old in the police car, this 6 foot 4, 200-pound officer of the law "felt like a five year old holding onto Hulk Hogan," a professional wrestler and Hollywood actor who was a popular TV figure when Wilson was a boy. Not only was Michael Brown physically intimidating, said Wilson, the demonic look in his eyes was positively terrifying. He had an "intense and psychotic look on his face," Wilson told the St. Louis County detective who had been called to assist at the scene of the shooting. "He was just staring at me, almost like to intimidate me or to overpower me." Wilson's fear did not subside even when the teen ran down the street after being hit by Wilson's first shot. As Michael Brown turned to face the officer again, apparently ready to surrender, he took a few steps toward Wilson, either stumbling from his first wound, or giving himself up, or running toward the officer—witnesses differ. Yet Wilson described the teen as "charging" toward him with superhuman strength and lunatic determination to kill him with his bare hands. "It looked like he was almost bulking up to run through the shots," Wilson testified. "Like it was making him mad that I was shooting at him. And the face that he had was looking straight through me, like I wasn't even there, like I wasn't even anything in his way."[45]

As social critic Jamelle Bouie explains, Wilson's vision of an enraged, animal-like Michael Brown is reminiscent of white supremacist rhetoric in the lynching era of the late 19th and early 20th centuries. The southern press at the time was "rife with articles attacking the 'Negro Beast' and the 'Big Black Brute,' a menacing, powerful creature who could withstand the worst punishment. Likewise, in northern papers, it was easy to find stories of 'giant negroes' who 'spread terror' and rampaged through urban centers."[46] One might think that racist images from America's past would have little meaning nowadays, since so few of us study our country's racial history in school, or read old newspapers in library archives, or even watch classic films like *The Birth of a Nation*, where depictions of the "black brute" are blatantly and unapologetically displayed. Yet powerful media images can have a striking lifespan. Movie buffs will recognize that over time, the image of the hulking, newly freed slave morphed into the giant gorilla who crushes cities and carries away helpless, highly sexualized, white women, only to be reborn as the black predator who lurks in the inner city: the mugger, the carjacker, the gangbanger. "That image never went away," says Bouie. "It lingers in crack-era stories of superpowered addicts and teenaged superpredators, as well as rhetoric around other victims of police brutality." It is not so surprising, then, that white police officers might experience genuine fear for their safety when confronted by a black suspect. Media images, highly suggestive words and phrases ("no angel"), social conditioning, implicit bias, hyper-militarization of law enforcement, and a culture of disrespect toward working-class communities of color all impinge on that split-second decision an officer makes when confronted by a teenage "brute" that he sees—or imagines—rushing toward him. And if, according to police department regulations, "reasonable fear" can justify the use of deadly force,[47] we can see how unacknowledged racial bias gets built in to laws and procedures that seem, on the face of it, objective and rational. Business as usual becomes white privilege by another name.

So given our country's racial history and the effect it can have on even the most well-intentioned law enforcement officers, why do we continue to

# RACISM AS A COMPLEX SYSTEM

allow police to "shoot first and ask questions later"? Why do we not insist that antibias training be a regular part of the departmental training of all police officers? For that matter, why do we not require police to be trained to confront dangerous situations without the use of deadly force at all, as they are in some other countries? In Britain, for example, "British police officers actually fired their weapons three times" in all of 2013. "The number of people fatally shot was zero." Even when adjusting for the difference in population size, this means British residents are 100 times less likely than Americans to be shot by a police officer.[48] Furthermore, why are the Ferguson police allowed to treat residents with blatant disrespect, regularly stopping them without cause, cursing them, physically abusing them, and interpreting their every reaction as a threat to their authority? Anyone with an inkling of race relations in this country could foresee that such practices are bound to increase the likelihood of deadly encounters between the largely white police force and the majority black community they presumably serve.

But since the 1970s, police tactics have become considerably more violent and intrusive than ever before. Officers across America are now being trained in a "stress-based regimen that's modeled on military boot camp, resulting in enforcers who believe policing is about kicking ass rather than working with the community to make neighborhoods safer."[49] SWAT[50] teams, originally formed to respond to extraordinarily dangerous situations like active shooters, hostage situations, or large-scale disturbances, have proliferated to the point where they now can be found in 80% of cities the size of Ferguson. As the number of these elite para-military units have increased, so have the number of violent intrusions into people's homes. "Every year now, there are approximately 50,000 SWAT raids in the United States," says Matthew Harwood of the American Civil Liberties Union—that's nearly 1,000 a week. "As a result, we have roving squads of drug cops, loaded with SWAT gear, who get money if they conduct more raids, make more arrests, and seize more property, and they are virtually immune to accountability if they get out of line." Eighty percent of these violent home invasions are routinely used against people who are only suspected of a crime.[51]

Who is most likely to be the target of these terrifying searches? By now, the answer should be obvious. According to an ACLU study, "on the other side of that broken-down door, more often than not, are blacks and Latinos." Indeed, the study found that "68% of the SWAT raids against minorities were simply executing a warrant in search of drugs. When it came to whites, that figure dropped to 38%, despite the well-known fact that blacks, white, and Latinos all use drugs at roughly the same rates."[52] Where do police departments get the idea that they can bash down doors in impoverished communities of color but leave white suspects alone? One can easily speculate what might happen if white, middle-class teenagers having a pot party in their basement suddenly became the target of flash-bang grenades and a battering ram wielded by officers with automatic weapons and an MRAP in the driveway. Whatever else might happen, we can be sure that the policy of militarized, forced entry in such cases wouldn't remain in place for long. Remember Tarika Wilson, the unarmed African American woman who was shot and killed in her home while holding her 1-year-old baby in her arms? Remember 7-year-old Aiyana Stanley-Jones, who fell asleep on the couch while watching TV and was killed by a flash grenade as officers stormed into her house with no warning? These are the human beings who suffer from the racially biased distribution of power. "We are now in a new era of American policing," says Harwood, "where cops increasingly see themselves as soldiers occupying enemy territory... and where even nonviolent crimes are met with overwhelming force and brutality."[53]

How did our country reach a point where communities of color are under military assault from the very authorities that are supposed to protect and serve them? And how did local police forces come by enough military gear to amaze even a state governor? I don't believe that our nation's police departments deliberately geared up in order to harass, imprison, and kill people of color. Militarization happened gradually, through a series of seemingly reasonable decisions to cut down on crime, keep drugs out of inner-city neighborhoods, and protect the country from terrorism. "In 1990," Harwood explains, "Congress authorized the Pentagon to transfer its surplus property free of charge to federal, state, and local police departments in order to fight the war on drugs. In 1997, Congress expanded the purpose of the program to include counterterrorism." Nearly 20 years later, the giveaway program has transferred $4.3 billion worth of battle equipment to domestic law enforcement, a 450-fold increase. Police recruiting videos "actively play up militarization as a way of attracting young men with the promise of Army-style adventure and high-tech toys. Policing, according to recruiting videos like these, isn't about calmly solving problems; it's about you and your boys breaking down doors in the middle of the night."[54] Add racial bias—both explicit and implicit—to that volatile mix and you have a hundred more Fergusons ready to explode.

But it is not only the volatile encounters between militarized police and the community that are causing the friction. Increasingly, cash-strapped cities like Ferguson have been relying on traffic tickets and other fines to fund their day-to-day operations. This has created a culture of constant, low-profile police surveillance: speed traps, stops for minor traffic offenses, and the bullying of residents for petty offenses like jaywalking that marked the beginning of the encounter between Darren Wilson and Michael Brown. Processing these citations has made Ferguson's municipal court "incredibly busy and extremely profitable." According to a report from a nonprofit lawyers group, ArchCity Defenders, "Fines and court fees for the year in this city of just 21,000 people totaled $2,635,400," or an average of three warrants per Ferguson household.[55] And because of department-wide assumptions, explicit and implicit, about black criminality, most of the municipal court cases come from vehicle stops that target black drivers. In fact, blacks are almost twice as likely as whites to be searched during these stops and twice as likely to be arrested, even though searches of whites actually turn up more contraband.[56] The result: African Americans in Ferguson, many of them unemployed—"do more to fund local government than relatively affluent whites."[57] As the ArchCity researchers found, "Impoverished defendants were frequently ordered to pay fines that were triple their monthly income. Some ended up with no income at all as they sat in jail for weeks, awaiting a hearing."[58] Given the number of cases—an incredible 1,500 for a typical three-hour court session—one can easily imagine the racial antagonism generated by such practices.

But looking closely at the history that created these dynamics, one finds even more ways that a toxic combination of personal and institutional racism has disenfranchised Ferguson's black majority. In the 1970s, when civil rights laws made segregation illegal, the more affluent blacks began relocating out of the ghettoes into formerly all-white spaces. Whites reacted by fleeing to the suburbs, abetted by unscrupulous realtors who bought up white homes for a song and sold them to blacks at an enormous profit. Whites took their businesses with them, leaving African Americans far from the employment they needed to fund their neighborhood schools and government services. As the inner city became more impoverished, and as disillusioned young people turned increasingly to the underground economy of drugs and crime, many black families who had the resources followed whites to the suburbs in search of jobs, green spaces, and a better life for their children. Whites reacted by moving even farther away, fearing "black crime" from the newcomers (even though the crime rates in black and white suburbs were often quite similar) and plunging property values. But in Ferguson, some longtime white residents stayed on, consolidating power, continuing to dominate the city councils and school boards, and retaining control of patronage jobs and municipal contracts. This is why the city has a white power structure: a white mayor, a school board with six white members and one Latino, a city council with just one black member, and 3 blacks among its 52 police officers.[59]

Why don't the black Ferguson residents just vote in candidates who promise to work in their interest? With nearly a 70% majority, one would think it would be relatively easy for black leaders to organize a get-out-the-vote campaign that would back African American candidates or any other politicians who were able to win the trust of the community. But here, too, we find institutional racism at work. Unions in the Ferguson area that control the good jobs, the municipal elections, and the political appointments have always been overwhelmingly white. Whites in the "skilled trades"—plumbers, pipe fitters, and electrical workers, for example—have benefited from their racial advantage both through their solid paychecks and through a city government that works in their interest. For blacks to upset this balance, they need campaign funding. But the more municipal contracts a labor organization receives, the more generously it can fund reelection campaigns.[60] In this way, some historically white unions have been able to effectively back white candidates over so-called black upstarts.

Under such circumstances, many blacks have chosen not to participate in a system that is stacked against them. Even a child can see that the racial power dynamics are skewed. Marquis Govan, an 11-year-old Ferguson resident, explained to reporter Jane Pauley on CBS Sunday Morning that the town needs more African American police officers.

"But who in your school aspires to be a cop?" asks Pauley. "Anyone?"

"Look, let me tell you why," says the boy. "From the beginning we felt abused by these people. Why would you grow up to serve among the abusers? It doesn't make any sense."[61]

Govan's perceptive comment helps us understand not only the antipathy of the black residents to the police but the effect of white power on the aspirations of so many black youth. "The people of Ferguson don't need tear gas thrown at them," Govan tells the city council. "I believe they need jobs." He is right. Forty-seven percent of blacks in Ferguson are unemployed. And those who are working are languishing in low-wage service jobs. Auto and aerospace plants that used to employ both blacks and whites at solid wages—$24 an hour in 1990—have radically downsized or closed, impoverishing both their former employees and the city itself.[62]

Ferguson, like all American cities, has its own unique character, history, and set of circumstances that fracture the relationships between whites and people of color. But the forces that drive racism and poverty in Ferguson are familiar to people of color across the nation. "Ferguson is what America looks like," says professor Marc Lamont Hill of Morehouse College. "Ferguson is not unusual. It is a reflection of American life in just about every way imaginable. High unemployment rates. High drop-out rates in schools. Underfunded education programs. Police harassment. Before you get to a Michael Brown death, before you get to an international outcry of protest, you still have a city that is wrestling with the very forms of inequality that every city in this nation is."[63]

Racial inequality across our nation may not be a planned and deliberate goal of white power holders and policy makers, but neither is it accidental.[64] The complex system of white racial advantage and inequity has been laid down, brick by brick, through historical precedent, implicit racial bias, a veiled belief in white superiority and entitlement, and a strong white grip on power and material resources. The workings of the system are all in plain sight, but they remain invisible to those who benefit from it—at least until a Michael Brown comes along.

Thank you, Mike. Your life has meant something. But how much your sacrifice will change this country depends on what we do next.

# · 7 ·

# THE WAY FORWARD

When the news broke in late November that the St. Louis County grand jury had declined to bring charges against Officer Darren Wilson for the killing of Michael Brown, activists of color and their allies stepped up the demonstrations and protests that had begun on the streets of Ferguson. The number and variety of actions that sprang up after the verdict were astonishing, especially since social critics had been claiming that the kind of protest that had characterized the civil rights and Vietnam eras no longer appealed to Americans, especially the young, who seemed too preoccupied with their own personal advancement to care. Yet everyone I met in the last two months of 2014 seemed energized to say or do something, whether to attend an event, sign a petition, discuss the situation with friends and coworkers, comment online, or simply watch the endless coverage of the demonstrations and political commentary on television. It didn't matter if they were in favor of or against the protests or whether they thought race had everything or nothing to do with the killing of unarmed black men and women by our nation's police—at last, Americans were talking about race. And not only about race, but all things connected to it: the militarization of police, the skewed criminal justice system, the claims and counterclaims about racial profiling and color-coded inequality, the decline of unions, the scandalously low minimum wage, the "stand your ground" laws, the pervasiveness of guns, the political attacks on voting rights, the cultural consequences of "thug music" and jail-house fashion statements, the madness of "black-on-black crime," the silence about "white-on-white crime,"[1] the street protests, the looting, the black rage and white denial about race and class privilege—the whole complex system of racism in America, all triggered by the death of one unarmed black teenager too many, Michael Brown.

"Michael was chosen by God to bring change to America," Brown's stepmother confided to a reporter from *Esquire* who spent days with the family, trying to get a sense of the agony that Michael Brown, Sr., and other black fathers felt when their children were targeted.[2] Indeed, signs of change were everywhere. Religious leaders were holding prayer vigils in houses of worship and on the street. Academics were putting together an online "Ferguson Syllabus"[3] to provide resources to teachers. Legal scholars were organizing teach-ins about racism in the criminal justice system. The NAACP, recalling the historic voting rights march from Selma to Montgomery, organized a 120-mile, seven-day "Journey for Justice" from the Canfield Green Apartments where Brown was shot to the Missouri governor's mansion in Jefferson City.[4] The American Civil Liberties Union proposed specific legal reforms and posted handouts on its website informing protesters and photographers of their rights.

Some of the most visible demonstrations were organized by young people of color using the power of social media to spread the word. On college campuses across the country, black and brown students organized "die-ins" where protesters of all ethnicities lay down in silence, sometimes for four and a half minutes, sometimes for hours, to symbolize the time that Mike Brown's body lay bleeding onto the Ferguson street. At sports arenas, black players risked censure to show their solidarity with the victims of police killings. Five players from the St. Louis Rams ran onto the field with their hands up in a "don't shoot" gesture, raising the ire of the St. Louis Police Officers Association, which called the players' display "tasteless, offensive, and inflammatory." "I just think there has to be a change," said Jared Cook, one of the protesting team members. "There has to be a change that starts with the people that are most influential around the world. No matter what happened on that day, no matter how the whole situation went down, there has to be a change."[5]

As the winter holidays approached, the opportunity for larger, more visible demonstrations was seized by activist groups of color that had formed spontaneously after the announcement of the verdict. Under the Twitter

# THE WAY FORWARD                                                137

hashtags #BlackLivesMatter and #BlackOutBlackFriday, organizers called for a nationwide boycott of business as usual for the day after Thanksgiving, one of the busiest shopping days of the year.

"African Americans have a current buying power of 1 trillion & it is forecast to reach $1.3 trillion by 2017," said one widely shared tweet.

"If a cheap Xbox matters more to you than police racism and Black lives you should re-think your priorities," said another.

Buoyed by their enthusiasm for massive, public protest and determined to convince the nation that black lives matter, activists chanting "hands up don't shoot" gathered by the thousands, urging people not to buy from major retailers and joining striking Walmart and convenience store employees in their demands for a higher minimum wage. "One of the few ways to be heard and have people listen to you is to have an economic impact," explained Alisha Sonnier, the 19-year-old president of Tribe X, a youth activist group that formed in the St. Louis region after the Michael Brown shooting. "If you want to really affect people, especially those who are in power, you got to hit their pocket. We as a people cannot allow people to keep making money and a business to go on when we can't even get justice when our people die."[6]

The protests gained even more momentum on December 3rd when another grand jury declined to indict Daniel Pantaleo, the white police officer who took down Eric Garner in an illegal chokehold for the petty crime of selling untaxed cigarettes. As Garner lay gasping for breath on the pavement with two officers sitting on his back, he managed to cry out "I can't breathe" 11 times before his heart failed. As outrage over the grand jury decision grew, hand-lettered signs emblazoned with Garner's last words began to appear at rallies, marches, sit-ins, and die-ins across the country. Demonstrations continued over the December holidays as more killings of young blacks by police were exposed on social media and in the mainstream press: Twelve-year-old Tamir Rice, playing with an authentic-looking toy gun in a city park, shot dead by white police officers within two seconds of their arrival on the scene; John Crawford, a young black man shopping at Walmart, gunned down by a SWAT team as he idly toyed with an air rifle in the firearms aisle while chatting on his cell phone; Ramarley Graham, 18 years old and unarmed, shot dead by police who found him flushing a small bag of marijuana down the toilet in his own home; Aura Rosser, a mentally ill African American woman armed with a fish knife, shot in the heart by police who had been called by her boyfriend to escort her out of his home. ("Why would you kill her?" asked the astonished boyfriend. "It was a woman with a knife. It doesn't make any sense."[7])

138  FRACTURED: RACE RELATIONS IN "POST-RACIAL" AMERICAN LIFE

By now, mainstream organizations and families with children had joined committed activists in protest. In New York City on December 13, 30,000 people marched on police headquarters demanding independent investigations into police shootings. Thousands more marched in solidarity in Washington, DC, Boston, Philadelphia, Chicago, San Antonio, San Diego, Los Angeles, and scores of other cities. Teachers came out of concern for their black and Hispanic students. Parents of teens who had been killed by police addressed the crowds. Labor unions came out in force. Young people who had been targeted by police marched with parents who were afraid to let their children out of the house. Everywhere, whites and people of color held hand-lettered signs saying "Black lives matter." "Am I next?" "End police impunity." "This stops today." "At previous protests for other similar causes, it's been only black faces," Los Angeles resident Aiesha Spires told *The Huffington Post*. "I appreciate the diversity and I appreciate that [the white allies] are taking cues from us and not taking over."[8]

The protests, demonstrations, educational events, and individual actions were so varied, and they sprang up so spontaneously, that one could discern no common goal, method, or central strategy. Demands ranged from specific, local actions—body cameras for city police, for example—to calls for broad systemic change. "Ferguson Action," a coalition of activist groups of color, called for "an end to police brutality, freedom from mass incarceration, full employment for all our people, and decent housing fit for the shelter of human beings."[9] Other groups had more modest goals for institutional reform: safeguarding voting rights, demilitarizing police, repealing "stand your ground" laws, building unions, reforming school suspension and expulsion policies that target black and brown children. Some of the older activists who had been part of the civil rights and antiwar movements in the 1960s warned that the lack of clear leadership might become a problem. How will all of these protests and demands turn into a national movement if there is no coherence, they wondered. Where is the core group of strategy makers? Without leadership, how can these isolated actions, massive as they are, be turned into real political power?

But as I listened to some of the college student organizers who came together to discuss the way forward, they did not seem terribly concerned. The civil rights movement also started as a scattering of unconnected actions, they pointed out. Sporadic protests went on for years throughout the South before they coalesced into a movement with enough power to force the federal government to write new laws and clamp down on abusive local practices. Even

THE WAY FORWARD 139

after civil rights leaders emerged, various factions continued to disagree over style, rhetoric, goals, and tactics. This is the nature of movements, they said. Ours is no different. In fact, they pointed out, we live in a new age, an age of social media organizing, where connections can instantly be forged, and people can fill the streets at a moment's notice. Perhaps Millennial activists will create their own form of politics, their own analysis, they said. True, each age has its particular challenges. Social media opens the door to so many voices that one can become overwhelmed with information. "You're up late at night watching the tweets roll in from the protests in hundreds of cities," said one student organizer. "You're elated by the incredible energy of all these voices. You can't sleep. You can't make total sense of it, since each post has a different opinion and everyone seems convinced of their own position. It's like everyone's a leader now!" How can we apply the lessons of the civil rights era to such fragmentation, the students asked themselves. Or is the wisdom of the elders no longer relevant? Only time will tell, they concluded. It's hard to make sense of a movement when you're right in the middle of it.

Regardless of any confusion they might have about the aims and direction of the protests, young activists of color across the country were united in their instructions to their white allies. At a die-in I attended at a Midwestern university, many of the white students held signs saying "I am Michael Brown," as if they, too, could have been the target of random police stops in their own neighborhoods, which was unlikely, as activists of color later pointed out in letters to the campus newspaper. When students lay down on the frigid pavement that November afternoon, several of the white protesters began checking their cell phones after a few minutes, while students of color lay still, as if dead, for long periods of time. "If you're here as an ally, behave like one," organizers tweeted.

At another rally, signs saying "Black Lives Matter" were interspersed with signs saying "All Lives Matter," almost always waved by non-black marchers. "Why is it wrong to say that all lives matter?" wondered a white protester, a bit hurt by the disapproving looks she was getting from some of the black demonstrators. "I'm here in solidarity. I just don't think it has to be a racial thing."

"It's not a racial thing? Really?" responded activists of color. "That is so painfully naïve."

"Telling us that all lives matter is redundant," explained African American blogger Julia Craven. "We know that already. But, just know, police violence disproportionately affects my people. Justice is not applied equally, laws are not applied equally, and neither is our outrage."[10] Some white allies caught on quickly. At a Midwestern university, a small group of white students who had started to organize a campus-wide die-in immediately handed over the reins to activists of color when it was explained to them that protests against racialized police violence should be led by the people most affected. "If you want to be an ally, don't pretend it doesn't matter who organizes an event," a black protester said bluntly. "If it's not obvious to you why black leadership is central, you need to spend the time educating yourself about your privilege."

While youth were organizing on campus and in the streets, other social justice advocates were protesting through more conventional means. Petitions and letter-writing campaigns implored the newly elected 114th Congress to work together, even though, as Florida Representative Alan Grayson pointed out, for the previous five months, every single elected Republican in Congress, all 250-plus of them, had been a white Christian, which hardly suggested that compromise, as a tactic, would lead to any significant change in the status quo.[11] Van Jones, an African American attorney and advisor on green jobs to the Obama White House, told youth organizers that the centers of power in this country include the "technocracy," the elite group that invents the technology that will rule our lives in years to come. "The future is being written by a tiny, narrow demographic slice of mostly white men who design and build these products," said Jones. People of color must become part of the industry, not merely as "digital cotton pickers" but as technologically savvy professionals who know how to write code. "We're already creative, communicative, and media-savvy," Jones told his largely black and brown audience. "There's no reason we can't take the next step. We're going to have to be just as sophisticated as the system we're trying to change."[12]

Other professionals of color emphasized local politics. When Ferguson Township's lone black committeewoman, Patricia Bynes, became disillusioned with the street protests, which on some nights had turned violent, she began urging residents to become more active in municipal elections instead:

"I know all the 'anti-system' talk sounds & feels good but to make change you have to use the system," Bynes tweeted. "Getting in office is a MAJOR step."

"The heavy lifting on these issues starts in the city halls across this country. LOCAL ELECTIONS and LOCAL BOARDS matter," she urged her followers. "The right people need to be in office to help usher in the changes we need in our communities. That means YOU have to run."[13]

President Obama also showed his concern—he, too, had been targeted as a black man—when he invited some of the most prominent young adult

THE WAY FORWARD 141

activists of color to the White House to share their perspectives and experiences. He chose an interesting, eclectic group: among them, Ashley Yates, organizer with "Millennial Activists United," a group that had taken the lead in many of the street protests; Tef-Poe and T-Dubb-O, rappers for social change; James Hayes, political director for the Ohio Student Association, and Jose Lopez, lead organizer at "Make The Road New York," both working on radical educational reform; and Phillip Agnew, head of the Florida-based Dream Defenders, the group that had occupied the Florida State House after George Zimmerman was exonerated for shooting Trayvon Martin, an unarmed black teen walking home from the store with a packet of Skittles and a soft drink. But although the president listened closely and respectfully to the young activists, he seemed to question their depiction of how dire the situation in this country really was.

"When I hear the young people talk about their experiences it violates my belief in what America can do. To hear young people feeling marginalized and distrustful even after they've done everything right,"[14] President Obama said, apparently to the press, during the meeting with the youth.

Yet as an *Ebony* editorial pointed out, the problem is not that youth of color are simply *feeling* marginalized, they *are* marginalized, hence their distrust of law enforcement, the state that emboldens them, and at times, the president himself.[15] President Obama even seemed to deny that the issues with police in cities across the country were entrenched or chronic. "[T]he kinds of ongoing problems we have with police and communities of color around the country are not of the sort that we saw in Selma [during the civil rights era]," he told George Stephanopoulos of ABC News. "We're not talking about systematic segregation or discrimination. They are solvable problems if in fact law enforcement officials are open to the kind of training and best practices that we've seen instituted in a lot of parts of the country."[16]

Eric Holder, the nation's first black attorney general, was not nearly as optimistic about the nation's ability or willingness to reform itself. When asked in an interview by *New York Magazine* why there is still the same sense of mistrust between black communities and the police that there has been for generations, Holder replied bluntly, "It means that we as a nation have failed. It's as simple as that. We have failed." Yet in that failure, Holder saw opportunity, though he expressed it tentatively, with many qualifiers: "We have a moment in time that we can, perhaps, come up with some meaningful change." He is committed to this change, he assured his interviewer. So is the administration. And the country seems ready for it, he said. But the change must be measured and gradual. We need to conduct more studies, collect more statistics, look for patterns, and document any deficiencies in how police departments are run. The Federal Bureau of Justice Statistics is trying to come up with a way in which we can start to gather this kind of information, Holder said. "And that'll give us a much better way in which we can get a handle on this problem."[17]

To activists, this kind of talk can be frustrating. "We don't need any more studies to discover that people in this country are experiencing injustice," said Mary Frances Berry, veteran civil rights activist and former chair of the U.S. Civil Rights Commission. "That's how politicians put you off when you propose specific reforms: 'Let's do a study first, and then we'll see.'" There is already ample evidence that shows how and why people are suffering, she told law students at the University of Michigan. "It's time to act. Society does not improve on its own. You have to make people do the right thing."[18]

One of the ways to make people do the right thing, some activists say, is to take the protests beyond awareness-raising events, beyond marches that minimally inconvenience the public, beyond pleasant, positive appeals for unity and comforting words about how far we've already come. Disruption is what gets people's attention, they say, sustained disruption that makes people uncomfortable. In California, for example, 14 protesters stopped service in a Bay Area rapid transit station by chaining themselves to a train while another 200 demonstrated outside, shutting down traffic across the system. Other protest groups targeted brunch spots in Oakland and New York in order to inconvenience people who are "blissfully unaffected by police brutality." "People who have money and privilege have the leisure to brunch. Other people don't," said organizer Carrie Leilam Love. Responding to annoyance of some of the customers who patronize these predominantly white spaces, Love said, "It is an inconvenience to us to be shot in the street.... We respectfully demand that people take five minutes of their time to look at what life is like for us every day."[19]

Most activists agree that citizen involvement is the key to systemic change. But the best way to sustain the protest is not yet clear. "What happens when the media stops paying attention?" they ask. "How can we continue to generate a compelling narrative?" "What will it take for white people to acknowledge black humanity?" Knowing that the white majority occupies the positions of greatest influence, many activists of color see the need to bring more white people into the movement. But regardless of the impressive numbers of whites at the demonstrations and protests of the two grand

THE WAY FORWARD 143

jury decisions, the majority of whites in this country are not convinced that a new civil rights movement is necessary or even that all of the unrest is fundamentally about race. Their bewilderment and resentment when race is mentioned, their claims of color blindness, and their insistence on the equivalency of black and white experience that I observed during the years before the Michael Brown shooting are all still depressingly widespread.

Here is a case in point: The day after Christmas 2014, a drive-by shooter wearing body armor was spotted firing multiple times at people and cars in Chattanooga, Tennessee. According to witnesses, the shooter pulled up to a car at a stop sign and fired into the vehicle, disabling the radiator. A few minutes later, the shooter was pointing a gun at pedestrians and firing at another car in the same area. Police gave chase, and when cornered, the suspect pointed a gun at one of the officers. "Surely this was not going to end well," said *New York Times* columnist Charles Blow of the encounter. "We've all seen in recent months what came of people who did far less. Surely in this case officers would have been justified in using whatever force they saw fit. Right?" But the episode did not end in the expected tragedy; instead, the suspect was arrested "without incident or injury." "Who was this shooter anyway?" asked Blow. "Julia Shields, a 45-year-old white woman."[20]

To the African American columnist, the story is about race, specifically, the implicit racial bias that is bound to affect officers' spilt-second decisions. "The American mind has been poisoned since this country's birth against minority populations," writes Blow. "People of color, particularly African American men, have been caught up in a twister of macroaggressions and micro ones. No amount of ignoring can alleviate it; no amount of achieving can ameliorate it."[21] Yet the online responses to Blow's piece indicated that his rather obvious interpretation had eluded the general readership of *The New York Times*. Yes, we know that racial prejudice is still a problem in America, commenters said. Yes, police need sensitivity training about race. Yes, we need more officers of color. But for the most part, they did not concede that the incident that had so alarmed Blow should be taken as an example of color-coded inequality. None of their comments were crass, or mean, or overtly racist. The writers just weren't convinced that there was a problem:

"Stop playing the race/gender card already."

"We shouldn't expect police to act with perfect consistency. Police are just human."

"The discrepancy you see is about gender, not race."

144  FRACTURED: RACE RELATIONS IN "POST-RACIAL" AMERICAN LIFE

"As grand juries have consistently found, the evidence that the police act criminally just isn't there."

"If you want to compare apples to apples—then find identical incidents handled by the same cops in the same district that involved a white man behaving exactly as a corresponding black man did. Then, and only then, would you have an argument."

One lone responder tries to explain: "As a black man, I get a bit frustrated reading comments from people who come up with rational explanations for the acknowledged racial disparities in the criminal justice system. Research study after research study shows that black men and boys are sentenced differently. Study after study indicates that black boys and men are incarcerated at higher rates. Study after study reflects that black boys and men are targeted at higher rates for drug infractions despite drug usage being similar in black and white communities. In spite of all of this, somehow it's difficult for people to extrapolate to the idea that perhaps—just perhaps—the policeman on the street also interacts with black boys and men differently than they do with others."[22]

As cultural critic Michael Eric Dyson put it, "These clashing perceptions underscore the physics of race, in which an observer effect operates: The instrument through which one perceives race—one's culture, one's experiences, one's fears and fantasies—alters in crucial ways what it measures."[23] Dyson's astute observation suggests that the widespread interest in race that is emerging in the wake of the Michael Brown affair does not amount to a real conversation—a "national conversation," as the media sometimes refer to it. It is talk, of course, and that is a start. But the kind of conversation this country needs is something more knowledgeable, more grounded in history and fact, more open to hearing the experiences and points of view of the people who continue to be dismissed, ignored, ridiculed, and targeted by the white majority. To have a real conversation, one needs basic racial literacy. Like the print and media literacy required to read a book, explore a website, post a video, or heed instructions on a bottle of medicine, the ability to decipher race relations in contemporary American life should be considered an essential life skill. Basic racial literacy, in my view, would include an understanding of many of the themes I've touched on in this book: the history of race and racism in this country; the changing definitions of race; an understanding of racism as an ideology and a system, rather than as isolated acts of prejudice or hatred; the experience of immigrants, historically and currently; a solid understanding of the Native American experience; the meaning of race and class privilege;

the research on implicit bias and the psychology of race; the facts about the economic and social disparities that continue to plague communities of color; the historical contributions of people of color to American culture, including invention, education, the arts, the national economy, and movements for social justice; and significant exposure to the lived experiences, emotions, and points of view of people who are the target of racism's complex system.

What is the way forward for our fractured nation? Many whites—I would say most—need a solid grounding in basic racial literacy before they can understand the society around them, much less act responsibly and effectively as allies with people of color. Because there is so little taught about race and racism in formal settings, and because whites should not burden their friends of color by asking them to explain their painful experience of race, whites of good will need to start by educating themselves.[24] They need to read everything about race that they can get their hands on: history, biography, novels, sociology, lived experience, points of view. They need to watch videos about race with others and talk about them afterward. They need to attend anti-racism trainings. They need to reflect on their own experiences as racialized beings in this country. They need to get past the denial, the guilt, and the self-serving explanations that blame people of color for their own condition. I am not suggesting that everyone who studies race and racism with an open heart will come to the same conclusions; no group of thinking people will interpret history, research, and personal testimony in the same way. But whatever conclusions they come to, the experience of thinking critically and deeply about race will make them either better allies or informed, principled critics. And that will make it possible to begin a sustained conversation that gets to the heart of the racial fracturing that plagues our country.

Those who become convinced, through study and reflection, that they must do something to challenge racial inequality can get involved in any number of ways. They might look into the regulations that govern police practices in their own community, for example, or advocate for more affordable housing, or help bring the minimum wage issue to their state legislature, or join a movement to end mass incarceration, or add their voice to any one of hundreds of racial justice issues that activists of color and their allies are already working on at local, state, and national levels. Teachers can help end the silence about race by incorporating a more complete history of this country into their curriculum. Students can form antiracist ally groups that promote informed conversations among their peers. Religious groups can organize antiracism trainings and promote racial justice activism in their faith communities. Everyone can talk to their friends, their coworkers, their children, their younger cousins, or their online pals about racial and economic justice. Sending a link to an article or blog about a racial issue along with a calm, reasonable comment can spark reflective conversation among a select group of online friends. Speaking up at meetings when a person of color is demeaned or ignored helps break the silent acquiescence to racism that so many people of good will indulge in out of reluctance to rock the boat.

In deciding where and how to act, creative ideas for radical change should not be off the table. The abysmal poverty and hopelessness that plague America's cities cannot be solved by timid adjustments to the status quo. "Equality" may sound like a fair and meaningful goal, but treating everyone equally does not address the economic, social, and educational consequences of historical injustice. Let us strive instead for *equity*, says legal scholar and veteran activist Mary Frances Berry. "To achieve equity, one needs to go beyond equality of opportunity, which continues to leave the poorest people behind. Equity requires remedies for past injustice; recourse to honorable principles that correct or supplement existing laws; a challenge to business as usual."[25]

In the current political climate, equity is difficult to talk about, much less achieve. "These days, you have to make it on your own or not at all—especially if you are poor," Berry told her audience of University of Michigan law students. "Voters are less willing to support policies that consider all people worthy of assistance and respect. It has become more difficult to get legal remedies for race discrimination. Conservative and liberal lawmakers alike have decided such protections are no longer necessary, despite the fact that bias is still rampant, especially against new immigrants and 'slave-descended African Americans'—the 'left-behind folks' who have remained impoverished since our country's founding."[26]

Despite attempts to promote diversity in education and corporate hiring over the last several decades, Berry says, these practices and policies, such as they are, have mostly benefited ethnic and racial groups that were already fairly well off. Whites have gained some advantages, especially white women. Some Latinos are better off now, and so are Asians who were already educated and doing reasonably well before they came to this country. African Americans and blacks from the Caribbean have also benefited from diversity policies to some extent, but only if they were already middle class. The "left behind folks" don't encounter "diversity" at all, she says. They see it on TV. But in their segregated, impoverished spaces, they neither experience it first-hand nor gain anything from it.[27]

# THE WAY FORWARD

147

Now, it's true that certain top colleges, "in guilt-induced enthusiasm," have recruited some poor students of color, Berry continues. But so many of these students were forced to drop out because of financial difficulties. Faculty presumed that students from impoverished backgrounds were just poorly educated and that they dropped out because they couldn't keep up with the work. But in fact, she says, they were just as smart as anyone else—what they needed in order to succeed was financial relief. The top private colleges are offering more full scholarships these days, but for the most part these colleges achieve diversity by recruiting middle-class African Americans, Asians, black international students, and Latinos from South America, many of whom have the financial resources to be able to concentrate fully on their studies. "The result looks like diversity," Berry says, "but it avoids the problems faced by 'the least of these,' the students from the most impoverished families who drop out or are pushed out of the educational system at every level."[28]

"The dispossessed of this nation—the poor, both white and Negro—live in a cruelly unjust society," said Martin Luther King, Jr. in 1967. "They must organize a revolution against that injustice, not against the lives of the persons who are their fellow citizens, but against the structures through which society is refusing to take means which have been called for, and which are at hand, to lift the load of poverty."[29] As Dr. King suggests, social and economic change must directly involve the people who are most at risk. Allies who want to contribute their ideas and skills need to venture out of their comfort zone, agrees Berry. "The elite—that's you folks," she said, smiling at her University of Michigan audience—"have to hang out with people at the grassroots." You can't expect to change society when you don't know the people who are most impacted by the problem of poverty and disenfranchisement, she says. In the civil rights movement it was ordinary people who filled the jails. It was the people at the grassroots who took the risks. And today, we're starting to see poor people organizing again. So the people who are doing well have to be willing to go to jail alongside poor people of color. "You have to put yourself at risk to create change."[30]

Young people who are thinking about their future careers that will allow them to live according to their social conscience have a great variety of professions to choose from, Berry continues. "In this sustained, long-term movement for social change, we're going to need people with a whole range of knowledge and skills. We're going to need legal strategies to address historical discrimination and more effectively prosecute individual acts of racial violence. That means we'll need courageous lawyers and policy makers, people who are willing to take risks in their careers that might compromise their livelihoods. We need writers who can reclaim the history of race and racism in this country and put it in an accessible form, so people from all backgrounds can understand it and come to terms with it. We need educators who have the courage to teach the youth the histories of people of color in this country, which often have been painful, but also are full of heroism and solidarity in the face of struggle. We need activists who are prepared to risk arrest through civil disobedience. We need funding agencies that are committed to generous, long-term support for the transformation of poor communities. We need everyone, no matter what their occupation, or age, or life circumstances, to be working on restoring a sense of community and empathy through their willingness to help each other and their intolerance of poverty and injustice."[31]

For their part, young activists of color may need to broaden their nascent movement to include people whose experiences with racism have been sidelined in many of the current protests: Native Americans, Asians, Muslims, and undocumented immigrants, especially those who are visibly brown. All of these groups might choose to organize separately, but since the complex system of racism includes everyone, it makes sense, I think, to look at the problem in its entirety. As Berry says, "It's critically important for people of color to deal with our own inter-group disagreements and rivalries. The Latin American groups, many of whom are seen as 'acceptable' by whites in this country, need to work in solidarity with the poorer, darker Hispanics who whites see as a threat. Middle class Asians need to work with the Asian groups that tend to be more impoverished in this country: the Laotians, Cambodians, Vietnamese and Khmer. It's true that all groups of color have been discriminated against so they're all somewhat in the same boat, but the problems of each group are different. Lumping groups together—all people of African descent, all Hispanics, all Asians, all women, for that matter—might not be the best idea. On the one hand those broad designations have been a positive force for change because they've increased the number of constituents in each group. Potentially, at least, larger groups are more politically powerful. But does lumping people together actually get things done? It seems that every oppressed group can find a way to oppress somebody else, even within their own identity group," says Berry. In her long experience as an activist, she has learned that it's not only whites who have blinders on at times: "We've learned that white females don't remember that all women aren't white. But black males don't remember that all blacks aren't men. Whites want to avoid the race problem by talking about poverty. Yet elites of color want to avoid the

THE WAY FORWARD                                                    149

class problem by talking about race. So it seems that there are always people who are left out and discriminated against. We need to work on that, both as activist groups of color, and as a country."[32]

Social change takes time. As President Obama said in his ABC News interview, "In a democracy, progress is incremental. You know, and it goes in stutter-steps and sometimes there is some backsliding. But the overall trajectory I think is positive."[33] Martin Luther King, Jr. expressed the same sentiment in spiritual terms: "The arc of the moral universe is long but it bends toward justice." So we need not be overwhelmed by the difficulty of the task, even where change seems most unlikely and the denial most debilitating. There are many such places in this country; the most obvious are the white conservative strongholds, whether they are genteel, gated neighborhoods, or meetings of gun-toting white nationalists. But some of the most disturbing spaces of resistance are the pleasant, well-meaning, politically liberal communities where "there is no such thing as race." For it may be "the appalling silence of good people," as King often said, that fractures our country the most.

It was with this thought in mind that I decided to return, one year later, to the lovely little East Coast town where the three high school students I interviewed in Chapter 1 had begun to grapple with the racism that, unbeknownst to most whites, had fractured their community. When I first interviewed the teens, Kay, the biracial daughter of college professors, and her two white friends, Emma and Troy, had begun conversations among themselves on the taboo topic of race. Emma and Troy were learning, to their dismay, about the systemic racism that frustrated and angered the students of color at their high school. It was not just the curriculum, which was blatantly Eurocentric, or the classes, which somehow ended up segregated by race, or the racial disparity in academic achievement that started back in middle school, but the silence about race that had most disturbed the three friends. And since there was no space in their school to talk about race across racial lines, they were reduced to telling "stupid racial jokes" just to broach the topic, or in Kay's case, carrying around books with provocative titles in a futile attempt to jolt her teachers and fellow students out of their complacency.

But a year later, all of that had changed. "Remember how last year we said that our town is so liberal there's no such thing as race?" Kay asks me when I arrive. "Well, that's no longer true."

The silence about race had been broken when an African American teacher who had taught successfully and without incident for years in a nearby town received several anonymous racial threats. "It was ironic that it all started that way," says Kay, "because that kind of racism is totally uncharacteristic of what goes on at our school. What we have here is more like microaggressions, tracking, self-segregation in the cafeteria, the silencing of student of color perspectives. That's the kind of stuff our school has allowed to go on for years, untouched. But when someone wrote the n-word on a teacher's door, *that's* when everyone got upset. First the students started talking, and then the parents heard about it, and pretty soon the news media picked it up."

"But the n-word on a teacher's door *is* kind of shocking, don't you think?" I ask her.

"Of course what happened wasn't trivial," Kay replies quickly. "But it's not the main problem, in my opinion. It's just a symptom of what lies underneath, which is the whole *ideology* of racism that creates the separation and inequality that is endemic in our school. But nobody's addressing that core issue in any meaningful way. They're just focusing on what looks bad—the racist words that were directed at this one teacher."

"I see. So then what happened?"

"Well, once the media got hold of it, people in town began taking sides, depending, in large part, on their race. And since then, there's been a lot of public meetings and hearings about it, all of which involve a lot of shouting. And now it's just a *mess*. There's a lot of adult agendas going on."

"What do you mean by adult agendas?" I ask Kay.

"The adults in our town, most of them, don't know how to have a real conversation about race with people they disagree with. Wherever the topic comes up, whether it's at a school committee meeting or over e-mail or in city council, the discussion is very binary. One side says the school is racist. The other side says it's not. And then it's 'Black lives matter.' 'No, all lives matter.' The discussion can get very rude, with people interrupting each other and not letting other people speak."

"People can get emotional about the subject of race," I say. "It's natural, I think, when they first start to talk about it."

"But there's got to be a way to educate people about what's going on so we can have a more productive discussion," says Kay. "The problem is, a lot of the white people in town—most, I would say—think they know all about racism already. So once the news reports started coming out about how racist our school is, some of the white students started saying, 'Well, that's not true! *I've* had a *great* time here.' Which is such a white person thing to say! It's not the *point* that you had a great time here. *You're* not held back by racism. *You're* not the one who's dismissed and ignored. But now there's a growing contingent of white moms and their children who are saying we have to focus on the positives. They keep saying, 'This school's not *all* bad!'"

"Which is probably true, right?"

"Yes, of course it's not *all* bad!" says Kay. "We have to acknowledge the good things too. But the thing is, the people who are leading the charge to support the school are all white! They don't understand racism. They've never thought deeply about why our school is so segregated or why students of color are so discouraged academically. And they're saying we need to focus on the *positives?* That's *completely* disregarding the stories and the experiences of the youth of color in our school! It's *so* disrespectful!"

I turn to Troy, who is listening intently. "What's your take on all this?" I ask him.

"I agree with Kay," says Troy, smiling at her across the kitchen table. "A lot of the talk about race at our school this year has been very frustrating to me, especially when I try to convince people to see things from the standpoint of the students of color. I feel like my white friends have this idea that what they know is right and that their opinions are like, the pinnacle of knowledge. And that can be pretty dangerous when dealing with an issue as personal and hurtful as racism."

"So the white students are set in their opinions?" I ask him.

"Well, not completely," Troy replies. "In fact, compared to last year, there's actually been this huge shift, where most of the white students have accepted that yes, there might be *some* racism or at least some racist *tendencies* in our school. But I think a lot of them have yet to grasp what that means for their peers of color."

Kay nods in agreement. "Even though this whole affair created a lot of controversy and angry words, at least it had the effect of getting our racial issues out in the open," she says. "And that gave the people of color in town the opportunity to speak out about what they thought racism really meant, which was the first time a lot of the white people had heard their point of view. And then Troy and I started making a documentary about the whole affair and we got a little press for that, and that increased the talk."

"Tell me about your documentary. What prompted you to do it?"

"Well, from what I've learned from teachers who have been here for a long time, our school has gone through periods of great racial strife before," says Kay. "Something will happen and everyone gets upset, and then it passes and everyone forgets about it until the next incident sets it off again. So Troy and another friend and I decided we had to at least document what people are thinking right now, when race is on everyone's mind. That way, in future years, students can see what we were talking about back in 2014, and hopefully, that will keep the conversation about race alive."

"So how are you going about it?"

"We're interviewing people across the racial spectrum about the events that have happened in our school over the past year," says Troy. "And it's going to be so obvious that there's a stark divide between the perception of white people and the perception of people of color."

"That's such a great idea," says Emma, who we're talking to on Skype from her college in the Midwest. "And, well, speaking from the experience I've had in my first year here, your video might also help white students who think they're good allies to hear some of the frustrations that students of color have with them."

"What do you mean?" asks Troy, looking a little concerned.

"Mmm, it's not that important," says Emma, waving her hands across the screen as if to erase her words. "Let's go on."

"Are you sure?" asks Kay.

"Well, okay," says Emma. "This is going to sound really bad, but I'll say it anyway. In my senior year in high school I was part of a group of students and administrators that were tasked with improving race relations at our school. So I was involved in a lot of big ideas. And I was thinking, wow, it's such a great feeling to be an ally! I had a lot of drive. I wanted to be an authority! I wanted to get involved in social change! But when I got to college and started taking classes about our country's racial history—which has been *amazing*, by the way—I started talking with students of color a lot more than I had previously. And what I realized was, as much as I wanted to be involved and to really be a part of creating change, I wasn't ready yet. So I had to tell myself, this is one area where you can't be a leader. You aren't even an effective ally. Not yet, anyway. So you can't have the power in this situation, even if it's coming from a well-intentioned place. And that was a really big thing for me."

"That's good, Emma," says Troy.

"So do you think Emma should stop working on racial issues altogether?" I ask Troy.

"No, not at all," interrupts Emma. "The thing is, I need to know a lot more than I thought I did. I realize now that I'm in the midst of a learning process. I have *so* much more to learn. So just listening has become a huge thing for me right now."

THE WAY FORWARD 153

"I can relate to that," says Troy. "And one thing I've realized is that, okay, I'm a white male in this society"—he glances over at Kay, who is trying to hide a smile—"and although I can listen and sort of see where a person of color is coming from, I cannot truly know what it is like to be them."

"But does that mean you can't empathize at all?" I ask. "If you can't know how someone feels, how can you relate? And if you can't relate...."

"I can relate. But only up to a point," says Troy. "You know, it's really easy to say, 'I know where you're coming from.' It *sounds* sympathetic. It sounds like I care. And I do care. But what I've learned is, caring is not enough. Recognizing my privilege is a lot more important. And there's something powerful in realizing that I don't know how a person of color feels or what their life is like that sort of highlights my privilege. I've *never* been held back because of my race. I've *always* known I would go to college, even when I wasn't such a great student. It's been so easy for me to bounce back from failures because of my race and probably my gender as well."

"That's one reason why it's important for whites to step back and let people of color lead this new social movement, or the new civil rights movement, as some call it," says Kay. "It doesn't mean we don't want white involvement. But like Emma says, white people need to repress their tendency to jump in until they've understood their privilege and learned how to be more effective allies."

"Kay, I understand that you led a walkout from your school today to protest the grand jury decision in the Michael Brown shooting," I say.

"Really, Kay? That's so awesome!" says Emma.

"I wish you could have seen it," says Kay. "Even though we had only three days to plan, we got about 350 students to walk out, including quite a few white students as well as students of color."

"That's impressive," I say. "How did you manage it?"

"Well, I think a lot of white students really want to have a chance to talk about race, even though it's pretty hushed up at our school," says Kay. "So that's what our walkout was about, an opportunity to talk together outside of class where we could say whatever we wanted without censorship."

"Censorship?"

"You know, the usual teacher restrictions. There was no one to say you can't swear, you can't say anything personal, you can't say this, you can't say that. But since we were in public space we got to say whatever we wanted. And that in itself was so awesome! People could say what was *authentic* to them, and what they felt from the heart."

"So your walkout was quite different from the other demonstrations and marches protesting the grand jury decisions."

"Well, we had several goals. We wanted it to symbolize our solidarity with people who are protesting Michael Brown's death and also to protest ways that discussion about race is silenced at our school. But mainly, we saw it as an opportunity to sit down together and talk about racial issues. We wanted to show our school that we think these conversations are *absolutely* essential to us. Not just *having* these conversations, but having them *well*. And that if the school can't provide this kind of education for us, we *will* take up school time to do it elsewhere."

"What did your school think about that?" I ask.

"We actually requested permission to walk out," says Troy. "And the administration agreed. All they said was that students had to sign out before they left the school."

"Some of my teachers were very supportive," adds Kay. "They know that most of the staff at our school are incapable of leading productive conversations about race. In fact, one of them told me, 'These discussions have to be student-led. Adults can't do this.' And she was right!"

"How did you organize the conversations?" I ask Kay.

"We thought it was essential to start by giving people some solid information," Kay replies. "So we gave them some statistics about police violence, the numbers of people killed, the over-representation of people of color in prison, the achievement gap, that sort of thing, just so everyone would have the opportunity to reflect on the same information. And then we gave them a chance to talk about the themes of Ferguson and how they relate to racism in our country in general."

"That's quite an agenda for one afternoon."

"Yeah, it really was! I can't say we accomplished all that, but the walkout is only the beginning."

"Tell me about it from start to finish."

"Well, first, we assembled all the students in front of the school and announced four and a half minutes of silence for the four and a half hours that Michael Brown's body lay in the street. Everyone respected that, which gave us confidence that we were going to be able to lead 350 people through town without losing too many of them. Because we were just astonished at how many people came out! We thought we'd get maybe a hundred, or a hundred and fifty, but we had more than twice that! So we all walked through our town center to the local library, and a couple of us gave some speeches on the front

THE WAY FORWARD 155

steps—that's where we read the statistics—and then we sent a large group of students, about 180 of them, into one big room in the library. And we broke up the rest of the students into groups of about 20 and sent them to the smaller library rooms and to coffee shops all around town and also to a couple of outdoor spaces, even though it was freezing. So each group went to their assigned space with a discussion facilitator who we had chosen beforehand."

"These were all students? The organizers, the facilitators, everyone?"

"All students. Everyone was under 18 years old."

"Impressive! So how did the discussions go?"

"Pretty well, I thought," says Kay. "What I found most amazing was that in that one large room we had a group of 180 kids speaking and listening to each other without the presence of adults. Just talking it out in our own way and asking each other, 'What can we do to make this better?' And at the end of the conversation, what the students came to was that we need to know each other. We need to *see* each other. We need to start being *people* with each other. We need to sit together in the cafeteria. We need to reach out and talk to each other."

"Did the white students need convincing that this was necessary?" I ask Kay. "The way you've described the atmosphere at the school, it seems as though they had no clue that there were any racial issues at all."

"It's interesting," says Kay. "Even though we'd never talked together about the racial separation, it has always been so obvious, even to white students."

"That's so true," says Troy. "Everyone *knows* the cafeteria is segregated. Everyone knows that tracking is segregation, basically, and that it's completely unfair. These things weren't surprises to people."

"But it used to be just the students of color who were ready to dive into those issues," says Emma. "White students didn't want to touch it."

"White students could see the patterns," says Kay. "But I don't think they realized that those patterns *mean* something to people of color and that what it means is—*painful*. Now, even though it's clear we have a long way to go, I think we have a start in a new direction."

Later that afternoon, Kay invites me to sit in on a meeting of the organizers of the walkout to discuss what happened and plan next steps. Ten or twelve high schoolers, mostly male, about half students of color and half white, pile into Kay's living room, talking avidly. The first item of business is a bit surprising: thank you notes to the library for providing the discussion space and to the small businesses around town that contributed the sandwiches, pizza, and sweets to fortify the marchers. Once volunteer letter writers are found, the teens move on to an item of immediate concern: Someone from the local press wrote a piece that distorted the purpose of the march, and letters critical of the student action were written by residents who read the misleading article. Shall we just ignore the miscommunication and move on, they ask each other? No. The march was too important. They decide to write a "reflection letter" to the editor, correcting the errors.

Next up: Kay has been invited by some college student organizers to help plan a large demonstration for the coming weekend. She reports that activists have already held a protest at a local mall where they encountered police dogs and zip ties, rather than the stares and admiring glances the high school students had gotten from passersby during their own walkout. "Taking the streets is the next level of activism by and for students of color," Kay says. The teen organizers laugh nervously; this is all very new to them. "What do you mean by 'take the streets?'" someone asks. "Does that mean they can arrest you?"

"It means the organizers are not asking permission," says Kay. "They might stop some traffic. They can arrest you for that. It all depends on how the police choose to respond."

The teens eye each other. "Are you going?" they ask Kay. "I'm thinking about it," she says. "This is something we need to do as individuals, not as a group. You'll need to decide for yourselves on your level of involvement. If white allies want to join in, you'll be expected to position yourselves on the edges of the march, linking arms, protecting the people of color from arrest," Kay says, looking into the eyes of each of the white student organizers, who nod reflectively, accepting their role. "As we know, whites are less likely to be arrested and better able to protect themselves if they are."

It's clear that Kay has taken charge, not only as the facilitator of this meeting but as the lead organizer of the walkout and the actions to come. Her authority in the group is palpable; her peers listen attentively as she fills them in on the details of an action; they volunteer quickly for roles and tasks. Kay's mom, who is white, tells me later how proud she is of her daughter for taking the lead. "As you know," she says, "one of the key things that happens with white people when they get involved in this kind of movement is that they can't listen. And they can't follow. They can't follow people of color. But what I observed during the march and the discussion at the library was that the white kids were really listening to the kids of color and particularly to the kids of color in leadership roles. And I thought, if just one thing comes out of the walkout, this is a significant shift. For that age range, there was some *serious* listening going on!"

It's getting on toward dinner time. Kay has provided a pitcher of water, which everyone downs with relish. Someone has brought a big bag of chips, which they all share. The organizers stand around the kitchen island to continue their discussion of tactics. A student of color tells the group that it's frustrating that white students don't know anything about race, but sometimes students of color don't know about race either, and that's even worse.

"Is it really worse though?" asks a white student. "I'm not so sure."

"What I really don't like," says another student of color, "is that some people of color pull the race card without having any understanding of racism at all." Many heads nod in agreement. This reminds Kay of something she's learned from W. E. B. Du Bois, that blacks need to understand and define their own condition.

"There's so much written about these issues by the most brilliant people, but we don't read any of it in school," Kay says to enthusiastic agreement among her peers. Kay talks for a moment about a class she is taking at the local college, where they are reading "not just fiction but actual theory that all students of color should be exposed to." Someone brings up the problem of trying to learn about race in high school without reading a single book by a person of color. "The history of organizing is so romanticized the way we learn about it in school," says Kay. "It seems so straightforward. But then you find out that successful organizers in the past paid a lot of attention to theory. If we learn from them we can be more effective."

"We need a sustained model of learning for our organizers—for us," the teens agree.

"We need a book club!" someone suggests.

"We need a book club where we read like, *real* shit," says another.

"Oh my god, let me show you!" Kay runs to the living room and returns with a stack of biographies of radical people of color. "There are so many books out there!" she says. "This course I'm taking has changed my life." Everyone starts thumbing through Kay's books with great interest. "Did you read ALL of these?" the students ask Kay, clearly impressed.

"Well, not all," she confesses. "We read excerpts. But I want to read them all."

The teens return to the living room, refreshed by food and conversation. They discuss how to get more information out to their community of peers. Someone suggests that they produce a countercurrent newspaper. There is discussion of the form, the content, and the distribution of a zine, as well as the availability of online graphics and the legalities of copyright. Anonymous publishing will keep our writers safe, they decide. And there would be no need or requirement for a teacher-advisor. They can say what they want without censorship.

Suddenly, a new idea emerges: The group could post on the walls of their school the names of all the people of color who have been killed by police in the past year, especially victims who are less commonly known. This will appeal to the adolescent sense of curiosity and one-upmanship, they say. "Everyone will wonder what those names mean. So then they'll start looking them up online. As soon as someone knows something that no one else knows it will spread like wildfire." Yes! They will do this. Tasks of researching the names, making the lists, and posting them throughout the school are all quickly assigned.

It's been a huge day, and the teens are getting punchy; it's hard for Kay to keep order. As they joke with each other, Kay joins in, laughing with them. Then, quietly, skillfully, she pulls the group back to the few remaining items of business. The teens quiet down and listen attentively. Someone asks, "If I get arrested, will it show up on my college report? Seriously, I need to know!" There is more nervous laughter as the group begins to disperse.

As the teens reassure each other and negotiate rides home, I am left with a feeling of buoyancy and hope. At age 17, these students, along with thousands of other young organizers who are meeting in living rooms and college dorms and virtual spaces across the country, are beginning what they hope will become a new chapter in our nation's racial history. They are ready to learn from activists before them. But at the same time, they believe they have found a new way forward. As for the rest of us, we all have a part to play in this new racial drama, some as teachers, some as listeners and learners, some as skeptics, some as principled critics, and some as stubborn deniers that there is any problem at all. As individuals, and as a nation, we choose our destiny.

# NOTES

## Chapter 2

1 Real Clear Politics, 2010, January 27.
2 Snopes.com.
3 Gregory, 2012, January 22.
4 New Politics Institute, 2007.
5 See Yancy, 2013, September 1.
6 McCoy, 2014, February 21.
7 Myers and Williamson, 2001, p. 4.
8 Myers and Williamson, 2001, p. 10.
9 Myers and Williamson, 2001, p. 11.
10 Myers and Williamson, 2001, p. 8.
11 Myers and Williamson, 2001, p. 11.
12 Myers and Williamson, 2001, p. 12.
13 Myers and Williamson, 2001, p. 12.
14 Myers and Williamson, 2001, p. 14.
15 Kurzman, 2014, February 13.
16 Greenwald and Hussain, 2014, July 9.
17 Huffington Post, 2014, July 11.
18 2010 Census Briefs, 2012, January.

## Chapter 3

1 Harris, 2013, December 10.
2 See, for example, Van Ausdale and Feagin, 2001.
3 See Roberts, 2009, December 17.
4 Harris, 2013, December 12.
5 Genius.com/Fox-news-santa-claus-should-not-be-white-annotated (no date)
6 Harris, 2013, December 10.
7 Genius.com/Fox-news-santa-claus-should-not-be-white-annotated (no date)
8 Genius.com/Fox-news-santa-claus-should-not-be-white-annotated (no date)
9 Genius.com/Fox-news-santa-claus-should-not-be-white-annotated (no date)
10 Harris, 2013, December 12.
11 Williams, 2013, December 4.
12 Cole, 2013, December 13.
13 Roediger, 2007, p. 133.
14 Ignatiev, 1995, p. 59.
15 *United States v. Bhagat Singh Thind*, 1923.
16 Roediger, 2007, p. 64.
17 Roediger, 2007, quoting Cubberley, 1909, pp. 14–15.
18 Roediger, 2007, p. 58.
19 Roediger, 2007, p. 58.
20 Roediger, 2007, p. 80.
21 Quoted in Roediger, 2005, p. 3.
22 Haley and Malcolm X, 1964, p. 459.
23 Roediger, 2005, p. 181.
24 Roediger, 2005, p. 181.
25 Roediger, 2005, p. 73.
26 Roediger, 2005, p. 171.
27 Roediger, 2005, p. 9.
28 Roediger, 2005, p. 14.
29 Roediger, 2005, p. 11.
30 Roediger, 2005, pp. 25–26.
31 Racebox.org, n.d.
32 Mackintosh, 1988.
33 As former Senator David Reed of Pennsylvania put it, cited in Stephenson, 1964, p. 90.
34 Muhammad, 2010, p. 4.
35 *Plessy v. Ferguson*, 1896.
36 *Plessy v. Ferguson*, 1896, p. 79.
37 Takaki, 1998, p. 101.
38 *Takao Ozawa v. United States*, 1922.
39 *United States v. Bhagat Singh Thind*, 1923.
40 *United States v. Bhagat Singh Thind*, 1923.
41 *United States v. Bhagat Singh Thind*, 1923.

NOTES 161

42 *Johnson & Graham's Lessee v. McIntosh*, 1823.
43 In 1971, the Indian Claims Commission finally agreed that the two tribes were owed $10 million in damages for being cheated in concessions they made under treaties ratified in the 1800s. But since the federal government could not agree on how to distribute the judgment fund among the plaintiffs, the money was tied up until 1996, when it was worth nearly $70 million.
44 http://www.juancole.com/images/2013/12/Screen-Shot-2013-12-13-at-4.11.13-AM.png.
45 http://www.juancole.com/2013/12/photo-nicholas-white.html.
46 Roediger, 2005, p. 29.
47 Roberts, 2011, p. 50.
48 Roberts, 2011, p. 51. See also Ventner's (2000) remarks at the Human Genome announcement. Today, with advances in technology, scientists can determine from DNA markers in a person's genome the regions of the world that their ancestors came from. However, the percentages of these markers cannot really determine a person's race, since "race" is a socially and politically constructed system that assigns people to broad categories that do not reflect the full diversity of an individual's actual ancestry. In fact, someone who knows only of "white" European ancestors (for example) may be surprised to discover, on having their genome mapped, that s/he has significant percentages of Asian, African, Native American, and/or Middle Eastern DNA markers. See, for example, the PBS television series "Finding Your Roots," where Dr. Henry Louis Gates, Jr., investigates the DNA and historical ancestry of various celebrities and other public figures.
49 Roberts, 2011, p. 52.
50 Roberts, 2011, p. 5.
51 Roberts, 2011, p. 5.

# Chapter 4

1 Van Ausdale and Feagin, 2001.
2 Van Ausdale and Feagin, pp. 104–105.
3 See, for example, Pewewardy (1997) on the "Pocahontas paradox."
4 Snowden, 1983.
5 Snowden, 1983, p. 108.
6 Snowden, 1983, p. 86.
7 Snowden, 1983, p. 63.
8 Snowden, 1983, p. 70.
9 Snowden, 1983, p. 69.
10 Snowden, 1983, p. 68.
11 Mills, 1997, p. 21.
12 Mills, 1997, p. 23.
13 Mills, 1997, p. 11.
14 Mills, 1997, p. 11.
15 Mills, 1997, p. 10.
16 Mills, 1997, p. 5.

162 FRACTURED: RACE RELATIONS IN "POST-RACIAL" AMERICAN LIFE

17 Marable, 2002, p. xiii.
18 See Lui, Robles, Leondar-Wright, Brewer, and Adamson (2006), Katznelson (2005), and Fox (2012) for details.
19 Moyers & Company, 2014, March 12.
20 Mills, 1997, p. 18.
21 Mills, 1997, p. 19.
22 Chait, 2014.
23 Coates, 2014, March 21.
24 Noonan, 2012, April 30.
25 Even though much has been improved in terms of getting permission from the subjects of medical experimentation, explaining the effects of treatment; and treating them with respect, questionable practices remain. For example, according to the *New York Times* (Murphy, 2014, June 9), doctors in Baltimore are eager to test a new procedure that would save lives on the battlefield, in extreme auto accidents, or when people have been shot or stabbed. The procedure, already favorably tested on animals, would involve draining all of the victim's blood from their body and replacing it with ice cold sea water, stopping the heart, lungs and brain function so that the patient essentially dies. This would give the surgeons time to stitch up the patient's wounds before replacing the blood and re-warming the body, hopefully as good as new. But how to test such a radical procedure on humans? Gunshot victims don't have time or consciousness to give their consent. So, the researchers say, we'll go ahead and do it anyway, which will likely save their life as well as give us the verification we need that the procedure works. And if it doesn't? The patient would likely be brain dead and need to be cared for by family members—who weren't consulted either. Why is this racial? Gunshot victims in Baltimore, the study acknowledges, are most likely to be men of color.
26 Bouie, 2014, May 16.
27 For a creative conversation starter see the interactive video feature "The N-Word" (*The Washington Post*), where viewers can create their own minivideos featuring three arguments of their choice.
28 Colorlines, 2013, August 5.
29 See, for example, Richard Wright's autobiographical novel *Black Boy* (1945/2007), for a personal account of the feelings of blacks about whites in the time before the civil rights era.
30 Roediger, 2007.
31 In a study of traffic psychology in Portland, Oregon (Rose, 2014, May 21), researchers recruited six research subjects, three white men and three black men in their 20s, and had them dress in identical clothing and approach a crosswalk in the same manner. When they activated the crosswalk signal, the study reported, "twice as many drivers failed to yield for black pedestrians than those who were white. Meanwhile, black pedestrians typically had to wait a third longer for cars to stop for them when they had the legal right of way." The researchers noted, "In a fast-paced activity like driving, where decisions may need to be made in a fraction of a second, people's actions can be influenced by these subtle attitudes." "These subtle attitudes" can have tangible, physical effects on people of color. Nationally, African Americans have a 60% and Hispanics a 43% higher rate of pedestrian

NOTES 163

deaths than whites. How many of these deaths are due to racism? We don't know, but we should be discussing it.

32  Bonilla-Silva, 2003.

33  Walker, 2013, June 19.

34  As seen in David Turnley's (2012) perceptive film about the murder, *Shenandoah*.

35  Bonilla-Silva, 2003, p. 2.

36  Of course, whites have been blaming blacks for their degraded condition since the days of slavery. But before the civil rights era it was more common for whites to claim that black poverty was due to their inherent physical and moral inferiority rather than their culture.

37  Bonilla-Silva, 2003, p. 4.

38  For many more examples of racism among college and university faculty and administrators, especially against women of color, see Gutiérrez y Muhs, Niemann, González, and Harris, 2013.

39  Coates, 2014, May 1.

# Chapter 5

1  See Borowski (2013, February 28) for a video of a white Millennial making this argument. See Finnegan (2014, September 15) for a very personal and comprehensive look at the fast food workers' campaign for raising the minimum wage.

2  For statistics on child poverty in America, see Children's Defense Fund (2013, September 17).

3  See, for example, the ABC News video on Huffington Post (2013, August 26) where columnist George Will argues that the rise in the number of children born to black, unwed mothers over the last 50 years is a bigger impediment to their progress than the absence of civil rights. But as the article points out, this "rise" in the number of black children born out of wedlock ignores the fact that the actual birthrate for black women is at the lowest point ever documented. For the history of this argument, see Massey (2007, pp. 172–173). As Massey explains, once civil rights legislation made it more difficult for states to deny relief to impoverished minorities, black women began to organize to gain access to their entitled benefits. Their success increased the number of women on welfare dramatically. But since most of these newly supported families were African American, relief for the poor became associated with lower class blacks in the minds of many Americans. These newly entitled black women were depicted by politicians and the media as undeserving, irresponsible "welfare queens" who bilked the system at the expense of "taxpayers," who were, presumably, upstanding whites.

4  For statistics on "the incredible shrinking American middle class," see Kamp (2013, September 20); for reasons the middle class is sliding into poverty, see Horowitz (2011, September 23).

5  See New Politics Institute (2007).

6  However, according to economist Joseph Stiglitz, economic mobility is lower in the United States than in almost every other industrialized country. "The life prospects of an American are more dependent on the income and education of his parents than in almost any other advanced country for which there is data" (Stiglitz, 2013, February 16).

7 Americans' attitudes toward people in poverty are complex. Although a "massive shift" in public opinion about the causes of poverty has been noted in the past 20 years, with more people across the generations now seeing poverty as the result of circumstances rather than personal failing, young people are more likely to be conservative on this point. And the increase in apparent sympathy for the poor among older people does not seem to translate into support for increased government assistance, but rather, for more education and job training opportunities. In other words, the majority still think that poor people need to work harder (albeit at different things) to solve their own financial problems. See Maloy (2014, June 20) and Wessler (2014, June 20).

8 Edsall, 2014, July 16.

9 Not to mention the plethora of conspiracy theories about President Obama's supposed origins, activities, and secret agenda. See Subasing and Gilson (n.d.) for a chart of these strange, racist imaginings and a bit of comic relief.

10 Tilove, 2008, January 31.

11 Regarding black-on-black racism, Ta-Nehisi Coates remarks, "Racism is a kind of fatalism, so seductive, that it enthralls even its victims" (Coates, 2014, January 20).

12 The ostensible purpose of requiring voters to show identification at the polls is to prevent voter fraud. But in fact, according to the American Civil Liberties Union, (2014, August 7) "Voter ID laws have the potential to deny the right to vote to thousands of registered voters who do not have, and, in many instances, cannot obtain the limited identification states accept for voting" (https://www.aclu.org/blog/tag/voter-id). These voters are disproportionately poor people of color.

13 Blow, 2014, April 11.

14 Fry and Taylor, 2012, August 1.

15 Blow, 2014, April 11.

16 Inzlicht and Obhi, 2014, July 25.

17 For an eye-opening personal account of "why poor people's bad decisions make perfect sense," see Tirado (2014, June 19).

18 For a history of how economic inequality was created in the United States, from the New Deal to the present, see Massey (2007), particularly Chapter 5, "Remaking the Political Economy."

19 For a fascinating and nuanced discussion of how and why blacks must play the role of "palatable" black in the workplace, see Carbado and Gulati (2013).

20 In fact, although "strivers" of color may be seen as acceptable by most of their white neighbors and colleagues, they are still vulnerable to racist attacks. See Graham (2014, November 6) for a personal account of the shock and dismay felt by a wealthy black parent who, try as he might, could not shield his son from racial insult.

21 According to a study from Florida State University College of Medicine, rich youth who abuse drugs are more likely to do so because of personality problems, while poor youth do so because of their hopeless economic situation. "One possible interpretation of these intriguing findings is that the stereotype of the drug using poor as feckless and unruly, is in fact the precise opposite of the truth. It's relatively richer people who suffer disorganized and undisciplined personality types, who are more drawn to drugs. When the poor are taking cocaine, it's much more likely to reflect their tough economic circumstances than

NOTES 165

their personality" (Persaud & Bruggen, 2013, June 12). Also, see Luthar (2013, November 5) for insight into why rich kids get involved in substance abuse.

22 A Stanford scholar found that talking about social class in a one-hour session helped first-generation college students reduce the social-class achievement gap by as much as 63 percent (*Stanford News*, 2014, April 22). However, Andrea's story suggests that solving the problem at other elite colleges will be more complicated than what a brief program can provide.

23 The idea that social class reflects biological endowment is still surprisingly prevalent, even among some social scientists. See Corak (2014, May 22).

# Chapter 6

1 Johnson's full account, as told to the Grand Jury on September 10, 2014, can be found here: https://www.documentcloud.org/documents/1370517-grand-jury-volume-4.html.

2 A recording of the shots was made unintentionally by a neighborhood resident as he was talking to someone by video chat. See Phillip (2014, August 26).

3 Eromosele, 2014, August 19. Accounts differ about the exact position of Brown's hands. Out of 29 witnesses that testified to the Grand Jury, 16 said he had his hands up. See Davey, Wines, Eckholm, and Oppel (2014, November 29) for a summary of the differing accounts throughout the Grand Jury hearing and the questions that remain.

4 Eromosele, 2014, August 19. My account of the entire interaction is based on Dorian Johnson's testimony and comments made to reporters by five witnesses who viewed the encounter from different vantage points (Kindy & Horwitz, 2014, October 23). The police and other witnesses have a different version of the events: that Brown intentionally slammed the police car door, trapping the officer in his vehicle; that Brown thrust his upper body into the vehicle in order to attack the officer; that during the struggle, Brown hit the officer in the face, grabbed for his gun, and let go only after it fired twice; and that after initially running away, Brown turned and approached Officer Wilson in a threatening manner, causing him to shoot the unarmed teen in self-defense. See Wilson's testimony to the Grand Jury (https://www.documentcloud.org/documents/1370518-grand-jury-volume-5.html).

5 Bosman and Goldstein, 2014, August 24.

6 The protests continued, waxing and waning for more than 100 days after the initial demonstrations died down.

7 Quigley, 2014, August 18. For more on the police overreaction from Human Rights Watch, see Morales (2014, August 18).

8 NBC Washington, 2014, August 14.

9 *The Wall Street Journal*, 2014, August 18.

10 MRAPS is an acronym for "mine-resistant ambush-protected vehicles."

11 Bell, 2014, August 17.

12 Rubin, 2014, August 20.

13 Blake, 2014, August 18.

# 166 FRACTURED: RACE RELATIONS IN "POST-RACIAL" AMERICAN LIFE

14 Pew Research Center, 2014, August 18. This split in attitudes is not confined to what happened in Ferguson. In a review of Gallup poll data of black and white attitudes toward police in general shows that "Blacks have significantly lower levels of confidence in the police as an institution, and lower assessments of the honesty and ethics of police officers specifically" (Newport, 2014, August 20).

15 In Ferguson, the reaction of white residents suggested that many had no idea that race relations in their city were in any way problematic. Even the mayor expressed shock that blacks experienced trouble with the police: "I keep a lot of African American friends— some of my dearest friends—but when we hang out at the brew house, we don't talk about these issues," he told *The Washington Post*. "A lot of residents are going, 'Damn, I never realized my friends felt that way or had these experiences'" (Samuels, 2014, October 7).

16 Wilkerson, 2014, August 25.

17 For a discussion on how often unarmed black men are shot by white police, see Lee (2014, August 15).

18 Fox 31 Denver, 2014, July 7.

19 White, 2014, August 12. For more instances of black women, teens, and children being brutalized by police, see Gross, 2014, December 11.

20 Parker, 2014, September 4.

21 Jahi, 2014, August 15.

22 ABC News, Good Morning America, 2014, August 18.

23 Ferguson, 2014, August 14. This Klan group also claims, bizarrely, that "black thugs" are "Jewish controlled" and that most white cops are "cowards" in fighting crimes against (presumably non-Jewish) whites.

24 Pearce, 2014, September 1.

25 Chemerinsky, 2014, August 26. The dean of the School of Law at the University of California, Irvine, wrote in a *New York Times* op-ed piece that the decision to hold Officer Darren Wilson accountable for Michael Brown's murder would be "severely restricted" by the U.S. Supreme Court. The court's decisions that stand in the way of prosecutions of civil rights violations "undermine the ability to deter illegal police behavior and leaves victims without compensation. When the police kill or injure innocent people, the victims rarely have recourse." Indeed, the Grand Jury that was convened to decide whether to bring Officer Wilson to trial voted on November 24, 2014, not to indict him. Protests broke out immediately after the verdict, which was widely considered by Ferguson residents of color, and people of color generally, to be biased toward Officer Wilson. See Davey and Bosman (2014, November 24).

26 Wilkerson, 2014, August 25.

27 King, 2014, August 18.

28 King, 2014, August 18. Indeed, studies show that, for example, whites are 45% more likely than blacks to deal drugs but far less likely to get arrested for it (Ingraham, 2014, September 30).

29 Eligon, 2014, August 24.

30 Waddell, 2014, August 25.

31 Makarechi, 2014, August 25.

32 Sullivan, 2014, August 25.

# NOTES

167

33 Staats, 2014.

34 Lang, 2014, August 17.

35 The best-known tests of implicit bias are computer based exercises where the viewer is asked to quickly associate some aspect of human identity such as race, gender, religion, skin tone, weight, age, sexuality, disability, and so on with positive or negative words. Readers can try these tests here: https://implicit.harvard.edu/implicit/research/

36 Staats, 2014.

37 In an article apologizing for the "ill-chosen phrase, 'he's no angel,'" Eligon says he is "attentive to many of the issues in the Ferguson case" and that he has been racially profiled himself (Sullivan, 2014, August 25).

38 Beckford, n.d. On the comments section on this blog post is this note: "Comments on this post have been closed. After receiving 1000 comments of various natures, it became impossible to monitor and the conversation became inhumane."

39 Powell, 2014, July 24.

40 Powell, 2014, July 24.

41 Lewin, 2012, March 6. Perhaps even more disturbing is a recent study showing that the darker a student's skin tone, the higher the likelihood that student has been suspended, especially for girls (Hing, 2014, October 8).

42 American Psychological Association, 2014, March 6.

43 American Psychological Association, 2014, March 6.

44 Harwood, 2014, August 14.

45 Testimony of Darren Wilson before the Grand Jury (*State of Missouri v. Darren Wilson*, 2014, September 16).

46 Bouie, 2014, November 26. Also see Bloom, 2014, November 26.

47 Wines and Robles, 2014, August 22.

48 Economist, 2014, August 15. Even though at times their lives are in serious jeopardy, British police "overwhelmingly" say they wish to remain unarmed (Kelly, 2012, September 19).

49 Harwood, 2014, August 14.

50 SWAT is an acronym for "Special Weapons and Tactics."

51 Harwood, 2014, August 14.

52 Harwood, 2014, August 14.

53 Harwood, 2014, August 14. A particularly shocking example of a military-style assault on a young black man shopping for a BB gun while talking on his cell phone can be seen on video (Harris-Perry, 2014, September 28).

54 Harwood, 2014, August 14.

55 Daly, 2014, August 22.

56 According to a study by *The Washington Post*, police are authorized under federal law to take cash and property from drivers without charging them with any crime. Owners must prove their money or property was acquired legally in order to get it back—not always an easy or cost-free process. Originally enacted to fight the War on Drugs, the law is now more likely to be used by local police departments to fund day-to-day operations: "Police agencies have used hundreds of millions of dollars taken from Americans under federal civil forfeiture law in recent years to buy guns, armored cars and electronic surveillance

168 FRACTURED: RACE RELATIONS IN "POST-RACIAL" AMERICAN LIFE

gear. They have also spent money on luxury vehicles, travel and a clown named Sparkles" (O'Harrow & Rich, 2014, October 11).

57 Smith, 2014, August 17.
58 Daly, 2014, August 22.
59 Smith, 2014, August 17.
60 Smith, 2014, August 17.
61 CBS Sunday Morning, 2014, September 21.
62 Carroll, 2014, August 21.
63 AJ+, 2014, August 21. According to *The New York Times* (Fausset, 2014, September 28), most American cities, though "mostly black," have "mostly white city halls" (http://www. nytimes.com/2014/09/29/us/mostly-black-cities-mostly-white-city-halls.html?_r=0).
64 Gillborn, 2005, as quoted in Vaught, 2011, p. 26.

# Chapter 7

1 Eighty-four percent of the murders of white people are committed by other whites. See Dyson, 2014, November 29.
2 Richardson, 2015, January 5.
3 #FergusonSyllabus.
4 NAACP, 2014, November 24
5 Boren, 2014, December 1.
6 Eligon, 2014, November 28.
7 Counts, 2014, November 11.
8 Workneh, McLaughlin, and Meinick, 2014, December 15.
9 http://fergusonaction.com/demands/.
10 Craven, 2014, November 25.
11 Powers, 2015, January 13.
12 Jones, 2014, November 15.
13 https://twitter.com/patricialicious.
14 Ebony, 2014, December 2.
15 Ebony, 2014, December 2.
16 ABC News, This Week, 2014, November 23.
17 Reid, 2014, December 17.
18 Berry, 2014, September 19.
19 Moyer and Kirkpatrick, 2015, January 5.
20 Blow, 2015, January 4.
21 Blow, 2015, January 4.
22 Blow, 2015, January 4.
23 Dyson, 2014, November 29.
24 The annotated bibliography in the second revised edition of my book, *When Race Breaks Out*, gives up-to-date information about hundreds of relevant books, articles, online blogs, videos, and other resources that can be used either for teaching others or educating one's self.

NOTES      169

25   Berry, 2014, September 19.
26   Berry, 2014, September 19.
27   Berry, 2014, September 19.
28   Berry, 2014, September 19.
29   King, December, 1967.
30   Berry, 2014, September 19.
31   Berry, 2014, September 19.
32   Berry, 2014, September 19.
33   ABC News, This Week, 2014, November 23.

# BIBLIOGRAPHY

ABC News, Good Morning America. (2014, August 18). Michael Brown's mother: "Justice" will restore the peace in Ferguson. Retrieved from http://abcnews.go.com/GMA/video/michael-browns-mother-justice-restore-peace-ferguson-25019429

ABC News, This Week. (2014, November 23). "This Week" transcript: President Obama. Retrieved from http://abcnews.go.com/ThisWeek/week-transcript-president-obama/story?id=27080731

ACLU. (2014, August 7). Blog of rights: Voter ID. Retrieved from https://www.aclu.org/blog/tag/voter-id

AJ+. (2014, August 21). Ferguson is America. Retrieved from https://www.youtube.com/watch?v=tGZTxNUXy-A&list=UUV3Nm3T-XAgVhKH9jT0ViRg#t=74

American Psychological Association. (2014, March 6). Black boys viewed as older, less innocent than whites, study finds. Retrieved from http://www.apa.org/news/press/releases/2014/03/black-boys-older.aspx

Beckford, K. (n.d.). Dear white moms. *Bonbon Break*. Retrieved from http://www.bonbonbreak.com/dear-white-moms/

Bell, B. (2014, August 17). Missouri Governor Jay Nixon "thunderstruck" by images of Ferguson police. *ABC News*. Retrieved from http://abcnews.go.com/blogs/politics/2014/08/missouri-gov-jay-nixon-thunderstruck-by-images-of-ferguson-police/

Berry, M. F. (2014, September 19). Keynote address. 20th Anniversary Symposium. University of Michigan Law School.

Blake, A. (2014, August 18). African Americans are very concerned about what's happening in Ferguson. Whites are not. *The Washington Post*. Retrieved from http://www.washingtonpost.

com/blogs/the-fix/wp/2014/08/18/racial-reactions-to-ferguson-even-stronger-than-to-trayvon-martin/

Bloom, P. (2014, November 26) Racial fearmongering and Ferguson: U.S. stereotype of "violent" African American men as old as slavery. Retrieved from http://www.juancole.com/2014/11/fearmongering-stereotype-american.html

Blow, C. (2014, April 11). The self-sort. *The New York Times*. Retrieved from http://www.nytimes.com/2014/04/12/opinion/blow-the-self-sort.html

Blow, C. (2015, January 4). Privilege of "arrest without incident." *The New York Times*. Retrieved from http://www.nytimes.com/2015/01/05/opinion/charles-blow-privilege-of-arrest-without-incident.html

Bonilla-Silva, E. (2003). *Racism without racists*. Lanham, MD: Rowman & Littlefield.

Boren, C. (2014, December 1). St. Louis police group demands punishment for Rams players in Ferguson protest (updated). *The Washington Post*. Retrieved from http://www.washingtonpost.com/blogs/early-lead/wp/2014/12/01/st-louis-police-group-demands-punishment-for-rams-players-in-ferguson-protest/

Borowski, J. (2013, February 28). Why a $9 minimum wage is a bad idea. Retrieved from https://www.youtube.com/watch?v=_jJQJRKnu2I

Bosman, J., & Goldstein, J. (2014, August 24). Delay in moving body fueled anger in Ferguson. *The Boston Globe*. Retrieved from http://www.bostonglobe.com/news/nation/2014/08/23/hour-delay-moving-body-added-anger-over-ferguson-slaying/CzmOODcjeaTBSfHoma8juL/story.html

Bouie, J. (2014, May 16). Why do Millennials not understand racism? *Slate*. Retrieved from http://www.slate.com/articles/news_and_politics/politics/2014/05/millennials_racism_and_mtv_poll_young_people_are_confused_about_bias_prejudice.html

Bouie, J. (2014, November 26). Michael Brown wasn't a superhuman demon. *Slate*. Retrieved from http://www.slate.com/articles/news_and_politics/politics/2014/11/darren_wilson_s_racial_portrayal_of_michael_brown_as_a_superhuman_demon.html

Carbado, D. W., & Gulati, M. (2013). *Acting white: Rethinking race in "post-racial" America*. New York, NY: Oxford University Press.

Carroll, R. (2014, August 21). Ferguson: A blue collar town made desperate by years on the edge. *The Guardian*. Retrieved from http://www.theguardian.com/world/2014/aug/21/ferguson-community-suffers-clashes-jobs-equality

CBS Sunday Morning. (2014, September 21). Marquis Govan, 11, talks of justice in Ferguson. Retrieved from http://www.youtube.com/watch?v=PIviFC475AU

Chait, J. (2014, March 28). Barack Obama vs. the culture of poverty. *New York Magazine*. Retrieved from http://nymag.com/daily/intelligencer/2014/03/barack-obama-vs-the-culture-of-poverty.html

Chemerinsky, E. (2014, August 26). How the Supreme Court protects bad cops. *The New York Times*. Retrieved from http://www.nytimes.com/2014/08/27/opinion/how-the-supreme-court-protects-bad-cops.html?_r=0

## BIBLIOGRAPHY

Children's Defense Fund. (2013, September 17). *Child poverty in America 2012: National analysis*. Retrieved from http://www.childrensdefense.org/library/data/child-poverty-in-america-2012.pdf

Coates, T. (2014, January 20). Richard Sherman's best behavior. *The Atlantic*. Retrieved from http://www.theatlantic.com/entertainment/archive/2014/01/richard-shermans-best-behavior/283198/

Coates, T. (2014, March 21). Black pathology and the closing of the progressive mind. *The Atlantic*. Retrieved from http://www.theatlantic.com/politics/archive/2014/03/black-pathology-and-the-closing-of-the-progressive-mind/284523/

Coates, T. (2014, May 1). This town needs a better class of racist. *The Atlantic*. Retrieved from http://m.theatlantic.com/politics/archive/2014/05/This-Town-Needs-A-Better-Class-Of-Racist/361443/

Cole, J. (2013, December 13). Photo of the day: Was St. Nicholas "white"? Retrieved from http://www.juancole.com/2013/12/photo-nicholas-white.html

Colorlines. (2013, August 5). Florida Congressman: Obamacare tax on tanning is racist. Retrieved from http://colorlines.com/archives/2013/08/florida_congressman_obamacare_tax_on_tanning_is_racist.html

Corak, M. (2014, May 22). Social mobility: Fixed forever? Retrieved from http://milescorak.com/2014/05/22/social-mobility-fixed-forever-gregory-clarks-the-son-also-rises-is-a-book-of-scholarship-and-of-scholastic-overreach/

Counts, J. (2014, November 11). 40-year old woman fatally shot by Ann Arbor police officer identified. *MLive*. Retrieved from http://www.mlive.com/news/annarbor/index.ssf/2014/11/ann_arbor_police_shooting_name.html

Craven, J. (2014, November 25). Please stop telling me that all lives matter. *The Huffington Post*. Retrieved from http://www.huffingtonpost.com/julia-craven/please-stop-telling-me--th_b_6223072.html

Cubberley, E. P. (1909). *Changing conceptions of education* (pp. 14–15). Boston, MA: Houghton Mifflin.

Daly, M. (2014, August 22). Ferguson feeds off the poor: Three warrants a year per household. *The Daily Beast*. Retrieved from http://www.thedailybeast.com/articles/2014/08/22/ferguson-s-shameful-legal-shakedown-three-warrants-a-year-per-household.html

Davey, M., & Bosman, J. (2014, November 24). Protests flare after Ferguson police officer is not indicted. *The New York Times*. Retrieved from http://www.nytimes.com/2014/11/25/us/ferguson-darren-wilson-shooting-michael-brown-grand-jury.html

Davey, M., Wines, M., Eckholm, E., & Oppel, R. A. (2014, November 29). Raised hands, and the doubts of a Grand Jury. *The New York Times*. Retrieved from http://www.nytimes.com/2014/11/30/us/raised-hands-and-the-doubts-of-a-grand-jury-.html

Dyson, M. E. (2014, November 29). Where do we go after Ferguson? *The New York Times*. Retrieved from http://www.nytimes.com/2014/11/30/opinion/sunday/where-do-we-go-after-ferguson.html?_r=0

Ebony. (2014, December 2). Millennial activists talk directly with Obama. Retrieved from http://www.ebony.com/news-views/millennial-activists-talk-directly-with-obama-987#axzz3OFSwOHSf

The Economist. (2014, August 15). "Trigger happy." Democracy in America. Retrieved from http://www.economist.com/blogs/democracyinamerica/2014/08/armed-police

Edsall, T. B. (2014, July 16). The coming Democratic schism. *The New York Times*. Retrieved from http://www.nytimes.com/2014/07/16/opinion/thomas-edsall-a-shift-in-young-democrats-values.html

Eligon, J. (2014, August 24). Michael Brown spent last weeks grappling with problems and promise. *The New York Times*. Retrieved from http://www.nytimes.com/2014/08/25/us/michael-brown-spent-last-weeks-grappling-with-lifes-mysteries.html

Eligon, J. (2014, November 28). Protesters united against Ferguson decision, but challenged in unity. *The New York Times*. Retrieved from http://www.nytimes.com/2014/11/29/us/protesters-united-against-ferguson-decision-but-challenged-in-building-movement.html

Eromosele, D. O. (2014, August 19). What they saw: 5 eyewitnesses to the Michael Brown shooting. *The Root*. Retrieved from http://www.theroot.com/articles/culture/2014/08/_5_eyewitness_accounts_of_michael_brown_s_shooting.html

Fausset, R. (2014, September 28). Mostly black cities, mostly white city halls. *The New York Times*. Retrieved from http://www.nytimes.com/2014/09/29/us/mostly-black-cities-mostly-white-city-halls.html?_r=0

Ferguson, D. (2014, August 14). KKK raising money for "hero" Ferguson cop who shot "Jewish controlled black thug." *Raw Story*. Retrieved from http://www.rawstory.com/rs/2014/08/14/kkk-raising-money-for-hero-ferguson-cop-who-shot-jewish-controlled-black-thug/

Finnegan, W. (2014, September 15). Dignity: Fast-food workers and a new form of labor activism. *The New Yorker*. Retrieved from http://www.newyorker.com/magazine/2014/09/15/dignity-4

Fox, C. (2012). *Three worlds of relief: Race, immigration, and the American welfare state from the progressive era to The New Deal*. Princeton, NJ: Princeton University Press.

Fox 31 Denver. (2014, July 7). Family of great-grandmother beaten by California highway patrol officer plans to sue. Retrieved from http://kdvr.com/2014/07/07/family-of-great-grandmother-beaten-by-california-highway-patrol-officer-plans-to-sue/

Fry, R., & Taylor, P. (2012, August 1). The rise of residential segregation by income. *Pew Research Social & Demographic Trends*. Retrieved from http://www.pewsocialtrends.org/2012/08/01/the-rise-of-residential-segregation-by-income/

Genius.com/Fox-news-santa-claus-should-not-be-white-annotated (no date)

Gillborn, D. (2005). Education policy as an act of white supremacy: Whiteness, critical race theory and education reform. *Journal of Education Policy, 20*(4), 485–505.

Graham, L. O. (2014, November 6). I taught my black kids that their elite upbringing would protect them from discrimination. I was wrong. *The Washington Post*. Retrieved from http://www.washingtonpost.com/posteverything/wp/2014/11/06/i-taught-my-black-kids-that-their-elite-upbringing-would-protect-them-from-discrimination-i-was-wrong/

## BIBLIOGRAPHY

Greenwald, G., & Hussain, M. (2014, July 9). Meet the Muslim-American leaders the FBI and NSA have been spying on. *The Intercept.* Retrieved from https://firstlook.org/theintercept/article/2014/07/09/under-surveillance/

Gregory, P. R. (2012, January 22). Is President Obama truly a socialist? *Forbes.* Retrieved from http://www.forbes.com/sites/paulroderickgregory/2012/01/22/is-president-obama-truly-a-socialist/

Gross, K. N. (2014, December 11). Demands for justice are failing black women and girls. *The Huffington Post.* Retrieved from http://www.huffingtonpost.com/kali-nicole-gross/demands-for-justice-are-failing-black-women-and-girls_b_6295744.html

Gutiérrez y Muhs, C., Niemann, Y. F., González, C. G., & Harris, A.P. (2013). *Presumed incompetent: The intersections of race and class for women in academia.* Logan: Utah State University Press.

Haley, A., & Malcolm X. (1964). *The autobiography of Malcolm X.* New York, NY: Random House.

Harris, A. (2013, December 10). Santa Claus should not be a white man anymore. *Slate.* Retrieved from http://www.slate.com/articles/life/holidays/2013/12/santa_claus_an_old_white_man_not_anymore_meet_santa_the_penguin_a_new_christmas.html

Harris, A. (2013, December 12). What Fox News doesn't understand about Santa Claus. *Slate.* Retrieved from http://www.slate.com/blogs/browbeat/2013/12/12/santa_claus_white_fox_news_megyn_kelly_thinks_so_but_santa_s_not_real.html

Harris-Perry, M. (2014, September 28). Video released of Wal-Mart shooting. *MSNBC.* Retrieved from http://www.msnbc.com/melissa-harris-perry/watch/video-relcased-of-wal-mart-shooting-334558787700

Harwood, M. (2014, August 14). Tomgram: Matthew Harwood, one nation under SWAT. Retrieved from http://www.tomdispatch.com/post/175881/tomgram%3A_matthew_harwood%2C_one_nation_nder_swat/#more

Hing, J. (2014, October 8) Study: For black students, skin color and suspensions linked. *Colorlines.* Retrieved from http://colorlines.com/archives/2014/10/study_for_black_students_skin_color_and_suspensions_linked.html

Horowitz, S. (2011, September 23). Welcome to middle-class poverty—Does anybody know the way out? *The Atlantic.* Retrieved from http://www.theatlantic.com/business/archive/2011/09/welcome-to-middle-class-poverty-does-anybody-know-the-way-out/245447/

The Huffington Post. (2013, August 26). Black single mothers are "biggest impediment" to progress, journalist George Will says. *The Huffington Post.* Retrieved from http://www.huffingtonpost.com/2013/08/26/black-single-mothers-biggest-impediment_n_3818824.html

The Huffington Post. (2014, July 11). Growing number of Americans say Barack Obama is a Muslim. Retrieved from http://www.huffingtonpost.com/2010/08/19/barack-obama-muslim_n_687360.html

Ignatiev, N. (1995). *How the Irish became white.* New York, NY: Routledge.

Ingraham, C. (2014, September 30). White people are more likely to deal drugs, but black people are more likely to get arrested for it. *The Washington Post.* Retrieved from http://www.washingtonpost.com/blogs/wonkblog/wp/2014/09/30/white-people-are-more-likely-to-deal-drugs-but-black-people-are-more-likely-to-get-arrested-for-it/

Inzlicht, M., & Obhi, S. (2014, July 25). Powerful and coldhearted. Sunday Review. *The New York Times*. Retrieved from http://www.nytimes.com/2014/07/27/opinion/sunday/powerful-and-coldhearted.html

Jahi, A. (2014, August 15). Cops just shot my cousin dead. Here's why talking about it is quietly destructive. *Salon*. Retrieved from http://www.salon.com/2014/08/15/cops_just_shot_my_cousin_dead_heres_why_talking_about_it_is_quietly_destructive/

Johnson & Graham's Lessee v. McIntosh, 21 U.S. (8 Wheat.) 543 (1823). Retrieved from http://press-pubs.uchicago.edu/founders/documents/a1_8_3_indianss9.html

Jones, V. (2014, November 15). Facing Race Conference 2014. Plenary: The next fifty. *Colorlines*. Retrieved from http://colorlines.com/archives/2014/11/facing_race_2014_plenary_livestream_the_next_fifty.html

Kamp, K. (2013, September 20). By the numbers: The incredibly shrinking American middle class. *Moyers & Company*. Retrieved from http://billmoyers.com/2013/09/20/by-the-numbers-the-incredibly-shrinking-american-middle-class/

Katznelson, I. (2005). *When affirmative action was white*. New York, NY: W.W. Norton.

Kelly, J. (2012, September 19). Why British police don't have guns. *BBC News Magazine*. Retrieved from http://www.bbc.com/news/magazine-19641398

Kennedy, R. (2003). *Nigger: The strange career of a troublesome word*. New York: Vintage Books.

Kindy, K., & Horwitz, S. (2014, October 23). Evidence supports officer's account of shooting in Ferguson. *The New York Times*. Retrieved from http://www.washingtonpost.com/politics/new-evidence-supports-officers-account-of-shooting-in-ferguson/2014/10/22/cf38c7b4–5964–11e4-bd61–346aee66ba29_story.html

King, J. (2014, August 18). Jesse Williams on Ferguson: We are not treated like human beings. *Colorlines*. Retrieved from http://colorlines.com/archives/2014/08/jesse_williams_on_ferguson_we_are_not_treated_like_human_beings.html

King, M. L., Jr. (1967). *The trumpet of conscience*. Canadian Broadcasting Corporation Massey Lecture Series. Boston, MA: Beacon Press.

Kurzman, C. (2014, February 13). Anti-Muslim sentiment rising in the U.S: What is happening to religious tolerance? *ISLAMiCommentary*. Retrieved from https://islamicommentary.org/2014/02/anti-muslim-sentiment-rising-in-the-u-s-what-is-happening-to-religious-tolerance/

Lang, C. (2014, August 17). On Ferguson, Missouri: History, protest, and "respectability." *LAWCHA*. Retrieved from http://lawcha.org/wordpress/2014/08/17/ferguson-missouri-history-protest-respectability/

Lee, J. (2014, August 15). Exactly how often do police shoot unarmed black men? *Mother Jones*. Retrieved from http://www.motherjones.com/politics/2014/08/police-shootings-michael-brown-ferguson-black-men

Lewin, T. (2012, March 6). Black students face more discipline, data suggests. *The New York Times*. Retrieved from http://www.nytimes.com/2012/03/06/education/black-students-face-more-harsh-discipline-data-shows.html?_r=0

## BIBLIOGRAPHY

Lui, M., Robles, B. J., Leondar-Wright, B., Brewer, R. M., & Adamson, R. (2006). *The color of wealth: The story behind the U.S. racial wealth divide*. New York, NY: The New Press.

Luthar, S. (2013, November 5). The problem with rich kids. *Psychology Today*. Retrieved from http://www.psychologytoday.com/articles/201310/the-problem-rich-kids

Mackintosh, P. (1988). *White privilege and male privilege: A personal account of coming to see correspondences through work in women's studies* (Working Paper No. 189). Wellesley College, Center for Research on Women, Massachusetts.

Makarechi, K. (2014, August 25). Besides Michael Brown, whom else does The New York Times call "no angel"? *Vanity Fair*. Retrieved from http://www.vanityfair.com/online/daily/2014/08/michael-brown-no-angel-new-york-times

Maloy, S. (2014, June 20). GOP's poverty poll problem: Changing public opinion upends their poverty sham. *Salon.com*. Retrieved from http://www.salon.com/2014/06/20/gops_poverty_poll_problem_changing_public_opinion_upends_their_poverty_sham/

Marable, M. (2002). *The great wells of democracy: The meaning of race in American life*. Cambridge, MA: BasicCivitas Books.

Massey, D. S. (2007). *Categorically unequal: The American stratification system*. New York, NY: Russell Sage.

McCoy, A. (2014, February 21). My remarks to the regents, 2–20. Retrieved from https://www.facebook.com/notes/austin-mccoy/my-remarks-to-the-regents-2–20/10152241833889349

Mills, C. W. (1997). *The racial contract*. Ithaca, NY: Cornell University Press.

Morales, A. (2014, August 18). Dispatches: On the ground in Ferguson, Missouri. *Human Rights Watch*. Retrieved from http://www.hrw.org/news/2014/08/18/dispatches-ground-ferguson-missouri

Moyer, J., & Kirkpatrick, N. (2015, January 5). #BlackBrunchNYC protests disrupt "white" N.T. breakfast spots. *The Washington Post*. Retrieved from http://www.washington-post.com/news/morning-mix/wp/2015/01/05/blackbrunchnyc-brings-police-brutality-protests-to-white-breakfast-spots/

Moyers & Company. (2014, May 21). Ta-Nehisi Coates on the case for reparations. Retrieved from http://billmoyers.com/episode/facing-the-truth-the-case-for-reparations/

Muhammad, K. G. (2010). *The condemnation of blackness: Race, crime, and the making of modern urban America*. Cambridge, MA: Harvard University Press.

Murphy, K. (2014, June 9). Killing a patient to save his life. *The New York Times*. Retrieved from http://www.nytimes.com/2014/06/10/health/a-chilling-medical-trial.html

Myers, K. A., & Williamson, P. W. (2001). Race talk: The perpetuation of racism through private discourse. *Race & Society, 4*, 3–26.

NAACP. (2014, November 24). NAACP announces march, "Journey for Justice: Ferguson to Jefferson City." Retrieved from http://www.naacp.org/press/entry/naacp-and-coalition-partners-announce-march-journey-for-justice-ferguson-to

NBC Washington. (2014, August 14). Howard University grad Mya Aaten-White shot in Ferguson, Missouri. Retrieved from http://www.nbcwashington.com/news/local/Howard-University-Grad-Mya-White-Shot-in-Ferguson-Missouri-271285081.html

New Politics Institute. (2007). The progressive politics of the Millennial generation. Retrieved from http://ndn-newpol.civicactions.net/sites/ndn-newpol.civicactions.net/files/NPI-Millennials-Final.pdf

Newport, F. (2014, August 20). Gallup review: Black and white attitudes toward police. Retrieved from http://www.gallup.com/poll/175088/gallup-review-black-white-attitudes-toward-police.aspx

Noonan, J. (2012, April 30). Black children less likely to get pain meds in E.R. *ABC News.* Retrieved from http://abcnews.go.com/Health/Wellness/black-children-pain-meds-er/story?id=16231146

O'Harrow, R., Jr., & Rich, S. (2014, October 11, 2014). Asset seizures fuel police spending. *The Washington Post.* Retrieved from http://www.washingtonpost.com/sf/investigative/2014/10/11/cash-seizures-fuel-police-spending/

Parker, D. D. (2014, September 4). A taxicab confession for a post-Ferguson America. *The Huffington Post.* Retrieved from http://www.huffingtonpost.com/dennis-d-parker/a-taxicab-confession_b_5767062.html

PBS Video. (n.d.). *Finding your roots.* Retrieved from http://video.pbs.org/program/finding-your-roots/

Pearce, M. (2014, September 1). Ferguson fundraiser mystery solved—or is it? *Los Angeles Times.* Retrieved from http://www.latimes.com/nation/la-na-ferguson-fundraisers-20140901-story.html#page=1

Persaud R., & Bruggen, P. (2013, June 12). The rich use cocaine for different reasons compared to the poor. *The Huffington Post.* Retrieved from http://www.huffingtonpost.co.uk/dr-raj-persaud/cocaine-use-uk_b_4391374.html

Pew Research Center. (2014, August 18). Stark racial divisions in reaction to Ferguson police shooting. Retrieved from http://www.people-press.org/2014/08/18/stark-racial-divisions-in-reactions-to-ferguson-police-shooting/

Pewewardy, C. (1997). The Pocahontas paradox: A cautionary tale for educators. *Journal of Navajo Education, 14*(1–2), 2–25. Retrieved from http://www.hanksville.org/storytellers/pewe/writing/Pocahontas.html

Phillip, A. (2014, August 26). Audio recording allegedly captures at least 10 shots fired in Michael Brown killing. *The Washington Post.* Retrieved from http://www.washington-post.com/news/post-nation/wp/2014/08/26/audio-recording-allegedly-captures-at-least-10-shots-fired-in-michael-brown-killing/

Plessy v. Ferguson, 163 U.S. 537 (1896). Retrieved from http://www.ourdocuments.gov/doc.php?flash=true&doc=52&page=transcript#judgement

Powell, T. (2014, July 24). My son has been suspended five times. He's 3. *The Washington Post.* Retrieved from http://www.washingtonpost.com/posteverything/wp/2014/07/24/my-son-has-been-suspended-five-times-hes-3/

Powers, S. (2015, January 13). Alan Grayson, the "monochromatic" GOP and white supremacists. *Orlando Sentinel.* Retrieved from http://www.orlandosentinel.com/news/politics/political-pulse/os-alan-grayson-the-monochromatic-gop-and-white-supremacists-20150112-post.html

## BIBLIOGRAPHY

Quigley, B. (2014, August 18). Ten facts about police violence in Ferguson Sunday night. *The Huffington Post*. Retrieved from http://www.huffingtonpost.com/bill-quigley/ten-facts-about-police-vi_b_5688146.html

Racebox.org. (n.d.). The census since 1790. Retrieved from http://www.racebox.org

Real Clear Politics. (2010, January 27). MSNBC's Matthews on Obama: "I forgot he was black tonight." Retrieved from http://www.realclearpolitics.com/video/2010/01/27/msnbcs_matthews_on_obama_i_forgot_he_was_black_tonight.html

Reid, J-A. (2014, December 17). Eric Holder on anti-police protests, Obama's legacy, and his final battle as attorney general. *New York Magazine*. Retrieved from http://nymag.com/daily/intelligencer/2014/12/exclusive-eric-holder-exit-interview.html

Richardson, J. H. (2015, January 5). Michael Brown Sr. and the agony of the black father in America. *Esquire*. Retrieved from http://www.esquire.com/features/michael-brown-father-interview-0115

Roberts, D. (2011). *Fatal invention*. New York, NY: The New Press.

Roberts, S. (2009, December 17). Projections put whites in minority in U.S. by 2050. *The New York Times*. Retrieved from http://www.nytimes.com/2009/12/18/us/18census.html

Roediger, D. R. (2005). *Working toward whiteness: How America's immigrants became white*. New York, NY: Basic Books.

Roediger, D. R. (2007). *The wages of whiteness: Race and the making of the American working class*. New York, NY: Verso.

Rose, J. (2014, May 21). Portland drivers "clearly" show racial bias at crosswalks, PSU study says (poll). *The Oregonian*. Retrieved from http://www.oregonlive.com/commuting/index.ssf/2014/05/portland_drivers_clearly_exhib.html

Rubin, L. J. (2014, August 20). A former Marine explains all the weapons of war being used by police in Ferguson. *The Nation*. Retrieved from http://www.thenation.com/article/181315/catalog-ferguson-police-weaponry

Samuels, R. (2014, October 7). For some Ferguson whites, racial fault lines exposed by shooting come as a surprise. *The Washington Post*. Retrieved from http://www.washingtonpost.com/national/for-some-ferguson-whites-racial-fault-lines-exposed-by-shooting-come-as-a-surprise/2014/10/07/a25d95c0–497f-11e4–891d-713f052086a0_story.html

Smith, J. (2014, August 17). In Ferguson, black town, white power. *The New York Times*. Retrieved from http://mobile.nytimes.com/2014/08/18/opinion/in-ferguson-black-town-white-power.html?ref=opinion&_r=0&referrer

Snopes.com. Birth certificate. Retrieved from http://www.snopes.com/politics/obama/birthers/birthcertificate.asp

Snowden, F. M., Jr. (1983). *Before color prejudice: The ancient view of blacks*. Cambridge, MA: Harvard University Press.

Staats, C. (2014). State of the science: Implicit Bias Review, 2014. *Kirwan Institute for the Study of Race and Ethnicity*. Retrieved from http://www.kirwaninstitute.osu.edu/implicit-bias-review

Stanford News. (2014, April 22). Stanford researcher: First generation college students benefit from discussing class differences. http://news.stanford.edu/news/2014/april/first-gen-resources-042214.html

State of Missouri v. Darren Wilson. (2014, September 10). Transcript of Grand Jury Vol. IV. Retrieved from https://www.documentcloud.org/documents/1370517-grand-jury-volume-4.html

State of Missouri v. Darren Wilson. (2014, September 16). Transcript of Grand Jury Vol. V. Retrieved from https://www.documentcloud.org/documents/1370518-grand-jury-volume-5.html

Stephenson, G. M. (1964). *A history of American immigration 1820–1924*. New York, NY: Russell & Russell.

Stiglitz, J. (2013, February 16). Equal opportunity, our national myth. *The New York Times*. Retrieved from http://opinionator.blogs.nytimes.com/2013/02/16/equal-opportunity-our-national-myth/

Subasing, A., & Gilson, D. (n.d.). Chart: Almost every Obama conspiracy theory ever. *Mother Jones*. Retrieved from http://www.motherjones.com/politics/2012/10/chart-obama-conspiracy-theories

Sullivan, M. (2014, August 25). An ill-chosen phrase, "no angel" brings a storm of protest. Public Editor's Journal. *The New York Times*. Retrieved from http://publiceditor.blogs.nytimes.com/2014/08/25/an-ill-chosen-phrase-no-angel-brings-a-storm-of-protest/?_php=true&_type=blogs&_r=0

Takaki, R. (1998) [1989]. *Strangers from a different shore: A history of Asian Americans*. Boston, MA: Little, Brown.

Takao Ozawa v. United States, 260 U.S. 178 (1922). Retrieved from http://caselaw.lp.findlaw.com/cgi-bin/getcase.pl?court=us&vol=260&invol=178

Tilove, J. (2008, January 31). "Pookie" keeps popping up in Obama's speeches. *Houston Chronicle*. Retrieved from http://www.chron.com/life/article/Pookie-keeps-popping-up-in-Obama-s-speeches-1788973.php

Tirado, L. (2014, June 19). This is why poor people's bad decisions make perfect sense. *The Huffington Post*. Retrieved from http://www.huffingtonpost.com/linda-tirado/why-poor-peoples-bad-decisions-make-perfect-sense_b_4326233.html

Turnley, D. (2012). *Shenandoah: The story of a working class town and the American dream on trial*. Retrieved from http://vimeo.com/43903604

2010 Census Briefs. (2012, January). The American Indian and Alaska Native population: 2010. Retrieved from http://www.census.gov/prod/cen2010/briefs/c2010br-10.pdf

United States v. Bhagat Singh Thind, 261 U.S. 204 (1923). Retrieved from http://supreme.justia.com/cases/federal/us/261/204/case.html

Van Ausdale, D., & Feagin, J. R. (2001). *The first R: How children learn race and racism*. Lanham, MD: Rowman & Littlefield.

Vaught, S. E. (2011). *Racism, public schooling, and the entrenchment of white supremacy*. Albany: State University of New York Press.

## BIBLIOGRAPHY 181

Ventner, J. C. (2000). Remarks at the Human Genome Announcement. *Celera*. Retrieved from https://www.celera.com/celera/pr_1056647999

Waddell, K. (2014, August 25). New York Times says Michael Brown was "No angel." Twitter: No one is. *National Journal*. Retrieved from http://www.nationaljournal.com/politics/new-york-times-says-michael-brown-was-no-angel-twitter-no-one-is-20140825

Walker, H. (2013, June 19). Paula Deen on her dream "southern plantation wedding." *TPM DC*. Retrieved from http://talkingpointsmemo.com/dc/paula-deen-on-her-dream-southern-plantation-wedding

The Wall Street Journal. (2014, August 18). Ferguson Timeline: What's happened so far. http://blogs.wsj.com/washwire/2014/08/18/ferguson-timeline-whats-happened-so-far/

The Washington Post. (n.d.). The N-word. Retrieved from http://www.washingtonpost.com/wp-dre/features/the-n-word

Wessler, S. F. (2014, June 20). Poll: Fewer Americans blame poverty on the poor. *NBC News*. Retrieved from http://www.nbcnews.com/feature/in-plain-sight/poll-fewer-americans-blame-poverty-poor-n136051

White, K. C. (2014, August 12). Black and unarmed: Women and girls without weapons killed by law enforcement. *Role Reboot*. Retrieved from http://www.rolereboot.org/cultureandpolitics/details/2014–08-black-unarmed-women-girls-without-weapons-killed-law-enforcement/

Wilkerson, I. (2014, August 25). Mike Brown's shooting and Jim Crow lynchings have too much in common. It's time for America to own up. *The Guardian*. Retrieved from http://www.theguardian.com/commentisfree/2014/aug/25/mike-brown-shooting-jim-crow-lynchings-in-common

Williams, M. E. (2013, December 4). A university's terrible black Santa question. *Salon*. Retrieved from http://www.salon.com/2013/12/04/a_universitys_terrible_black_santa_question/

Wines, M., & Robles, F. (2014, August 22). Key factor in police shootings: "Reasonable fear." *The New York Times*. Retrieved from http://mobile.nytimes.com/2014/08/23/us/ferguson-mo-key-factor-in-police-shootings-reasonable-fear.html?_r=0

Workneh, L., McLaughlin, M., & Meinick, M. (2014, December 15). "Everyone has a stake in this": Tens of thousands mobilize across America to protest police killings. *The Huffington Post*. Retrieved from http://www.huffingtonpost.com/2014/12/13/millions-march-oakland_n_6321046.html

Wright, R. (2007). *Black boy: A record of childhood and youth*. New York, NY: Harper Perennial Modern Classics. (Original work published 1945)

Yancy, G. (2013, September 1). Walking while black in the "white gaze." *The New York Times*. Retrieved from http://opinionator.blogs.nytimes.com/2013/09/01/walking-while-black-in-the-white-gaze/